Vessel Collisions in the Law of the Sea

Alfredo C. Robles Jr.

Vessel Collisions in the Law of the Sea

The South China Sea Arbitration

DE LA SALLE UNIVERSITY
RELIGIO MORES CULTURA
MANILA

palgrave
macmillan

Alfredo C. Robles Jr.
De La Salle University
Manila, Philippines

ISBN 978-981-16-9795-1 ISBN 978-981-16-9793-7 (eBook)
https://doi.org/10.1007/978-981-16-9793-7

Jointly published with De La Salle University Publishing House
The print edition is not for sale on the Philippines. Customers from the Philippines please order the print book from: De La Salle University Publishing House.
ISBN of the Co-Publisher's edition: 978-971-555-700-9

This Palgrave Macmillan imprint is published by the registered company Springer Nature Singapore Pte Ltd.
The registered company address is: 152 Beach Road, #21-01/04 Gateway East, Singapore 189721, Singapore

Preface

It was not without trepidation that I embarked on the study of the decisions of the Tribunal in the *South China Sea Arbitration* on the Philippine submission that the conduct of China's vessels at Scarborough Shoal in April and May 2012, by creating a risk of collision with Philippine official vessels, had violated the Convention on the International Regulations for Preventing Collisions at Sea 1972 (COLREGS 1972) and the United Nations Convention on the Law of the Sea. The first hurdle to be overcome, one that initially seemed to be well-nigh insuperable, was the technical nature of the COLREGS. The second hurdle, probably resulting from the first, was the notable lack of scholarly commentary on the subject with which I could engage. The most detailed commentary available so far, the extended critique undertaken by the Chinese Society of International Law, was published only in mid-2018, just as I was starting my research.

Yet it is precisely for these same reasons that a full-length study of the Tribunal's decisions is necessary. To cope with these twin hurdles, I undertook research that encompassed not just the documentation submitted by the Philippines to the Tribunal and the independent expert's report, but also handbooks, commentaries, histories, and videos on the COLREGS, navigation, and yes, major collisions, by and for mariners. While I remain a landlubber, I hope to have acquired sufficient understanding of the COLREGS to explain to specialists of the law of the sea the Tribunal's decisions relating to Philippine Submission No. 13. At the same time, I hope to have explained to professional mariners some of the international legal issues that were raised by the Tribunal's decisions and that may be unfamiliar to them.

While my research was completed in early 2019, I have not deemed it necessary to update my conclusions. On the contrary, the last Chapter's characterization of collisions as instruments of China's foreign policy seems to have been confirmed by the passage in January 2021 of China's Coast Guard Law.

One cannot underestimate the significance of China's violations of the COLREGS in the South China Sea in 2012, before 2012, and after 2012. It is largely through such violations that China asserts on the ground—or to be more accurate, on the water—its claims to sovereignty over maritime features and to "historic rights" in the South China Sea. As long as China persists in these violations, the operation of its vessels will continue to threaten human life and the safety of navigation in the South China Sea.

Manila, Philippines Alfredo C. Robles Jr.

Acknowledgments

It is my pleasure to acknowledge the assistance that I received in the writing of this book.

Dr. Thaemar Tana of the University of the Philippines helped me obtain access to a wide range of materials in various languages.

Kareff Rafisura's gift of the *Commentary* on the United Nations Convention on the Law of the Sea edited by Alexander Proelss is the gift that keeps on giving.

Benjie Lelis very kindly provided me a copy of Carlos Espaliú Berdud's book, *Le passage inoffensif des navires de guerre étrangers dans la mer territoriale*.

Darren Mangado came to the rescue during the revision process by offering me a copy of Cameron Moore's *Freedom of Navigation and the Law of the Sea*.

Dr. David Jonathan Bayot, Director of De La Salle University Publishing House (DLSUPH), expressed interest in my manuscript, sought to keep the review process going in the Philippines even during the prolonged quarantine, and established contact with Palgrave Macmillan for the publication of an international edition of the book.

Two anonymous reviewers for Palgrave Macmillan gave me very welcome feedback and suggestions for improvement of the manuscript.

Last but not least, the production staffs of Palgrave Macmillan and the DLSU Publishing House deserve thanks for their painstaking work in preparing the book for publication.

Contents

About the Author

Alfredo C. Robles Jr. is a University Fellow at De La Salle University. He holds doctorate degrees from the Université Paris 1 (Panthéon-Sorbonne) and Syracuse University. He is the author of *French Theories of Regulation and Conceptions of the International Division of Labour* (Macmillan, 1994), *The Political Economy of Interregional Relations: ASEAN and the EU* (Ashgate, 2004), *The Asia-Europe Meeting: The Theory and Practice of Interregionalism* (Routledge, 2008), *The South China Sea Arbitration: Understanding the Awards and Debating with China* (De La Salle University Publishing House and Sussex Academic Press, 2018), and *Endangered Species and Fragile Ecosystems in the South China Sea: The Philippines v. China Arbitration* (Palgrave Macmillan, 2020).

Abbreviations, Acronyms, and Terms

AFDI	*Annuaire Français de Droit International* [French Yearbook of International Law]
AJIL	*American Journal of International Law*
Allen Opinion	Opinion of Craig H. Allen, Judson Falknor Professor of Law, University of Washington (19 March 2014)
BFAR	Bureau of Fisheries and Aquatic Resources (Philippines)
BRP	*Barko ng Republika ng Pilipinas* [Ship of the Republic of the Philippines]
CMS	China Marine Surveillance
COLREGS	International Convention on the International Regulations for Preventing Collisions at Sea, adopted at London on 20 October 1972, entered into force 15 July 1977, consolidated text as amended in 1981,1987, 1989, 1993, 2001 and 2007
Convention	United Nations Convention on the Law of the Sea, signed at Montego Bay on 10 December 1982, entered into force 16 November 1994
CSIL	Chinese Society of International Law
CSIS	Center for Strategic and International Studies
EEZ	Exclusive Economic Zone
FLEC	Fisheries Law Enforcement Command (China)
FRPLEU/QRT	Fishery Resource Protection and Law Enforcement Unit/Quick Response Team (Philippines)
ICJ	International Court of Justice
ILC	United Nations International Law Commission
IMCO	Intergovernmental Maritime Consultative Organization
IMO	International Maritime Organization

ITLOS	International Tribunal for the Law of the Sea
JON	*Journal of Navigation*
MCS	Monitoring, Control, and Surveillance Vessel (Philippines)
MLE	Maritime Law Enforcement (China)
MP	*Memorial of the Philippines* (30 March 2014)
PCA	Permanent Court of Arbitration
REDI	*Revista Española de Derecho Internacional* [Spanish Journal of International Law]
SARV	Search and Rescue Vessel (Philippines)
SDP	*Supplemental Documents of the Philippines* (19 November 2015)
Singhota Report	Report of the International Navigational Safety Expert Appointed by the Permanent Court of Arbitration [sic], The Hague, The Netherlands, 15 April 2016, by Captain Gupreet S. Singhota
SOLAS	International Convention for the Safety of Life at Sea, adopted at London, 1 November 1974, entered into force 25 May 1980
SWSP	*Supplemental Written Submissions of the Philippines* (16 March 2015)
UNCLOS	United Nations Conference on the Law of the Sea, Geneva, 24 February–27 April 1958
UNCLOS III	Third United Nations Conference on the Law of the Sea, 1973–82
UNTS	*United Nations Treaty Series*

CHAPTER 1

Introduction

I. The Safety of Navigation in the South China Sea

The South China Sea, a semi-enclosed sea in the Western Pacific spanning approximately 3.5 million square kilometers, is a crucial shipping lane.[1] China graphically described it as a maritime area where shipping lanes criss-cross.[2] The Philippines more prosaically described it as a maritime area offering the shortest route between the Indian Ocean and Northeast

[1] *South China Sea Arbitration (Philippines v. China)*, Award on Jurisdiction and Admissibility (29 October 2015), 1, para. 2 ("Award on Jurisdiction"), https://pcacases.com/web/sendAttach/2579, accessed 29 May 2019. Article 122 of the United Nations Convention on the Law of the Sea 1982 ("the Convention") defines an "enclosed or semi-enclosed sea" as "a gulf, basin or sea surrounded by two or more States and connected to another sea or the ocean by a narrow outlet or consisting entirely or primarily of the territorial seas and exclusive economic zones of two or more coastal States." *United Nations Convention on the Law of the Sea*, concluded at Montego Bay on 10 December, entered into force 16 November 1994, http://www.un.org/Depts/los/convention_agreements/texts/unclos/closindx.htm, accessed 21 March 2019.

[2] *South China Sea Arbitration, Supplemental Documents of the Philippines* (19 November 2015), Annex 624, Ministry of Foreign Affairs, People's Republic of China, *Foreign Ministry Spokesperson Hua Chunying's Regular Press Conference* (9 April 2015), vol. I, 165, http://www.pcacases.com/pcadocs/The%20Philippines%27%20Supplemental%20Documents%20-%20Volume%20I%20%28Annexes%20607-667%29.pdf, accessed 29 May 2019; quoted in *South China Sea Arbitration*, Award of 12 July 2016, 410, para. 1022 ("Award of 12 July 2016"), http://www.pcacases.com/pcadocs/PH-CN%20-%2020160712%20-%20Award.pdf, accessed 30 May 2019.

A. C. Robles Jr., *Vessel Collisions in the Law of the Sea*,
https://doi.org/10.1007/978-981-16-9793-7_1

Asia, through which most of the world's oil tankers and merchant ships, carrying a quarter of world trade and including 75 percent of China's energy needs, passed.[3] A major insurance company simply states that the South China Sea represents around a third of global shipping trade.[4]

Unfortunately, the South China Sea (covering South China, mainland Southeast Asia, Indonesia, and the Philippines) is also the maritime area where the highest number of ships is lost. In 2019, it accounted for 12 out of 41 ships lost in the world.[5] The sad record is confirmed by the statistics for the decade between 2010 and 2019, during which the South China Sea represented 228 out of the total ship losses of 951.[6] An analysis of the statistics for the year 2019 revealed that in 30 percent of the cases in Southeast Asia, the ship "foundered," i.e., it sunk or was submerged due to causes such as rough weather, leaks, or breaking in two, excluding collisions. Among types of vessels, most cargo vessels lost in the world were lost in Southeast Asia.[7] The high number of ship losses is attributed to high levels of local and international trade, congested ports, busy shipping lanes, older fleets, exposure to typhoons, and ongoing safety problems on some domestic ferry routes.[8] To these factors might be added the incidence of certain practices. The predominant type of vessel in the region is the general cargo ship, which makes many port calls, navigates

[3] *South China Sea Arbitration, Memorial of the Philippines* (30 March 2014), vol. I, 21, para. 2.14 ("*MP*"), http://www.pcacases.com/pcadocs/Memorial%20of%20the%20Philippines%20Volume%20I.pdf, accessed 30 May 2019.

[4] Allianz Global Corporate and Specialty, *Safety and Shipping Review 2018: An Annual Review of Trends and Developments in Shipping Losses and Safety* (Munich: Allianz Global Corporate and Specialty SE, 2018), 43, https://www.agcs.allianz.com/assets/PDFs/Reports/AGCS_Safety_Shipping_Review_2018.pdf, accessed 7 November 2018.

[5] Allianz Global Ciorporate and Specialty, *Safety and Shipping Review 2020: An Annual Review of Trends and Developments in Shipping Losses and Safety* (Munich: Allianz Global Corporate and Specialty SE, 2020), 9, https://www.agcs.allianz.com/content/dam/onemarketing/agcs/agcs/reports/AGCS-Safety-Shipping-Review-2020.pdf, accessed 18 October 2021.

[6] *Ibid*., 9.

[7] *Ibid*., 13.

[8] *Ibid*., 6.

in congested coastal areas, and confronts hydrogeographic risks such as submerged reefs and rocks.[9]

Since these statistics were compiled for insurance purposes, it seems likely that they do not take into account incidents that are associated with the territorial and maritime disputes among the littoral States and the growing military presence of States from within and outside the region. These incidents may result in collisions between vessels, the ramming of one vessel by another, and occasionally the sinking of a vessel; even when they do not lead to collisions, ramming, or sinking, they raise tensions among the littoral States involved. Between 2010 and 2020, there were 64 incidents involving different types of vessels (navy, maritime law enforcement, maritime surveillance, coast guard, and fishing) from China, Taiwan, Indonesia, Malaysia, the Philippines, Thailand, or Vietnam.[10] Chinese vessels of all types were involved in all but twelve incidents; in five of these twelve incidents, vessels from Taiwan were involved.[11] In forty incidents, Chinese coast guard, maritime law enforcement, and/or navy vessels blocked or pursued fishing vessels from Indonesia, the Philippines, and Vietnam, boarded them, seized catch, and destroyed equipment; occasionally, they pointed guns at the vessels, fired water cannon at them, beat the captain and crew members, and rammed them, causing some of them to sink. The remaining incidents saw Chinese coast guard, maritime law enforcement, and navy vessels face off navy, maritime law enforcement, and maritime surveillance vessels from these Southeast Asian countries.[12]

[9] Nickie Butt et al., *15 Years of Shipping Accidents: A Review for WWF* (Southampton: Southampton Solent University, School of Maritime [sic] and Technology, 2013), 27, http://awsassets.panda.org/downloads/15_years_of_shipping_accidents_a_review_for_wwf_.pdf, accessed 14 June 2019.

[10] The following discussion concerns only incidents involving littoral States in the South China Sea.

[11] Reporting an incident involving Chinese coast guard and fishing vessels, on the one hand, and an official vessel from an unnamed NATO country, on the other, McLaughlin argued that Chinese fishing vessels act, at least temporarily, as maritime militia, under the direction of the Chinese Coast Guard. Rob McLaughlin, "An Incident in the South China Sea," *International Law Studies* 96 (2020): 505–28, https://digital-commons.usnwc.edu/cgi/viewcontent.cgi?article=2930&context=ils, accessed 13 October 2021.

[12] Figures calculated by the author from Center for Strategic and International Studies ("CSIS"), "Are Maritime Law Enforcement Forces Destabilizing Asia?" *China Power Project* (2021), https://chinapower.csis.org/maritime-forces-destabilizing-asia/, accessed 13 October 2021.

Most of these incidents prompted an exchange of diplomatic protests, sometimes accompanied by demands for investigation of the incident. Two incidents involving Chinese and Philippine official vessels in April and May 2012, in which Chinese official vessels operated in a manner that created serious risk of collision with Philippine vessels, retrospectively assumed greater prominence, as they formed the basis of Philippine Submission No. 13 to the Arbitral Tribunal constituted under Annex VII of the United Nations Convention on the Law of the Sea ("Convention"). A few words are in order about the *Arbitration*, to enable the reader to understand the context of the dispute relating to China's compliance with the International Convention on the Regulations for Preventing Collisions at Sea 1972 ("COLREGS 1972") and the Convention.[13]

II. Overview of the *South China Sea Arbitration*

The Convention accords States the flexibility to resolve disputes in the manner of their choosing, a principle that is enshrined in Article 279. At the same time, it provides for dispute settlement procedures that may be initiated by only one of the parties to the dispute, and that entail binding decisions for both parties. These procedures are subject to very specific limitations and exceptions that are set out in the Convention itself.[14]

Upon signature, ratification, or accession to the Convention or at any time thereafter, a State may declare that it accepts one or more means for the compulsory settlement of disputes entailing binding decisions that are identified in Article 287(1) of the Convention. These are the International Tribunal for the Law of the Sea ("ITLOS"), established by Annex VI of the Convention, the International Court of Justice ("ICJ"), arbitration under Annex VII of the Convention, or special arbitration under

[13] *International Convention on the International Regulations for Preventing Collisions at Sea*, adopted at London on 20 October 1972, entered into force 15 July 1977, consolidated text as amended in 1981, 1987, 1989, 1993, 2001 and 2007, http://www.ecolregs.com/index.php?option=com_k2&view=itemlist&layout=category&Itemid=505&lang=en, accessed 31 May 2019. It was only in 1972 that the International Regulations for Preventing Collisions at Sea were placed in the annex of an international convention. Hence, for much of their history, they were known simply as the International Regulations for Preventing Collisions at Sea and were referred to in the plural. This usage will be followed here.

[14] Award on Jurisdiction, 7, para. 107.

Annex VIII of the Convention. A State that does not make such a declaration will not be exempt from the obligation to participate in dispute settlement proceedings entailing binding decisions, as it will be deemed to have accepted arbitration under Annex VII.[15] If two States parties to a dispute have not chosen the same means of dispute settlement, they will also be deemed to have accepted arbitration under Annex VII of the Convention.[16]

By ratifying the Convention, the Philippines and China both gave their consent to the Convention's dispute settlement mechanisms.[17] Neither has made a declaration accepting the compulsory jurisdiction of any of the international courts or tribunals listed in Article 287(1). It follows that both are deemed to have given their consent in advance to arbitration as the compulsory procedure entailing binding decisions for the settlement of their disputes. As the Tribunal succinctly put it in its Award on Jurisdiction and Admissibility, the dispute was therefore "correctly" submitted to arbitration by a tribunal constituted under Annex VII.[18]

International arbitration is defined by the Convention for the Pacific Settlement of International Disputes 1907 as "the settlement of disputes between States by judges of their own choice and on the basis of respect for law."[19] Arbitration is ad hoc: an Arbitral Tribunal is created to hear a dispute and is dissolved once it has issued an award (judgment). This ad hoc character differentiates it from permanent international tribunals, such as the ICJ, the ITLOS, and the International Criminal Court ("ICC"). The tribunal's award is binding on the parties. The binding character of the award differentiates arbitration from diplomatic forms of dispute settlement (negotiation, good offices, mediation, and conciliation), whose results are not binding on the parties. Arbitration under

[15] Convention, Article 287(3).

[16] *Ibid.*, Article 287(5).

[17] The Convention was ratified by the Philippines on 8 May 1984 and by China on 7 June 1996. United Nations Office of Legal Affairs, Treaty Section, Treaty Collection, *Multilateral Treaties Deposited with the Secretary-General, Chapter XXI: Law of the Sea*, https://treaties.un.org/Pages/ViewDetailsIII.aspx?src=TREATY&mtdsg_no=XXI-6&chapter=21&Temp=mtdsg3&clang=_en, accessed 4 April 2019.

[18] Award on Jurisdiction, 38, para. 109.

[19] *Convention for the Pacific Settlement of International Disputes*, done at The Hague, 18 October 1907, Article 37, https://pca-cpa.org/wp-content/uploads/sites/6/2016/01/1907-Convention-for-the-Pacific-Settlement-of-International-Disputes.pdf, accessed 4 April 2019.

Annex VII of the Convention is noteworthy in that it is an integral part of a compulsory system of dispute settlement. In this system, consent to arbitration is implicitly given upon ratification of the Convention if the State has not made a choice among the different means of dispute settlement entailing binding decisions. The recourse to compulsory dispute settlement is subject only to the conditions set out in Sections I and III of Part XV of the Convention.

Arbitration under Annex VII of the Convention was initiated by the Philippines by a Notification and Statement of Claim dated 22 January 2013 and addressed to China.[20] The Philippines clarified that it was not seeking a determination of which of the two States enjoyed sovereignty over the islands in the South China Sea that they claimed.[21] This clarification reflected an awareness that at the Third United Nations Conference on the Law of the Sea ("UNCLOS III"), no State considered that a long-standing dispute over territorial sovereignty would ever be considered a dispute "concerning the interpretation or application of the Convention."[22] China returned the Notification and Statement of Claim and rejected the invitation to participate in the arbitration. The Arbitral Tribunal was constituted in June 2013 in accordance with Annex VII of the Convention and was composed of five members: Judge Thomas A. Mensah (president), member (1996–2005) and first President (1996–1999) of the ITLOS; Judge Jean-Pierre Cot, member (2002–2020) and President of the Chamber for Marine Environment Disputes (2008–2011) of the ITLOS; Judge Stanisław Pawlak, member (since 2005) of the ITLOS; Professor Alfred A.H. Soons, President of the Arbitral Tribunal in *Duzgit Integrity Arbitration (Malta v. São Tomé and Príncipe,*

[20] Notification and Statement of Claim of the Republic of the Philippines, 22 January 2013, http://www.philippineembassy-usa.org/uploads/pdfs/embassy/2013/2013-0122-Notification%20and%20Statement%20of%20Claim%20on%20West%20Philippine%20Sea.pdf, accessed 3 May 2019.

[21] *Ibid.*, 3, para. 7.

[22] *Chagos Marine Protected Area Arbitration* (Mauritius v. UK), Award of 18 March 2015, 89, paras. 215–16, http://www.pcacases.com/pcadocs/MU-UK%2020150318%20Award.pdf, accessed 3 May 2019. United Nations Codification Division, *Diplomatic Conferences, Third United Nations Conference on the Law of the Sea (1973–1982)*, http://legal.un.org/diplomaticconferences/1973_los/, accessed 14 June 2019.

2013–2019); and Judge Rüdiger Wolfrum, member (1996–2017), Vice-President (1996–1999), and President (2005–2008) of the ITLOS.[23] The Permanent Court of Arbitration ("PCA"), with headquarters in The Hague, was designated as the Registry in the case. The Philippines submitted its *Memorial* on 30 March 2014.

In December 2014, a week before the date that had been set for China's submission of its *Counter-Memorial*, China issued a Position Paper in which it challenged the jurisdiction of the Tribunal.[24] The latter treated the Position Paper as a preliminary objection and held a Hearing on Jurisdiction and Admissibility at The Hague in July 2015. The Tribunal issued an Award on Jurisdiction and Admissibility on 29 October 2015, in which it declared that it had jurisdiction over certain of the Philippine claims and decided to reserve consideration of its jurisdiction over other claims to the merits phase of the proceedings. A Hearing on the Merits and Remaining Issues of Admissibility was held at The Hague in November 2015. The Tribunal issued its Award on the merits on 12 July 2016.[25]

[23] International Tribunal for the Law of the Sea ("ITLOS"), *New Arbitrator and President Appointed in the Arbitral Proceedings Instituted by the Republic of the Philippines Against the People's Republic of China*, Doc. ITLOS/Press 197 (24 June 2013), https://www.itlos.org/fileadmin/itlos/documents/press_releases_english/PR_197_E.pdf, accessed 26 March 2019.

[24] *South China Sea Arbitration, Supplemental Written Submission of the Philippines* (16 March 2015), Annex 467, People's Republic of China, Position Paper of the Government of the People's Republic of China on the Matter of Jurisdiction in the South China Sea Arbitration Initiated by the Republic of the Philippines (7 December 2014), vol. VIII, 19–33 ("*SWSP*"), https://files.pca-cpa.org/pcadocs/The%20Philippines%27%20Supplemental%20Written%20Submission%20-%20Volume%20VIII%20%28Annexes%20466-499%29.pdf, accessed 4 April 2019.

[25] The procedural history of the arbitration is summarized in the Award of 12 July 2016, 11–28, paras. 26–111. For a summary of the Award on Jurisdiction, see the Press Release issued by the PCA, *Arbitration between the Republic of the Philippines and the People's Republic of China: Tribunal Renders Award on Jurisdiction and Admissibility; Will Hold Further Hearings*, 29 October 2015, http://www.pcacases.com/web/sendAttach/1503, accessed 26 March 2019. For a summary of the Award of 12 July 2016, see the Press Release issued by the PCA, *The South China Sea Arbitration The Republic of the Philippines v. the People's Republic of China: The Tribunal Renders Its Award*, 12 July 2016, https://pcacases.com/web/endAttach/1801, 26 March 2019. The documents relating to the case may be found on the PCA website, https://pca-cpa.org/en/cases/7/, accessed 26 March 2019.

China's refusal to appear before the Tribunal did not empower the Tribunal to render automatically a default judgment in favor of the Philippines. Article 9 on "Default of Appearance" of Annex VII of the Convention requires that "[b]efore making its award, the arbitral tribunal must satisfy itself not only that it has jurisdiction over the dispute but also that the claim is well founded in fact and law." Following China's rejection of the Philippine Notification and Statement of Claim, and in anticipation of China's failure to appear before the Tribunal, the latter instituted a procedure through which it would request further submissions from or pose questions to the Philippines on matters that in the Tribunal's view had not been canvassed, or had been inadequately canvassed, in the pleadings submitted by the Philippines. The Tribunal was also empowered to take any steps that it deemed necessary in order to provide each of the parties a full opportunity to present its case.[26]

Despite the fact that the Philippine *Memorial*, a copy of which had been sent to China, elaborated on Philippine Submission No. 13 that China had operated its law enforcement vessels in such a way as to create a risk of collision with Philippine official vessels, China's Position Paper did not raise any jurisdictional objection on this issue and, *a fortiori*, did not present any arguments on the merits of the Philippine claims. The Philippines submitted an expert report, the "Allen Opinion," as an annex to its *Memorial* but did not request Professor Allen to present testimony to the Tribunal during the Hearing on the Merits.[27]

The Arbitral Tribunal went to great lengths to ensure itself that Philippine Submission No. 13 was well founded in fact and in law, at the jurisdictional and merits phases of the proceedings. Following China's publication of its Position Paper, the Tribunal, in its Request for Further Written Argument, posed a question on the applicability of the exceptions to jurisdiction provided for in the Convention to Submission

[26] *South China Sea Arbitration*, Rules of Procedure, 27 August 2013, Article 25(1), 12, https://pcacases.com/web/sendAttach/233, accessed 7 April 2019.

[27] *MP*, Annex 239, Opinion of Craig H. Allen, Judson Falknor Professor of Law, University of Washington (19 March 2014), vol. VII, 371–88, https://files.pca-cpa.org/pcadocs/The%20Philippines%27%20Memorial%20-20Volume%20VII%20%28Annexes%20222-255%29.pdf, accessed 31 May 2019.

No. 13, among others.[28] The Philippine response to this question, insofar as it related to Submission No. 13, seems to have satisfied the Tribunal, as it did not pose any further question to the Philippines on the matter during the Hearing on Jurisdiction and Admissibility. On 10 November 2015, two weeks prior to the Hearing on the Merits, the Tribunal provided the Philippines an "Annex of Issues the Philippines May Wish to Present" as guidance for the Hearing.[29] The document contained, among others, a number of questions concerning Philippine Submission No. 13. The Philippines answered them during the Hearing itself, although the Philippine legal counsel did not identify the questions he was answering at any particular point.[30]

Following the closure of the Hearing on the Merits, the Tribunal decided, in February 2016, to appoint an expert to review the available documents on Submission No. 13 concerning navigational safety and to draw independent conclusions as to whether there had been violations of the navigational safety provisions covered by the Convention.[31] Later in the same month, the Tribunal informed the parties that it proposed to appoint Captain Gurpreet Singh, a UK national, as expert on navigational safety. The Philippines approved the appointment and made no further comments; China did not respond to the Tribunal.[32] In March 2016, Captain Singh's appointment was confirmed.[33] On 15 April 2016, he submitted his report, which was transmitted to the Philippines and China for their comments. The Philippines had no comments, presumably because the independent expert's report confirmed the Allen Opinion. China did not respond to the Tribunal.[34]

[28] *SWSP*, vol. I, 43–50, paras. 9.1–9.26, https://files.pca-cpa.org/pcadocs/Supplemental%20Written%20Submission%20Volume%20I.pdf, accessed 31 May 2019. The text of the Request for Further Written Argument is not available. One can only obtain it by reading the *SWSP*.

[29] Award of 12 July 2016, 21, para. 63.

[30] *South China Sea Arbitration*, Hearing on the Merits and Remaining Issues of Jurisdiction and Admissibility, Day 3 (26 November 2015), 56, https://pcacases.com/web/sendAttach/1549, accessed 2 June 2019.

[31] Award of 12 July 2016, 29, para. 84.

[32] *Ibid.*, paras. 85–86.

[33] *Ibid.*, 30, para. 88.

[34] *Ibid.*, 31, para. 91.

The Tribunal found that "China's operation of its law enforcement vessels on 28 April 2012 and 26 May 2012 created serious risk of collision and danger to Philippine ships and personnel" and that "China's operation of its law enforcement vessels on 28 April 2012 and 26 May 2012 violated Rules 2, 6, 7, 8, 15, and 16 of the Convention on the International Regulations for Preventing Collisions at Sea, 1972." Consequently, declared the Tribunal, China had breached its obligations under Article 94 of the Convention.[35] Two years after the issuance of the Award, the Chinese Society of International Law ("CSIL") published a critique of the Tribunal's decisions on jurisdiction and admissibility and on the merits relating to Philippine Submission No. 13 as part of an overall critique of the two Awards.[36] Although the critique was described as the output of a research group of the CSIL, in reality it was carried out "under the supervision and leadership of the Foreign Ministry."[37] For this reason, the CSIL's study may be taken as the expression of official Chinese views, despite its claim to being an academic study.

The Tribunal's decisions on Philippine Submission No. 13 are noteworthy, as this seems to be the first occasion in which the COLREGS, which play a central role in ensuring the safety of maritime navigation,[38] have been invoked as the legal basis for a decision on an inter-State claim concerning (near-)collision of vessels. It must be said that inter-State cases having as the central issue the responsibility of a State for the conduct of its vessels triggering a (near-)collision with the vessels of another State are not only very rare but also quite ancient indeed. In 1872, an award was

[35] *Ibid.*, 476, para. 1203.

[36] Chinese Society of International Law ("CSIL"), "The South China Sea Arbitration Awards: A Critical Study," *Chinese Journal of International Law* 17 (2018): 207–748. For an initial response to the "Critical Study," see Douglas Guilfoyle, "A New Twist in the South China Sea Arbitration: The Chinese Society of International Law's Critical Study," *ejil.talk*, 25 May 2018, ejiltalk.org/a-new-twist-in-the-south-china-sea-arbitration-the-chinese-society-of-international-laws-critical-study/, accessed 7 February 2019.

[37] Professor Bing Ling of the University of Sydney, quoted in Douglas Guilfoyle, "Taking the Party Line on the South China Sea Arbitration," *ejil.talk*, 28 May 2018, ejiltalk.org/taking-the-party-line-on-the-south-china-sea-arbitration/, accessed 16 July 2021. CSIL, "The South China Sea Arbitration Awards," 218, para. 6.

[38] Tullio Treves, "La navigation [Navigation]," in René-Jean Dupuy and Daniel Vignes (eds.), *Traité du Nouveau droit de la mer* [Treatise on the New Law of the Sea] (Paris: Éditions Économica, 1985), 728.

issued by the Portuguese envoy to Brazil in a case arising from a collision between a vessel flying the flag of Sweden-Norway anchored at the port of Asunción, in Paraguay, and a Brazilian vessel coming down the River Paraguay at full steam. The lone arbitrator, who rejected the claim for damages put forward on behalf of the first vessel, referred vaguely to a "general rule of maritime law" and "good jurisprudence."[39] He seemed to be unaware of the existence of the International Regulations for Preventing Collisions at Sea 1863, the ancestor of COLREGS, or of the fact that Brazil and Sweden-Norway were among the States that had recognized the applicability of the International Regulations to their vessels.[40]

A collision between a Spanish man-of-war and a British merchant vessel, which took place near Belize in 1884, was submitted to an arbitral commission composed of the British consul at Madrid, a lieutenant in the Spanish navy, and the Italian minister at Madrid. However, the umpire did not intervene, as the first two arbitrators managed to reach a settlement; the 1887 award was not published.[41]

[39] Albert Geouffre de Lapradelle and Nicolas Politis, *Recueil des arbitrages internationaux* [Compilation of International Arbitrations], vol. II, *1856–1872* (Paris: A. Pedone Éditeur, 1923), 706–12, https://ia802607.us.archive.org/3/items/recueildesarbitr02lapruoft/recueildesarbitr02lapruoft.pdf, accessed 6 June 2019. The Portuguese text of the award may be found in Henri La Fontaine, *Pasicrisie Internationale: Histoire documentaire des arbitrages internationaux 1794–1900* [Compendium of International Case Law: A Documentary History of International Arbitrations 1794–1900] (Berne: Imprimerie Stämpfli & Cie., 1902), 155–56, https://ia600205.us.archive.org/9/items/pasicrisieinter00fontgoog/pasicrisieinter00fontgoog.pdf, accessed 6 June 2019.

[40] Reginald Godfrey Marsden, *A Treatise on the Law of Collisions at Sea, with an Appendix Containing Extracts from the Merchant Shipping Acts, the International Regulations (of 1863 and 1880) for Preventing Collisions at Sea and Local Rules for the Same Purpose in Force in the Thames, The Mersey and Elsewhere* (London: Stevens and Sons, 1880), 135, https://ia800205.us.archive.org/26/items/cu31924022403897/cu31924022403897.pdf, accessed 6 June 2019.

[41] John Bassett Moore, *History and Digest of International Arbitrations to Which the United States Has Been a Party*, vol. V (Washington, DC: Government Printing Office, 1898), 5017, https://ia801403.us.archive.org/15/items/historyanddiges07moorgoog/historyanddiges07moorgoog.pdf, accessed 6 June 2019; A. M. Stuyt, *Survey of International Arbitrations 1794–1938* (N.p.: Springer Netherlands, 1939), 156. At the time, it was still accepted practice that the umpire intervened only when the arbitrators appointed by the two parties failed to reach agreement. Albert Geouffre de Lapradelle and Nicolas Politis (eds.), *Recueil des arbitrages internationaux* [Compilation of International Arbitrations], I, *1798–1855* (Paris: A. Pedone Éditeur, 1905), xvii–xxiv, https://ia600309.us.archive.org/19/items/recueildesarbit01lapr/recueildesarbit01lapr.pdf, 6 June 2019.

Two other circumstances should lead to increased interest in the contribution of the *South China Arbitration* to the case law relating to the COLREGS. First, the Philippines was not a party to the COLREGS 1972 at the time of the incidents that were the object of its submission. The Philippines acceded to COLREGS only in June 2013, nearly six months after the initiation of the *Arbitration*.[42] Nevertheless, the Arbitral Tribunal held that the COLREGS were binding on the Philippines, as they were "generally accepted international regulations" within the meaning of Article 94 of the Convention.[43] Consequently, the Philippines could invoke them in the dispute with China. Second, a post-arbitration rationalization of China's conduct in the two incidents is available, formulated by the CSIL. This post-arbitration rationalization obviates the disadvantages for the commentator of China's refusal to appear before the Arbitral Tribunal. The CSIL challenged the Tribunal's jurisdiction, based on the alleged absence of a provision in the Convention that enabled the application of the COLREGS to the territorial sea of Scarborough Shoal, and the Tribunal's decision on the merits, on the grounds that the law enforcement activities carried out by the Chinese vessels constituted exceptions to the application of the COLREGS.

Scholarly commentary devoted to the Tribunal's decisions on Philippine Submission No. 13 is quite thin, perhaps because of the perceived technical nature of the COLREGS. Overviews are provided by Oxman,[44]

[42] International Maritime Organization ("IMO"), *Status of IMO Treaties: Comprehensive Information on the Status of Multilateral Conventions and Instruments in Respect of Which the International Maritime Organization or Its Secretary-General Performs Depositary or Other Functions* (London: IMO, 2019), 95, http://www.imo.org/en/About/Conventions/StatusOfConventions/Documents/Status%20-%202018.pdf, accessed 14 June 2019; Republic of the Philippines, Maritime Industry Authority, *List of IMO Conventions Ratified by the Philippines* (July 2018), 2, http://marina.gov.ph/wp-content/uploads/2018/07/LIST-OF-IMO-CONVENTIONS-RATIFIED-BY-THE-PHILIPPINES.pdf, accessed 14 June 2019.

[43] Award of 12 July 2016, 422, para. 1063.

[44] Bernard H. Oxman, "The South China Sea Arbitration Award," *University of Miami International and Comparative Law Review* 24 (2017): 274–77, https://repository.law.miami.edu/cgi/viewcontent.cgi?article=1294&context=umiclr, accessed 2 June 2019. Oxman was a member of the Philippine legal team in the case.

Paik,[45] and Tanaka.[46] As we shall see, the CSIL undertook an extended critique of the Tribunal's decisions on Submission No. 13.[47] These decisions, together with the Tribunal's decisions regarding the escort by Chinese official vessels of Chinese fishing vessels engaged in illegal activity in the Philippine EEZ (Submission No. 9), and China's action to prevent the rotation and resupply of Philippine personnel stationed at Second Thomas Shoal (Submission No. 14(a), (b), and (c)), were analyzed by Moore from the broader perspective of their implications for the freedom of navigation and the use of force.[48] In other commentaries on the *Arbitration*, the subject is dealt with quite briefly,[49] if not neglected altogether.[50] There has thus been no full-length scholarly study devoted

[45] Jin-Hyun Paik, "South China Sea Arbitral Awards: Main Findings and Assessment," *Max Planck Yearbook of United Nations Law* 20 (2017): 398–99.

[46] Yoshifumi Tanaka, *The South China Sea Arbitration: Toward an International Legal Order in the Oceans* (Oxford: Hart, 2019), 148–51.

[47] CSIL, "The South China Sea Arbitration Awards," 794–806, paras. 827–57.

[48] Cameron Moore, "The Arbitral Award in the Matter of the South China Sea between the Philippines and China: What are the Implications for Freedom of Navigation and the Use of Force?" *Asia-Pacific Journal of Ocean Law and Policy* 2 (2017): 117–39, and *Freedom of Navigation and the Law of the Sea: Warships, States and the Use of Force* (Kindle edition; London: Routledge, 2021), Chapter 1, 52, Chapter 4, 110–14.

[49] The COLREGS are mentioned in a footnote in Vincent P. Cogliati-Bantz, "Current Legal Developments: The South China Sea Arbitration (The Republic of the Philippines v. The People's Republic of China)," *International Journal of Marine and Coastal Law* 31 (2016): 771. Submission No. 13 is discussed in two paragraphs in María Teresa Infante Caffi, "Arbitraje Filipinas c. China en el Mar del Sur de China [Philippines v. China Arbitration in the South China Sea]" *Anuario de Derecho Público* [Yearbook of Public Law, Diego Portales University] (2017): 152, https://derecho.udp.cl/cms/wp-content/uploads/2020/06/Anuario-Derecho-Publico-2017.pdf, accessed 15 July 2021, and in two sentences in Elena Pineros Polo, "Arbitraje del mar del sur de China. la estrategia procesal de la República Popular de China [The South China Sea Arbitration. The Procedural Strategy of the People's Republic of China]," *Revista Electrónica de Estudios Internacionales* [Electronic Journal of International Studies] 35 (2018): 19–20, www.reei.org/index.php/revista/.../09_Nota_PINEROS_Elena.pdf, accessed 9 February 2019.

[50] There is no discussion at all in Romain Le Bœuf, "Différend en Mer de Chine méridionale. Sentence arbitrale du 12 juillet 2016 [The South China Sea Dispute: Arbitral Award of 12 July 2016]," *Annuaire Français de Droit International* [French Yearbook of International Law] 52 (2016): 159–81, and in Jean-Paul Pancracio, "La sentence arbitrale sur la mer de Chine méridionale du 12 juillet 2016 [The South China Sea Arbitral Award of 12 July 2016]," *Annuaire Français de Relations Internationales* [French Yearbook

exclusively to the Tribunal's decisions concerning Submission No. 13. It is this gap in the scholarly literature that this book aims to fill.

III. Overview of the Book

Chapter 2 presents the uncontested factual background of Philippine Submission No. 13. On 28 April 2012, two Philippine vessels, *Barko ng Republika ng Pilipinas* (Ship of the Republic of the Philippines, "BRP") *Pampanga* and BRP *Edsa II*, nearly collided with Chinese vessel Fisheries Law Enforcement Command ("FLEC") 310 in the waters around Scarborough Shoal, as a result of the dangerous maneuvers of the latter. On 26 May 2012, Philippine vessel Monitoring, Control and Surveillance ("MCS") 3008 was involved in near-collisions with several Chinese vessels, resulting from the dangerous maneuvers of the latter, again in the waters around Scarborough Shoal. The factual background was uncontested by China, an attitude that contrasted with its vigorous efforts to present its own version of the facts in relation to the Philippine Submissions on the protection and preservation of the marine environment. The chapter suggests that China refrained from contesting the Philippine account in order to avoid the embarrassing experience of 2009, when the US charged Chinese vessels with provoking near-collisions with USNS *Impeccable*. China's strenuous denial of the facts was proven to be wrong when the US published video footage of the incident.

Since the COLREGS are incorporated into the Convention as "generally accepted international regulations," it is incumbent on us to understand the historical process whereby they became "generally accepted international regulations," binding even on States that are parties to the Convention but are not parties to the COLREGS. Chapter 3 will trace the historical process that began in the second half of the nineteenth century, by which mariners and a large number of States accepted that the International Regulations for Preventing Collisions at Sea, which were addressed to vessels, were binding on States. Chapter 3 argues that mariners accepted the COLREGS, also known as the "Rules of the Road," because the latter were drawn from their own practice and were characterized by relative simplicity. States realized that regulations to prevent collisions had to be international in scope to be effective and

of International Relations] 18 (2017): 639–57, http://www.afri-ct.org/wp-content/uploads/2018/06/Article-Pancracio.pdf, accessed 5 February 2019.

accepted the obligation to take measures to give effect to the Rules of the Road.

Chapter 4 will determine the scope of the jurisdiction conferred on the Arbitral Tribunal by the "generally accepted international regulations" clause in Article 94 of the Convention. After summarizing scholarly interpretations of the clause, it sets out to prove, by examining the preparatory work of the United Nations International Law Commission ("ILC") for the Geneva Convention on the High Seas 1958 that the COLREGS are the paradigmatic "generally accepted international regulations." Chapter 4 will also seek to determine whether the jurisdiction of tribunals constituted under the Convention is circumscribed, in disputes involving the COLREGS, by one exception set out in Part XV of the Convention, the "law enforcement activities" exception or by the lack of an enabling clause, as the CSIL argues.

Chapter 5 concentrates on the Arbitral Tribunal's analysis of the conduct of China's vessels that constituted breaches of the COLREGS and consequently, of the Convention, for which China was held responsible. The COLREGS rules that were breached by China are classified into three groups: the general rule of responsibility (Rule 2), rules applicable to the conduct of vessels in any condition of visibility (Rules 6, 7, and 8), and rules applicable to the conduct of vessels in sight of one another (Rules 15 and 16). Under each heading, the scope of the rules is explained before violations of the rules by the Chinese vessels are described in detail.

Chapter 6 examines the CSIL's post-arbitration critique of the conduct of China's vessels, which amounts to the claim that collisions are legitimate instruments of China's foreign policy. The justifications offered by the CSIL are analyzed under three separate headings: the existence or absence of special circumstances; the legality of the use of force against warships; and the legality of the use of force in maritime law enforcement. It is argued that the alleged violation of the human rights of Chinese fishermen on a separate incident, which took place on 10 April 2012, could not possibly constitute "special circumstances" that justified the dangerous conduct of Chinese vessels on 28 April and on 26 May 2012. It is further argued that the Philippine vessels as warships enjoyed sovereign immunity and that State practice prohibits the use of force against such vessels and condemns the deliberate resort to collisions against them. Finally, even assuming that China was authorized to use force in a maritime law enforcement operation, international case law requires the firing of warning shots and the use of force having in mind considerations of humanity, while State practice demonstrates that States draw the line at deliberately provoking collisions and prosecute State officials that fail to comply with the COLREGS in maritime law enforcement operations. In particular, it discusses a little-known judgment of the Italian Supreme Court in 2014 that wholly contradicts the CSIL's argument.

After summarizing the arguments of the book, Chapter 7 concludes that China's resort to collisions as instruments of foreign policy violates the COLREGS, the United Nations Convention on the Law of the Sea, and international law; expresses the hope that a major disaster will not be required to convince China to change its conduct; and regrets that there are few grounds for being so sanguine.

References

Allianz Global Corporate and Specialty. *Safety and Shipping Review 2018: An Annual Review of Trends and Developments in Shipping Losses and Safety*. Munich: Allianz Global Corporate and Specialty SE, 2018, https://www.agcs.allianz.com/assets/PDFs/Reports/AGCS_Safety_Shipping_Review_2018.pdf, accessed 7 November 2018.

———. *Safety and Shipping Review 2020: An Annual Review of Trends and Developments in Shipping Losses and Safety*. Munich: Allianz Global Corporate and Specialty SE, 2020, https://www.agcs.allianz.com/content/dam/onemarketing/agcs/agcs/reports/AGCS-Safety-Shipping-Review-2020.pdf, accessed 18 October 2021.

Butt, Nickie et al. *15 Years of Shipping Accidents: A Review for WWF*. Southampton: Southampton Solent University, School of Maritime [sic] and Technology, 2013, http://awsassets.panda.org/downloads/15_years_of_shipping_accidents_a_review_for_wwf_.pdf, accessed 14 June 2019.

Center for Strategic and International Studies. "Are Maritime Law Enforcement Forces Destabilizing Asia?" *China Power Project*, 2021, https://chinapower.csis.org/maritime-forces-destabilizing-asia/, accessed 13 October 2021.

Chagos Marine Protected Area Arbitration (Mauritius v. UK). Award of 18 March 2015, http://www.pcacases.com/pcadocs/MU-UK%2020150318%20Award.pdf, accessed 3 May 2019.

Chinese Society of International Law. "The South China Sea Arbitration Awards: A Critical Study." *Chinese Journal of International Law* 17 (2018): 207–748.

Cogliati-Bantz, Vincent P. "Current Legal Developments: The South China Sea Arbitration (The Republic of the Philippines v. The People's Republic of China)." *International Journal of Marine and Coastal Law* 31 (2016): 759–74.

Convention for the Pacific Settlement of International Disputes. Done at The Hague, 18 October 1907, https://pca-cpa.org/wp-content/uploads/sites/6/2016/01/1907-Convention-for-the-Pacific-Settlement-of-International-Disputes.pdf, accessed 4 April 2019.

Convention on the International Regulations for Preventing Collisions at Sea. Adopted at London on 20 October 1972. Entered into force 15 July 1977. Consolidated text as amended in 1981, 1987, 1989, 1993, 2001 and 2007, http://www.ecolregs.com/index.php?option=com_k2&view=itemlist&layout=category&Itemid=505&lang=en, accessed 31 May 2019.

Guilfoyle, Douglas. "A New Twist in the South China Sea Arbitration: The Chinese Society of International Law's Critical Study." *ejil.talk*, 25 May 2018, ejiltalk.org/a-new-twist-in-the-south-china-sea-arbitration-the-chinese-society-of-international-laws-critical-study/, accessed 7 February 2019.

———. "Taking the Party Line on the South China Sea Arbitration." *ejil.talk*, 28 May 2018, ejiltalk.org/taking-the-party-line-on-the-south-china-sea-arbitration/, accessed 7 February 2019.

Infante Caffi, María Teresa. "Arbitraje Filipinas c. China en el Mar del Sur de China [Philippines v. China Arbitration in the South China Sea]." *Anuario de Derecho Público* [Yearbook of Public Law, Diego Portales University] (2017): 117–56, https://derecho.udp.cl/cms/wp-content/uploads/2020/06/Anuario-Derecho-Publico-2017.pdf, accessed 15 July 2021.

International Maritime Organization (IMO). *Status of IMO Treaties: Comprehensive Information on the Status of Multilateral Conventions and Instruments in respect of Which the International Maritime Organization or Its Secretary-General Performs Depositary or Other Functions*. London: IMO, 2018, http://www.imo.org/en/About/Conventions/StatusOfConventions/Documents/Status%20-%202018.pdf, accessed 21 October 2018.

International Tribunal for the Law of the Sea (ITLOS). *New Arbitrator and President Appointed in the Arbitral Proceedings Instituted by the Republic of the Philippines Against the People's Republic of China*. Doc. ITLOS/Press 197 (24 June 2013), https://www.itlos.org/fileadmin/itlos/documents/press_releases_english/PR_197_E.pdf, accessed 26 March 2019.

La Fontaine, Henri. *Pasicrisie Internationale: Histoire documentaire des arbitrages internationaux 1794–1900* [Compendium of International Caselaw: Documentary History of International Arbitrations 1794–1900]. Berne: Imprimerie Stämpfli & Cie., 1902, https://ia600205.us.archive.org/9/items/pasicrisieinter00fontgoog/pasicrisieinter00fontgoog.pdf, accessed 6 June 2019.

Lapradelle, Albert Geouffre de, and Nicolas Politis (eds.). *Recueil des arbitrages internationaux* [Compilation of International Arbitrations]. Vol. I, *1798–1855*. Paris: A. Pedone Éditeur, 1905, https://ia600309.us.archive.org/19/items/recueildesarbit01lapr/recueildesarbit01lapr.pdf, accessed 6 June 2019.

———. *Recueil des arbitrages internationaux* [Compilation of International Arbitrations]. Vol. II. *1856–1872*. Paris: A. Pedone Éditeur, 1923, https://ia802607.us.archive.org/3/items/recueildesarbitr02lapruoft/recueildesarbitr02lapruoft.pdf, accessed 6 June 2019.

Le Bœuf, Romain. "Différend en Mer de Chine méridionale: Sentence arbitrale du 12 juillet 2016 [The South China Sea Dispute: Arbitral Award of 12 July 2016]." *Annuaire Français de Droit International* [French Yearbook of International Law] 52 (2016): 159–81.

Marsden, Reginald Godfrey. *A Treatise on the Law of Collisions at Sea, with an Appendix Containing Extracts from the Merchant Shipping Acts, the International Regulations (of 1863 and 1880) for Preventing Collisions at Sea and Local Rules for the Same Purpose in Force in the Thames, The Mersey and Elsewhere*. London: Stevens and Sons, 1880, https://ia800205.us.archive.org/26/items/cu31924022403897/cu31924022403897.pdf, accessed 9 June 2019.

McLaughlin, Rob. "An Incident in the South China Sea." *International Law Studies* 96 (2020): 505–28, https://digital-commons.usnwc.edu/cgi/viewcontent.cgi?article=2930&context=ils, accessed 13 October 2021.

Moore, Cameron. "The Arbitral Award in the Matter of the South China Sea between the Philippines and China: What are the Implications for Freedom of Navigation and the Use of Force?" *Asia-Pacific Journal of Ocean Law and Policy* 2 (2017): 117–39.

———. *Freedom of Navigation and the Law of the Sea: Warships, States and the Use of Force*, Kindle edition. London: Routledge, 2021.

Moore, John Bassett. *History and Digest of International Arbitrations to Which the United States Has Been a Party*. Vol. V. Washington, DC: Government Printing Office, 1898, https://ia801403.us.archive.org/15/items/historyanddiges07moorgoog/historyanddiges07moorgoog.pdf, accessed 9 June 2019.

Oxman, Bernard H. "The South China Sea Arbitration Award." *University of Miami International and Comparative Law Review* 24 (2017): 235–84, https://repository.law.miami.edu/cgi/viewcontent.cgi?article=1294&context=umiclr, accessed 2 June 2019.

Paik, Jin-Hyun. "South China Sea Arbitral Awards: Main Findings and Assessment." *Max Planck Yearbook of United Nations Law* 20 (2017): 367–407.

Pancracio, Jean-Paul. "La sentence arbitrale sur la mer de Chine méridionale du 12 juillet 2016 [The South China Sea Arbitral Award of 12 July 2016]." *Annuaire Français de Relations Internationales* [French Yearbook of International Relations] 18 (2017): 639–57, http://www.afri-ct.org/wp-content/uploads/2018/06/Article-Pancracio.pdf, accessed 5 February 2019.

Permanent Court of Arbitration. *Arbitration Between the Republic of the Philippines and the People's Republic of China: Tribunal Renders Award on Jurisdiction and Admissibility; Will Hold Further Hearings*, 29 October 2015, http://www.pcacases.com/web/sendAttach/1503, accessed 26 March 2019.

———. *The South China Sea Arbitration (The Republic of the Philippines v. the People's Republic of China). The Tribunal Renders Its Award*, 12 July 2016, https://pcacases.com/web/endAttach/1801, 26 March 2019.

Philippines, Republic of the. Maritime Industry Authority. *List of IMO Conventions Ratified by the Philippines* (July 2018), http://marina.gov.ph/wp-content/uploads/2018/07/LIST-OF-IMO-CONVENTIONS-RATIFIED-BY-THE-PHILIPPINES.pdf, accessed 14 June 2019.

Pineros Polo, Elena. "Arbitraje del mar del sur de China: la estrategia procesal de la República Popular de China [The South China Sea Arbitration: The Procedural Strategy of the People's Republic of China]." *Revista Electrónica de Estudios Internacionales* [Electronic Journal of International Studies] 35 (2018): 1–23, www.reei.org/index.php/revista/.../09_Nota_PINEROS_Elena.pdf, accessed 9 February 2019.

South China Sea Arbitration. Award of 12 July 2016, http://www.pcacases.com/pcadocs/PH-CN%20-%2020160712%20-%20Award.pdf, accessed 30 May 2019.

———. Award on Jurisdiction and Admissibility (29 October 2015), https://pcacases.com/web/sendAttach/2579, accessed 29 May 2019.

———. Hearing on the Merits and Remaining Issues of Jurisdiction and Admissibility. Final Transcript, Day 3 (26 November 2015), https://pcacases.com/web/sendAttach/1549, accessed 2 June 2019.

———. *Memorial of the Philippines* (30 March 2014). Vol. I, http://www.pcacases.com/pcadocs/Memorial%20of%20the%20Philippines%20Volume%20I.pdf, accessed 30 May 2019.

———. Annex 239. Opinion of Craig H. Allen, Judson Falknor Professor of Law, University of Washington (19 March 2014). Vol. VII, 371–88, https://files.pca-cpa.org/pcadocs/The%20Philippines%27%20Memorial%20-20Volume%20VII%20%28Annexes%20222-255%29.pdf, accessed 31 May 2019.

———. Annex 467. People's Republic of China, Position Paper of the Government of the People's Republic of China on the Matter of Jurisdiction in the South China Sea Arbitration Initiated by the Republic of the Philippines (7 December 2014). Vol. VIII, 19–33, https://files.pca-cpa.org/pcadocs/The%20Philippines%27%20Supplemental%20Written%20Submission%20-%20Volume%20VIII%20%28Annexes%20466-499%29.pdf, accessed 4 April 2019.

———. Notification and Statement of Claim of the Republic of the Philippines, 22 January 2013, http://www.philippineembassy-usa.org/uploads/pdfs/embassy/2013/2013-0122-Notification%20and%20Statement%20of%20Claim%20on%20West%20Philippine%20Sea.pdf, accessed 3 May 2019.

———. Rules of Procedure, 27 August 2013, https://pcacases.com/web/sendAttach/233, accessed 7 April 2019.

———. *Supplemental Documents of the Philippines* (19 November 2015). Annex 624. Ministry of Foreign Affairs, People's Republic of China, *Foreign Ministry Spokesperson Hua Chunying's Regular Press Conference* (9 April 2015). Vol. I, 165, http://www.pcacases.com/pcadocs/The%20Philippines%27%20Supplemental%20Documents%20-%20Volume%20I%20%28Annexes%20607-667%29.pdf, accessed 29 May 2019.

———. *Supplemental Written Submission of the Philippines* (16 March 2015). Vol. I, https://files.pca-cpa.org/pcadocs/Supplemental%20Written%20Submission%20Volume%20I.pdf, accessed 31 May 2019.

Stuyt, A. M. *Survey of International Arbitrations 1794–1938*. N.p.: Springer Netherlands, 1939.

Tanaka, Yoshifumi. *The South China Sea Arbitration: Toward an International Legal Order in the Oceans*. Oxford: Hart, 2019.

United Nations Convention on the Law of the Sea. Concluded at Montego Bay on 10 December 1982. Entered into force 16 November 1994, http://www.un.org/Depts/los/convention_agreements/texts/unclos/closindx.htm, accessed 21 March 2019.

United Nations. Codification Division. *Diplomatic Conferences: Third United Nations Conference on the Law of the Sea (1973–1982)*, http://legal.un.org/diplomaticconferences/1973_los/, accessed 14 June 2019.

———. Office of Legal Affairs. Treaty Section. Treaty Collection. *Multilateral Treaties Deposited with the Secretary-General: Chapter XXI: Law of the Sea*, https://treaties.un.org/Pages/ViewDetailsIII.aspx?src=TREATY&mtdsg_no=XXI-6&chapter=21&Temp=mtdsg3&clang=_en, accessed 4 April 2019.

CHAPTER 2

The Uncontested Factual Background

Philippine Submission No. 13 to the Arbitral Tribunal constituted under Annex VII of the United Nations Convention on the Law of the Sea ("Convention") alleged that:

> China has breached its obligations under the Convention by operating its law enforcement vessels in a dangerous manner causing serious risk of collision to Philippine vessels navigating in the vicinity of Scarborough Shoal.[1]

The Philippine account of the incidents that occurred in the waters around Scarborough Shoal on 28 April and 26 May 2012 was uncontested, not because China failed to appear before the Arbitral Tribunal, but because China, from the first moment that the Philippines protested over the conduct of the Chinese vessels, did not contest it. It is suggested here that China's somewhat surprising failure to deny the facts is linked to the public unraveling of its denials of the conduct of Chinese vessels in an encounter with the US vessel USNS *Impeccable* in 2009.

[1] *South China Sea Arbitration*, Award of 12 July 2016, 42, para. 113, http://www.pcacases.com/pcadocs/PH-CN%20-%2020160712%20-%20Award.pdf, accessed 2 June 2019. *United Nations Convention on the Law of the Sea*, concluded at Montego Bay on 10 December, entered into force 16 November 1994, http://www.un.org/Depts/los/convention_agreements/texts/unclos/closindx.htm, accessed 21 March 2019.

A. C. Robles Jr., *Vessel Collisions in the Law of the Sea*,
https://doi.org/10.1007/978-981-16-9793-7_2

I. The Philippine Account

The near-collisions on 28 April 2012 and 26 May 2012 are recounted in confidential Philippine documents that would not have been made accessible to the public had it not been for the *Arbitration*.

A. The Incidents of 28 April 2012: The Near-Collisions of BRP Pampanga *and BRP* Edsa II *with FLEC 310*

A report on the incidents was submitted on the very day that it took place by the commanding officer of the Philippine Coast Guard Vessel *Barko ng Republika ng Pilipinas* (Ship of the Republic of the Philippines, "BRP") *Pampanga* (identified as Search and Rescue Vessel ["SARV"]-003 in the report), one of the two Philippine vessels that nearly collided with the Chinese vessel Fisheries Law Enforcement Command ("FLEC") 310.[2] The brief report was followed a few days later by a more detailed account from personnel of the Bureau of Fisheries and Aquatic Resources ("BFAR") who were on board the BRP *Edsa II* (identified as SARV-002 in the report).[3]

The specifications of FLEC 310 are provided by China's own Ministry of Agriculture. FLEC 310

> has a gross tonnage of 2,580 tonnes, measures 108 meters long and 14 meters wide. It has a range of 6,000 nautical miles and can sail for 60 days and nights and go to international unrestricted navigation areas. The vessel has a maximum speed up to 22 knots. It is equipped with an onboard Z-9A helicopter, a modernized surface broadband satellite communication system, a photoelectric tracer evidence collection system, a maritime

[2] *South China Sea Arbitration, Memorial of the Philippines* (30 March 2014), Annex 78, Report from Commanding Officer SARV-003 Philippine Coast Guard to Commander, Coast Guard District, Northwestern Luzon, Philippine Coast Guard (28 April 2012), vol. IV, 147–58 ("*MP*"), https://files.pca-cpa.org/pcadocs/The%20Philippines%27%20Memorial%20-%20Volume%20IV%20%28Annexes%2061-102%29.pdf, accessed 2 June 2019.

[3] *MP*, Annex 80, Report from Relly B. Garcia et al., FRPLEU/QRT [Fishery Resource Protection and Law Enforcement/Quick Response Team] Officers, Bureau of Fisheries and Aquatic Resources, Republic of the Philippines (2 May 2012), vol. IV, 163–95, https://files.pca-cpa.org/pcadocs/The%20Philippines%27%20Memorial%20-%20Volume%20IV%20%28Annexes%2061-102%29.pdf, accessed 2 June 2019. The correct name of the vessel is "Edsa Dos" but it is referred to as "Edsa II" in the *Memorial* as well as in the Award of 12 July 2016.

ultraviolet imager and a color fish finder. In China's current fisheries law enforcement fleets, this ship is the fastest and most advanced ship in overall performance and has the most comprehensive special equipment.[4]

In its written and oral submissions, the Philippines did not describe the features of the Philippine Coast Guard vessels, but we know from other sources that each weighed 540 tons, about one-fifth of the tonnage of FLEC 310.[5]

On 28 April 2012, BRP *Pampanga*, which was on maritime patrol and law enforcement in the area of Scarborough Shoal, established contact with BRP *Edsa II*, which was to relieve it and take over from its duty.[6] BRP *Edsa II* was positioned at approximately 500 yards from BRP *Pampanga*; the captain and commander of the first boarded the second for briefing and turnover. At around 0900H, while BRP *Pampanga* was lying to (stationary), it was approached by FLEC 310 from port (left) to dead ahead, at a distance of about 600 yards, with a speed of 20.3 knots.[7] At 0915H, FLEC 310 passed from the starboard (right) quarter to the port (left) side of BRP *Edsa II* at a distance of 200 yards with a speed of

[4] *MP*, Annex 111, People's Republic of China, Ministry of Agriculture, "More Powerful Equipment Added to Enforce Rights and Protect Fisheries" (9 March 2010), vol. V, 77, https://files.pca-cpa.org/pcadocs/The%20Philippines%27%20Memorial%20-%20Volume%20V%20%28Annexes%20103-157%29.pdf, accessed 2 June 2019; quoted in *MP*, vol. I, p. 206, https://files.pca-cpa.org/pcadocs/Memorial%20of%20the%20Philippines%20Volume%20I.pdf, accessed 2 June 2019. A nautical mile is equivalent to 1852 meters or 6076.115 feet; one degree of latitude corresponds to 60 nautical miles. George K. Walker, *Definitions for the Law of the Sea: Terms Not Defined by the Convention* (Leiden: Martinus Nijhoff Publishers, 2012), 52.

[5] Center for Strategic and International Studies (CSIS), "Are Maritime Law Enforcement Forces Destabilizing Asia?", *China Power Project* (2018), https://chinapower.csis.org/maritime-forces-destabilizing-asia/, accessed 16 June 2019.

[6] *MP*, Annex 80, 189. There are two photographs of this part of the incident at 190, but the quality of the photographs leaves much to be desired.

[7] *MP*, Annex 78, 155; *MP*, vol. I, 206–07; *South China Sea Arbitration*, Award of 12 July 2016, 418, para. 1047, http://www.pcacases.com/pcadocs/PH-CN%20-%2020160712%20-%20Award.pdf, accessed 2 June 2019. "Dead ahead" means "exactly ahead on the ships fore and aft line." C. W. T. Layton et al., *Dictionary of Nautical Words and Terms* (2nd ed; Glasgow: Brown, Son & Ferguson Ltd., Naval Publishers, 1982), 119. A knot is a nautical unit of velocity representing a speed of 6080 feet per hour, 101.3 feet per minute, 1.69 ft. per second. Nearly equal to .5 meters per second. One meter per second = 3.944 knots. It is the only unit of velocity in existence. The name is derived from the knots in the common log line. *Ibid.*, 216.

20.6 knots. While the Philippine vessels did not suffer any damage, the maneuvers of FLEC 310 generated two-meter-high waves in its wake, battering two Philippine rubber boats that were transferring personnel.[8] The incidents were "properly documented with video footage covered by PAO [Public Affairs Office] personnel" on board the BRP *Pampanga*, which arrived safely at Pier 13 of South Harbor, Manila, at 2045H.[9]

The Philippine Coast Guard described the conduct of FLEC 310 as "bullying" and as a "violation of the International Code of Conduct [sic] placing at hazard/great risk the safety of the vessels and the personnel on board in such close call or near collision situations" and recommended that the Philippine government, preferably the Department of Foreign Affairs ("DFA"), issue a statement in response to the bullying.[10] On 30 April, the DFA expressed its "grave concern" to China's Embassy in Manila over the "provocative and extremely dangerous maneuvers" undertaken by FLEC 310 on 28 April.[11] The Philippines pointed out that its vessels had not instigated any action that would necessitate the provocative actions of FLEC 310 and that they had not reacted to the latter's maneuvers. The Philippines requested that "for the safety of vessels" China should "instruct its ships to observe" the COLREGS 1972.[12] No reference was made in the Philippine protest to the video footage of the incidents.

[8] *MP*, Annex 78, 55; *MP*, vol. I, 206–07; Award of 12 July 2016, 418, para. 1049. The "wake" refers to the water immediately astern of a moving vessel. It is disturbed by vessel's motion through it and by the subsequent filling up of the cavity made. Layton et al., *Dictionary*, 425.

[9] *MP*, Annex 78, 156.

[10] *Ibid.*, 157. It may be presumed that the authors of the report who referred to the "International Code of Conduct" had in mind the COLREGS, as it was the latter expression that was used by the DFA in its Note Verbale to China's Embassy in Manila.

[11] The Philippines also registered a protest concerning an incident on 26 April 2012, which was not included in the Philippine Submission to the Arbitral Tribunal.

[12] *MP*, Annex 209, Note Verbale from the Department of Foreign Affairs of the Philippines to the Embassy of the People's Republic of China in Manila, No. 12–1222 (30 April 2012), vol. VI, 394, https://files.pca-cpa.org/pcadocs/The%20Philippines%27%20Memorial%20-%20Volume%20VI%20%28Annexes%20158-221%29.pdf, accessed 2 June 2019. *International Convention on the International Regulations for Preventing Collisions at Sea*, adopted at London on 20 October 1972, entered into force 15 July 1977, consolidated text as amended in 1981, 1987, 1989, 1993, 2001 and 2007, http://www.ecolregs.com/index.php?option=com_k2&view=itemlist&layout=category&Itemid=505&lang=en, accessed 31 May 2019.

China's response in May 2012 to the Philippine protest made no allusion whatsoever to the COLREGS. Whether or not the Chinese government gave instructions to its vessels to comply with them, Chinese vessels again engaged, nearly a month later, in dangerous maneuvers that could have resulted in collisions with a Philippine vessel.

B. The Incidents of 26 May 2012: The Near-Collisions of MCS 3008 with Several Chinese Vessels

The series of near-collisions of 26 May 2012, which were reported by BFAR personnel on board the Philippine vessel, saw on the Philippine side, a BFAR Monitoring, Control, and Surveillance ("MCS") 3008 vessel, and on the Chinese side, FLEC 306 and China Marine Surveillance ("CMS") 71 and 84.[13] The MCS 3008 is a small, 90-ton vessel, measuring 30 meters in length. CMS 71 is significantly larger, at 1111 tons and 74 meters.[14] The CMS 84 is a 1500-ton vessel, 88 meters long, 12 meters wide, with molded depth of 5.6 meters, draft of 3.581 meters, displacement of 1740 tons, 50-person crew, and cruising endurance of 5000 nautical miles.[15] FLEC 306 is reported to be 56 meters long, 7.8

[13] *MP*, Annex 82, Report from Angelito A. Arunco, et al., FRPLEU-QRT Officers, Bureau of Fisheries and Aquatic Resources, Republic of the Philippines, to Director, Bureau of Fisheries and Aquatic Resources, Republic of the Philippines (28 May 2012), vol. IV, 201–08, https://files.pca-cpa.org/pcadocs/The%20Philippines%27%20Memorial%20-%20Volume%20IV%20%28Annexes%2061-102%29.pdf, accessed 2 June 2019.

[14] *MP*, vol. I, 203, paras. 6.115, 6.116.

[15] *MP*, Annex 315, "China Marine Surveillance 84 Boat Out into the South China Sea", Xinhua (8 May 2011), vol. X, 103, https://files.pca-cpa.org/pcadocs/The%20Philippines%27%20Memorial%20-%20Volume%20X%20%28Annexes%20307-343%29.pdf, accessed 2 June 2019. "Molded depth" means the vertical distance amid ships between the following points: (a) from the line of the upper deck at the vessel's side or, if the vessel has rounded gunwales, from the intersection of the line of the upper deck extended to the molded line of the shell plating as though the gunwales were of angular design; (b) to the top of the flat keel, to the lower edge of the keel rabbet if the vessel is of wood or composite structure, or to the point where the line of the flat of the bottom extended inward cuts the side of the keel if the vessel's lower part is hollow or has thick garboards. *Code of Federal Regulations*, Volume 2, Title 46—Shipping, Section 69.53—Definitions (Washington, DC: Government Printing Office, 2010), https://www.gpo.gov/fdsys/pkg/CFR-2010-title46-vol2/xml/CFR-2010-title46-vol2-sec69-53.xml, accessed 9 November 2018. "Displacement" refers to the amount of

meters wide, and 3.85 meters high, with a maximum speed of 18 knots and a range of 2000 nautical miles.[16]

On 26 May 2012, at approximately 1550H, MCS 3008 began to traverse the territorial sea of Scarborough Shoal to supply BRP *Corregidor*, a Philippine Coast Guard vessel. At a distance of approximately seven nautical miles from Scarborough Shoal, CMS 71 advanced toward MCS 3008. After a few minutes, CMS 71 increased speed at less than 100 yards from MCS 3008 and attempted to cross its port bow.[17] MCS 3008 increased its speed to 20 knots, altered course to starboard, and then passed through the rear of CMS 71 in order to evade possible impact.[18] CMS 71 immediately swung to its starboard and attempted to cross MCS 3008's starboard bow. To avoid a collision, MCS 3008 immediately maneuvered hard port and then passed through the rear of CMS 71.[19] After MCS 3008 had twice steered clear from possible collisions, another Chinese vessel, FLEC 306, steered toward MCS 3008 and aimed to cross its starboard bow. A collision was avoided only because MCS 3008 increased speed to 22 knots and swerved toward the rear of FLEC 306.[20]

MCS 3008 was then pursued by CMS 84, CMS 71, and FLEC 306 until MCS 3008 approached BRP *Corregidor*.[21] At around 1652H, nearly an hour after the first near-collision, while MCS 3008 was alongside the BRP *Corregidor*, CMS 84 passed through its starboard side at less than 100 yards. CMS 84 eventually stopped and positioned itself on the port

water displaced by a floating vessel in a given condition. It may be expressed in tons, or volume in cubic feet; tons being weight of vessel and contents, volume being that of the immersed part of vessel. Layton et al., *Dictionary*, 128. "Draft" ("draught" in British English) refers to the depth in water at which a ship floats. *Ibid.*, 134.

[16] *MP*, Annex 317, Liang Ganghua, "China's First Large Fishery Law Enforcement Vessel Permanently Stationed at the Xisha Islands Is Officially Placed Into Service", Xinhua (2 September 2011), vol. X, 115, https://files.pca-cpa.org/pcadocs/The%20Philippines%27%20Memorial%20-%20Volume%20X%20%28Annexes%20307-343%29.pdf, accessed 2 June 2019.

[17] The front part of a ship is called the "bow" or the "bows." *Collins English Dictionary* (Glasgow: HarperCollins Publishers, 2019), https://www.collinsdictionary.com/dictionary/english/bow, accessed 16 June 2019.

[18] *MP*, Annex 82, 204, para. 1.A.

[19] *Ibid.*, para. 1.B.

[20] *Ibid.*, para. 1.C.

[21] *Ibid.*, 205–06, para. 1.D.

quarter of MCS 3008 at a distance of less than 100 yards. FLEC 301 was stationed at the port beam at a distance of 1000 yards.[22]

At 1715H, after checking that the highest tide had dropped by only a few meters, MCS 3008 decided to proceed to the Scarborough Shoal lagoon.[23] As MCS 3008 pulled away from BRP *Corregidor*, CMS 84 again began to chase it. Sensing that the latter was aiming to cross through its front bow, MCS 3008 increased speed, which eventually caused CMS 84 to be left behind by a few yards.[24] As MCS 3008 continued toward the lagoon entrance, FLEC 303, CMS 71, and FLEC 306 approached it. When FLEC 306 was 50 yards from MCS 3008, it immediately altered course as if to cross the starboard bow of MCS 3008. When FLEC 306 was already dead ahead of MCS 3008, it reduced speed and established a blocking position. MCS 3008 then swerved toward the rear of FLEC 306 to evade a possible impact.[25] MCS 3008 then sighted CMS 71 moving fast toward it. However, because of the speed of the former vessel, the latter was only able to get near its position from a distance of 70 yards on its port side. Behind MCS 3008 were the two vessels chasing it, CMS 84 and FLEC 306.[26]

At the lagoon entrance, MCS 3008 sighted FLEC 306 and three Chinese fishing vessels, which were in blocking position. MCS 3008 was able to position itself a few yards from the entrance of Scarborough Shoal and entered the Shoal's basin by passing between the three Chinese fishing vessels and FLEC 306, which was fast moving toward it. On its way toward the basin, MCS 3008 sighted two mooring lines that had been planted by the Chinese fishing vessels, to impede movement toward the Shoal's basin. MCS 3008 stopped its engines and maneuvered backward to avoid the lines, at which point the crew of the Chinese fishing vessels and of FLEC 306 burst into cheers and clapped their hands. FLEC 306 was already in a blocking position ahead of MCS 3008.[27]

The mooring lines and the three Chinese ships positioned at the rear of MCS 3008 made it evident that they intended to obstruct the entry

[22] *Ibid.*, 206, para. 1.E.

[23] *Ibid.*, para. 1.F.

[24] *Ibid.*, para. 1.G.

[25] *Ibid.*, para. 1.H.

[26] *Ibid.*, para. 1.I.

[27] *Ibid.*, para. 1.K.

of MCS 3008 to the Shoal's basin. The latter increased its speed, maneuvered hard to starboard, and swerved hard astern of FLEC 306.[28] The latter then started all engines back, determined to ram MCS 3008, which increased speed, maneuvered left, and managed to dodge FLEC 306 by only approximately 10 meters on its port side, while attempting to keep the vessel safe from a shallow area 25 yards away on the starboard side.[29] After avoiding the "chase, harassment and intended sabotage," MCS 3008 was able to enter Scarborough Shoal's basin safely.[30] As in the case of the incidents of the previous month, the events were captured in photographs and videos.[31]

The incidents of May 2012 did not elicit any protest on the part of the Philippines. Consequently, there was no further statement from China.

China's failure to deny the facts of the incidents is so remarkable as to merit attention.

II. China's Failure to Deny the Facts

The contrast between China's noticeable failure to deny the facts relating to the near-collisions between Chinese and Philippine official vessels and its consistent attempts to present its own version of the facts concerning its construction activities in the Spratly Islands cannot but appear striking to the observer. It is likely that China's attitude reflects caution borne out of the embarrassing experience of seeing its strident denials of the facts relating to the conduct of its vessels in the 2009 *Impeccable* incident collapse in the face of incontrovertible evidence.

A. A Remarkable Contrast

It may be recalled that the Philippines alleged that China, through its construction activities, had caused damage to the marine environment of the South China Sea, particularly to coral reefs, thus violating its obligation under the Convention to protect and preserve the marine

[28] *Ibid.*, para. 1.L.

[29] *Ibid.*, para. 1.M.

[30] Award of 12 July 2016, 421, para. 1058.

[31] *MP*, Annex 82, para. 2.

environment.[32] Although China refused to appear before the Arbitral Tribunal, Chinese officials and institutions attempted on several occasions to contradict the Philippine presentation of the facts. Beyond the stress on the civilian, rather than military, purposes of the construction activities, they made numerous factual claims that contributed to a more sanguine vision of the reality on the ground, completely at odds with the assessment by the Philippines, the experts presented by the Philippines, and the independent experts appointed by the Tribunal of the harm caused to the marine environment by China's island-building.

For instance, a Foreign Ministry spokesperson declared that China adopted a "natural simulation" approach, which simulates the natural process of sea storms blowing away and moving biological scraps that eventually evolve into oasis on the sea.[33] A brief statement by the State Oceanic Administration ("SOA"), entitled "Construction work at Nansha Reefs Will Not Harm Oceanic Ecosystems" and published on 18 June 2015, claimed that construction projects were planned on bank-inset reefs, made of dead corals; that the cutter suction dredger method collected loose coral fragments and sands from flat lagoon basins, which are not hospitable environment for corals; that a new "dig, cutter, suction, blow and fill" land reclamation method integrated digging, transporting, and filling into the construction work; that a slope model was used to build permanent protective banks and walls around the land area to fend off waves; and that the duration of construction for each land reclamation

[32] According to Submission No. 11, China "has violated its obligations under the Convention to protect and preserve the marine environment at Scarborough Shoal, Second Thomas Shoal, Cuarteron Reef, Fiery Cross Reef, Gaven Reef, Johnson Reef, Hughes Reef and Subi Reef." Submission No. 12(b) alleged that China's occupation of and construction activities on Mischief Reef "violate China's duties to protect and preserve the marine environment under the Convention." Award of 12 July 2016, 41–42, para. 112.

[33] Ministry of Foreign Affairs, People's Republic of China, Foreign Ministry Spokesperson Hong Lei's Regular Press Conference (6 May 2016), quoted in the Award of 12 July 2016, 365–66, para. 921.

project was only several months.[34] A somewhat longer SOA Report, entitled "Construction Activities at Nansha Reefs Did Not Affect the Coral Reef Ecosystem" and published on 10 June 2015, stated that the extent of the reclamation and dredging areas was minimized; that trash collecting screens had been set; that construction was timed to avoid the spawn periods of red snapper, tuna, and bonito; that the change of the grain size of sand sediments was monitored regularly to maintain the water quality of coral reefs; that the construction intensity was reduced during the peak of growth of the coral reefs; that the growth and health of coral reefs in construction areas as well as indicators in coral reef areas were regularly monitored; that waste water and solid waste produced from life and construction were centrally collected to be sent for treatment at land facilities of harbors; that newer vessels were used to ensure no oil spills happened; and that weather and marine condition forecasts were regularly listened to.[35]

One searches in vain for factual claims that contradict the Philippine account concerning the near-collisions of 28 April and 26 May 2012 in China's response to the Philippine protest. China, surprisingly, referred to an incident that occurred on 10 April 2012, when a Philippine warship allegedly harassed Chinese fishermen in the waters around Scarborough Shoal. It alleged that in attempting to arrest and prosecute the fishermen, the warship "infringed" their human rights.[36] For the rest, China simply declared that the activities of the government public service ships

[34] *The Philippines' Annexes cited during Merits Hearing (Annexes 820–859)* (30 November 2015), Annex 821, China State Oceanic Administration, "Construction Work at Nansha Reefs Will Not Harm Oceanic Ecosystems" (18 June 2015), 13–14, https://files.pca-cpa.org/pcadocs/The%20Philippines'%20Annexes%20cited%20during%20Merits%20Hearing%20(Annexes%20820-859).pdf, accessed 2 June 2019; quoted in the Award of 12 July 2016, 368, para. 923.

[35] *The Philippines' Written Responses* (11 March 2016), Annex 872, China State Oceanic Administration, "Construction Activities at Nansha Reefs Did Not Affect the Coral Reef Ecosystem" (10 June 2015), 207–8, https://files.pca-cpa.org/pcadocs/The%20Philippines%27%20Written%20Responses%20%2811%20March%202016%29%20%28Annexes%20864-892%29.pdf, accessed 2 June 2019; quoted in the Award of 12 July 2016, 367, para. 922.

[36] *MP*, Annex 211, Note Verbale from the Embassy of the People's Republic of China in Manila to the Department of Foreign Affairs of the Republic of the Philippines, No. (12) PG-239 (25 May 2012), vol. VI, 403–4, https://files.pca-cpa.org/pcadocs/The%20Philippines%27%20Memorial%20-%20Volume%20VI%20%28Annexes%20158-221%29.pdf, accessed 16 June 2019.

were "completely within China's sovereignty" and that the Philippines therefore had "no right to make accusations and representations." China demanded that the Philippines pull out all Philippine ships from the area and desist from disturbing the operations of Chinese fishing and law enforcement vessels.[37]

During the Hearing on the Merits, it was only too easy for counsel for the Philippines to point out the obvious to anyone who would read the Note Verbale. Not only did China confine itself to reasserting its territorial claims and blaming the Philippines for allowing its vessels in the waters of Scarborough Shoal. China also failed to deny the allegations of "provocative and extremely dangerous maneuvers." Even worse, it simply ignored the Philippine request that China instruct its ships to comply with the COLREGS. Clearly, China did not contemplate taking any remedy. In effect, China displayed "deliberate disregard for the safety of navigation, and its reaction fell short of what one would expect from a flag State complying with its obligations under Article 94 of the Convention."[38]

The more elaborate rationalizations of the conduct of China's vessels developed by the CSIL will be discussed in the last chapter. At this point, China's failure to deny the allegations of "provocative and extremely dangerous maneuvers" will be explained by reference to its embarrassing experience when denying similarly dangerous maneuvers of Chinese vessels in 2009.

B. The Risks of Denying Facts: The Impeccable *Incident*

The USNS *Impeccable*, like other US Naval Ships, is not commissioned—placed in active duty in military service—and is a predominantly civilian-manned ocean surveillance vessel. Along with several other ships, it tows the sonar array system (SURTASS) that performs acoustic collection surveillance to help locate and identify submarines. Such operations would be applied to any future antisubmarine warfare.[39] In March 2009,

[37] *Ibid.*, 404.

[38] *South China Sea Arbitration*, Hearing on the Merits and Remaining Issues of Jurisdiction and Admissibility, Final Transcript, Day 3 (26 November 2015), 72–73, https://pcacases.com/web/sendAttach/1549, accessed 2 June 2019.

[39] Eric A. McVadon, "The Reckless and the Resolute: Confrontation in the South China Sea," *China Security* 5 (Spring 2009): 1, http://space-library.com/0905ChinaSecurity_Issue14_extract.pdf, accessed 2 June 2019.

the USNS *Impeccable* was conducting a military survey in China's Exclusive Economic Zone ("EEZ"). The US, which is not a party to the Convention, is of the view that:

> Customary international law, as reflected in articles 58 and 87 of the 1982 United Nations Convention on the Law of the Sea, guarantees to all nations the right to exercise within the EEZ, high seas freedoms of navigation and overflight, as well as the traditional uses of the ocean related to those freedoms.[40]

China, on the other hand, is of the view that military activities conducted by foreign naval vessels in a coastal State's EEZ require the coastal State's permission.[41]

On 5 March 2009, a Chinese frigate approached the *Impeccable* and crossed its bow at a range of approximately 100 yards. Less than two hours later, a Chinese Y-12 aircraft conducted 11 flybys of the ship at an altitude of 60 feet and a range from 100 to 300 feet. The frigate then crossed *Impeccable*'s bow again, this time at a range of about 400–500 yards. On 7 March, a Chinese intelligence collection ship directed *Impeccable* to leave the area or "suffer the consequences." On 9 March, three official Chinese vessels and two small Chinese trawlers surrounded the *Impeccable*, two of them closing to within fifty feet, waving Chinese flags and telling it to leave the area. In order to protect itself, *Impeccable* sprayed its fire hoses at one of the vessels. The Chinese crew members inexplicably disrobed to their underwear while their vessel continued

[40] Testimony of Deputy Assistant Secretary of Defense Robert Scher, Asian and Pacific Security Affairs, Office of the Secretary of Defense, before the Subcommittee on East Asian and Pacific Affairs, Senate Committee on Foreign Relations, United States Senate, 15 July 2009, in U.S. Congress, Senate, *Maritime Issues and Sovereignty Disputes in East Asia*, Senate Hearing 111–135, 111th Cong., 1st session, 2009, 8, https://www.gpo.gov/fdsys/pkg/CHRG-111shrg53022/html/CHRG-111shrg53022.htm, accessed 16 June 2019.

[41] Of the 167 parties to the Convention, only 26 other States agree with China. These are Bangladesh, Brazil, Burma, Cambodia, Cape Verde, Egypt, Haiti, India, Iran, Kenya, Malaysia, the Maldives, Mauritius, North Korea, Pakistan, Portugal, Saudi Arabia, Somalia, Sri Lanka, Sudan, Syria, Thailand, the United Arab Emirates, Uruguay, Venezuela, and Vietnam. Ronald O'Rourke, *Maritime Territorial and Exclusive Economic Zone (EEZ) Disputes Involving China: Issues for Congress*, Congressional Research Service R42784 (Washington, DC: Congressional Research Service, 9 August 2013), 4, https://www.everycrsreport.com/files/20130809_R42784_0cb0b5c25c7d13af56a56d1c13b776b166ccd25f.pdf, accessed 3 June 2019.

closing to within twenty-five feet. The *Impeccable*'s master informed the Chinese ships by radio that it was leaving the area and requested a safe path to navigate. Shortly afterward, two of the Chinese official vessels stopped directly ahead of the *Impeccable*, forcing it to conduct an emergency "all stop" in order to avoid collision. The Chinese vessels then dropped pieces of wood in the water directly in front of *Impeccable*'s path.[42] The US government, calling the behavior of the Chinese vessels "unprofessional," declared that they should "act responsibly and refrain from provocative activities that could lead to miscalculation or a collision at sea, endangering vessels and the lives of U.S. and Chinese mariners."[43]

In response to the US official statement, China's strategy consisted of outright and increasingly strident denials of the facts. Initially, a Chinese Foreign Ministry spokesman declared the claims by the US to be "flatly inaccurate and unacceptable to China."[44] The US statement that vessels that were not part of the Chinese Navy were involved in the incident was described in exactly the same terms.[45] In an indirect reference to the role of fishing vessels in the incident, a press release asserted on 11 March that "[t]he Chinese government always handles such activities strictly in accordance with [relevant] laws and regulations." The US claims, which had been initially described as "flatly inaccurate," had now become "gravely in contravention of the facts."[46] On the same day, a Chinese Defense Ministry statement, repeating the press release claim that the incident

[42] *Raw Data: Pentagon Statement on Chinese Incident With U.S. Navy*, 9 March 2009, http://www.foxnews.com/politics/2009/03/09/raw-data-pentagon-statement-chinese-incident-navy.html, accessed 3 June 2019.

[43] *Ibid.*

[44] Ma Zhaoxu, *P.R.C. Foreign Ministry Regular Press Conference*, 10 March 2009, http://www.fmprc.gov.cn/eng/xwfw/s2510/2511/t541713.htm, quoted in Jonathan G. Odom, "The True 'Lies' of the Impeccable Incident: What Really Happened, Who Disregarded International Law, and Why Every Nation (Outside of China) Should Be Concerned," *Michigan State University College of Law Journal of International Law* 18 (2010): 417, https://digitalcommons.law.msu.edu/cgi/viewcontent.cgi?article=1025&context=ilr, accessed 2 June 2019. This article was subsequently published, with photographs, as "The Case of USNS *Impeccable* versus 5 Chinese Ships: A Close Examination of the Facts, the Evidence and the Law," in Jon M. Van Dyke et al. (eds.), *Governing Ocean Resources: New Challenges and Emerging Regimes: A Tribute to Judge Choon-Ho Park* (Leiden: Martinus Nijhoff Publishers, 2013), 307–43.

[45] Ma Zahoxu, quoted in Odom, "The True 'Lies'," 417.

[46] Xinhua News Agency, *China Lodges Representation as U.S. Naval Ship Breaks Int'l, Chinese Laws*, 11 March 2009, quoted in Odom, "The True 'Lies'," 417.

involved "normal activities of law enforcement," transformed the US claims into "groundless accusations."[47] By 24 March, the "groundless accusations" had metamorphosed into "sheer lies."[48]

Unfortunately for China, the crew members of the USNS *Impeccable* had taken photographs and videos during the incident. All the US Navy had to do to counter China's denials was to release the photographs and post the videos on its website as well as on YouTube.[49] The photographs and/or videos show that two Chinese vessels stopped directly head of USNS *Impeccable* and forced it to conduct an emergency "all stop" in

[47] Xinhua News Agency, *Defense Ministry Urges U.S. to Respect China's Security Concern,* 11 March 2009, quoted in Odom, "The True 'Lies'," 418.

[48] Qin Gang, *P.R.C. Foreign Ministry Regular Press Release*, 24 March 2009, quoted in Odom, "The True 'Lies'," 419.

[49] The photographs and videos are still available on-line, although they are now found on different websites.

1. GHSRArchives, *East Asia—China vs US—20,090,309—Chinese Ships Approach USNS Impeccable—1.*, 0.25, published on 7 August 2011, https://www.youtube.com/watch?v=GfgGLvplLAQ, accessed 2 June 2019.
2. GHSRArchives, *East Asia—China vs US—20,090,309—Chinese Ships Approach USNS Impeccable—2.*, 0.10, published on 7 August 2011, https://www.youtube.com/watch?v=7fCZmIjXo6Q, accessed 2 June 2019; also available at https://vimeo.com/3782008, accessed 2 June 2019.
3. GHSRArchives, *East Asia—China vs US—20,090,309—Chinese Ships Approach USNS Impeccable—3.*, 2.18, published on 7 August 2011, https://www.youtube.com/watch?v=j-arbx9pRKM, accessed 2 June 2019; see also RAW VIDEO #3, https://vimeo.com/3782052, accessed 2 June 2019.
4. GHSRArchives, *East Asia—China vs US—20,090,309—Chinese Ships Approach USNS Impeccable—4.*,1.03, published on 7 August 2011, https://www.youtube.com/watch?v=peyuF05wR5c, accessed 2 June 2019.
5. GHSRArchives, *East Asia—China vs US—20,090,309—Chinese Ships Approach USNS Impeccable—5.*, 1.21, published on 7 August 2011, https://www.youtube.com/watch?v=jq-NgfQ1CwA, accessed 2 June 2019.
6. GHSRArchives, *East Asia—China vs US—20,090,309—Chinese Ships Approach USNS Impeccable—6.*, 3.00, published on 7 August 2011, https://www.youtube.com/watch?v=OvIwxjtQAog, accessed 2 June 2019.
7. GHSRArchives, *East Asia—China vs US—20,090,309—Chinese Ships Approach USNS Impeccable—7.*, 1.18, published on 7 August 2011, https://www.youtube.com/watch?v=aE0XUL_bxU8, accessed 2 June 2019.
8. GHSRArchives, *East Asia—China vs US—20,090,309—Chinese Ships Approach USNS Impeccable—8.*, 2.25, published on 7 August 2011, https://www.youtube.com/watch?v=BGTBP9fLZ_8, accessed 2 June 2019.

order to avoid collision[50]; that Chinese vessels closed to within 50 feet of the *Impeccable*, waved the Chinese flag and told it to leave the area[51]; that *Impeccable* sprayed its fire hoses at one of the vessels[52]; and that the Chinese crew members used poles to try to snag the *Impeccable*'s acoustic equipment in the water.[53] From the photographs and videos, one can conclude that it was the Chinese denials that were "inaccurate," "gravely in contravention of the facts," "groundless," and "sheer lies." Three years later, China's response to the Philippine protest following the incidents of 28 April and 26 May with Philippine vessels in the waters of Scarborough Shoal spared it the risk of its denials being described in the same terms.

In the wake of the *Impeccable* incident, the US exerted pressure on China to engage in a dialogue on freedom of navigation. By July 2009, a mere four months after the incident, the US Department of State was able to report to Congress that China had agreed to discuss freedom of navigation in a special session of the China-US military and maritime consultative agreement.[54] The Philippines obviously did not have the same means of exerting pressure on China as the US—one only has to

[50] Odom, "The True 'Lies'," 423, referring to U.S. Navy, "Image 090,308-N-0000X-003.jpg. Two Chinese Trawlers Stop Directly in Front of the Military Sealift Command Ocean Surveillance Ship USNS Impeccable (T-AGOS-23), Forcing the Ship to Conduct an Emergency 'All Stop' in order to Avoid Collision," (photograph), http://www.navy.mil/management/photodb/photos/090308-N-0000X-003.jpg, or http://www.navy.mil/view_single.asp?id=69478, accessed 2 June 2019.

[51] Odom, "The True 'Lies'," 424, referring to U.S. Navy, "Image 090,308-N-0000X-004.jpg. A Crewmember on a Chinese Trawler Uses a Grapple Hook in an Apparent Attempt to Snag the Towed Acoustic Array of the Military Sealift Command Ocean Surveillance Ship USNS Impeccable (T-AGOS-23)," (photograph), http://www.navy.mil/management/photodb/photos/090308-N-0000X-004.jpg, or https://commons.wikimedia.org/wiki/File:USNS_Impeccable_090308-N-0000X-004.jpg, accessed 2 June 2019.

[52] Odom, "The True 'Lies'," 424, referring to GHSRArchives, *East Asia—China vs US—20,090,309—Chinese Ships Approach USNS Impeccable—3.*

[53] Odom, "The True 'Lies'," 424, referring to U.S. Navy, "Image 090,308-N-0000X-004.jpg, Chinese Ships Approach USNS Impeccable—RAW VIDEO #2" (in its entirety); GHSRArchives, *China vs US—20,090,309—Chinese Ships Approach USNS Impeccable—2. 0*; GHSRArchives, *Chinese Ships Approach USNS Impeccable—RAW VIDEO #3* (at the 1:01 mark).

[54] Statement of Hon. Scot Marciel, Deputy Assistant Secretary of State, Bureau of East Asian and Pacific Affairs, Ambassador for ASEAN Affairs, Department of State, before the Subcommittee on East Asian and Pacific Affairs, Senate Committee on Foreign Relations, United States Senate, 15 July 2009, in U.S. Congress, Senate, *Maritime Issues and Sovereignty Disputes in East Asia*, 3.

recall the differences in the tonnage of the Chinese and Philippine vessels that nearly collided on 28 March and 26 April to realize how powerless the Philippines was when facing China. One also gets a sense from reading the Philippine *Memorial* that it perceived China's call on it to withdraw its ships from Scarborough Shoal as a thinly veiled threat to comply or "face the consequences."[55] Perhaps acting on the principle that prudence is the better part of valor, the Philippines preferred to refrain from sending its vessels to the area of Scarborough Shoal. However, it did decide to add a submission on the incidents of 28 April and 26 May 2012 to the other disputes that it submitted to compulsory dispute settlement.[56] In its written and oral pleadings, the Philippines systematically invoked the COLREGS. Thus, while US commentators contributed to an assessment of the conduct of China's vessels by identifying the specific rules of the COLREGS that the Chinese vessels had breached during the *Impeccable* incident,[57] it was the Philippine submission of the dispute to arbitration under Annex VII of the Convention that would ultimately result in what appears to be an unprecedented international judgment concerning the responsibility of a State party to the Convention for breaches of the COLREGS.

Despite the fact that the Philippines was not a party to the COLREGS 1972 at the time of the two incidents, the Arbitral Tribunal had no trouble finding that the COLREGS, "as generally accepted international regulations," were binding on the Philippines; the implication was that the Philippines had the right to invoke them in a dispute with China. The next Chapter will survey the historical process whereby the COLREGS were generally accepted by mariners and States.

[55] *MP*, vol. I, 207, para. 6.127.

[56] *Ibid.*

[57] Odom, "The True 'Lies'," 429–30, analyzed the specific rules of COLREGS that were breached by the Chinese vessels. See also McVadon, "The Reckless and the Resolute," 2, and Raul Pedrozo, "Close Encounters at Sea: The USNS *Impeccable* Incident," *Naval War College Review* 62 (Summer 2009): 110, n. 4, http://www.dtic.mil/dtic/tr/fulltext/u2/a519335.pdf, accessed 2 June 2019. On the results of the China-US dialogue on the freedom of navigation, see Chapter 3.

References

Center for Strategic and International Studies. "Are Maritime Law Enforcement Forces Destabilizing Asia?" *China Power Project* (2018), https://chinapower.csis.org/maritime-forces-destabilizing-asia/, accessed 26 October 2018.

Collins English Dictionary. Glasgow: HarperCollins Publishers, 2019, https://www.collinsdictionary.com/dictionary/, accessed 9 November 2019.

GHSRArchives. *East Asia—China vs US—20090309—Chinese Ships Approach USNS Impeccable—1.*, 0.25. Published on 7 August 2011, https://www.youtube.com/watch?v=GfgGLvplLAQ, accessed 2 June 2019.

———. *East Asia—China vs US—20090309—Chinese Ships Approach USNS Impeccable—2.*, 0.10. Published on 7 August 2011, https://www.youtube.com/watch?v=7fCZmIjXo6Q, accessed 2 June 2019; also available at https://vimeo.com/3782008, accessed 2 June 2019.

———. *East Asia—China vs US—20090309—Chinese Ships Approach USNS Impeccable—3.*, 2.18. Published on 7 August 2011, https://www.youtube.com/watch?v=j-arbx9pRKM, accessed 2 June 2019; see also RAW VIDEO #3, https://vimeo.com/3782052, accessed 2 June 2019.

———. *East Asia—China vs US—20090309—Chinese Ships Approach USNS Impeccable—4.*,1.03. Published on 7 August 2011, https://www.youtube.com/watch?v=peyuF05wR5c, accessed 2 June 2019.

———. *East Asia—China vs US—20090309—Chinese Ships Approach USNS Impeccable—5.*, 1.21. Published on 7 August 2011, https://www.youtube.com/watch?v=jq-NgfQ1CwA, accessed 2 June 2019.

———. *East Asia—China vs US—20090309—Chinese Ships Approach USNS Impeccable—6.*, 3.00. Published on 7 August 2011, https://www.youtube.com/watch?v=OvIwxjtQAog, accessed 2 June 2019.

———. *East Asia—China vs US—20090309—Chinese Ships Approach USNS Impeccable—7.*, 1.18. Published on 7 August 2011, https://www.youtube.com/watch?v=aE0XUL_bxU8, accessed 2 June 2019.

———. *East Asia—China vs US—20090309—Chinese Ships Approach USNS Impeccable—8.*, 2.25. Published on 7 August 2011, https://www.youtube.com/watch?v=BGTBP9fLZ_8, accessed 2 June 2019.

International Convention on the International Regulations for Preventing Collisions at Sea. Adopted at London on 20 October 1972. Entered into force 15 July 1977. Consolidated text as amended in 1981, 1987, 1989, 1993, 2001 and 2007, http://www.ecolregs.com/index.php?option=com_k2&view=itemlist&layout=category&Itemid=505&lang=en, accessed 31 May 2019.

Layton, C. W. T. et al. *Dictionary of Nautical Words and Terms*, 2nd ed. Glasgow: Brown, Son & Ferguson Ltd., Naval Publishers, 1982.

McVadon, Eric A. "The Reckless and the Resolute: Confrontation in the South China Sea." *China Security* 5 (Spring 2009): 1–28, http://space-library.com/0905ChinaSecurity_Issue14_extract.pdf, accessed 2 June 2019.
Odom, Jonathan G. "The True 'Lies' of the Impeccable Incident: What Really Happened, Who Disregarded International Law, and Why Every Nation (Outside of China) Should Be Concerned." *Michigan State University College of Law Journal of International Law* 18 (2010): 411–52, https://digitalcommons.law.msu.edu/cgi/viewcontent.cgi?article=1025&context=ilr, accessed 2 June 2019.
———. "The Case of USNS *Impeccable* versus 5 Chinese Ships: A Close Examination of the Facts, the Evidence and the Law." *Governing Ocean Resources: New Challenges and Emerging Regimes. A Tribute to Judge Choon-Ho Park*, 307–43. Eds. Jon M. Van Dyke et al. Leiden: Martinus Nijhoff Publishers, 2013.
O'Rourke, Ronald. *Maritime Territorial and Exclusive Economic Zone (EEZ) Disputes Involving China: Issues for Congress*. Congressional Research Service R42784. Washington, DC: Congressional Research Service, 9 August 2013, https://www.everycrsreport.com/files/20130809_R42784_0cb0b5c25c7d13af56a56d1c13b776b166ccd25f.pdf, accessed 3 June 2019.
Pedrozo, Raul. "Close Encounters at Sea: The USNS *Impeccable* Incident." *Naval War College Review* 62 (Summer 2009): 100–11, http://www.dtic.mil/dtic/tr/fulltext/u2/a519335.pdf, accessed 2 June 2019.
Raw Data: Pentagon Statement on Chinese Incident with U.S. Navy, 9 March 2009, http://www.foxnews.com/politics/2009/03/09/raw-data-pentagon-statement-chinese-incident-navy.html, accessed 3 June 2019.
South China Sea Arbitration. Award of 12 July 2016, http://www.pcacases.com/pcadocs/PH-CN%20-%2020160712%20-%20Award.pdf, accessed 2 June 2019.
———. Hearing on the Merits and Remaining Issues of Jurisdiction and Admissibility. Final Transcript, Day 3 (26 November 2015), https://pcacases.com/web/sendAttach/1549, accessed 2 June 2019.
———. *Memorial of the Philippines* (30 March 2014). Vol. I, https://files.pca-cpa.org/pcadocs/Memorial%20of%20the%20Philippines%20Volume%20I.pdf, accessed 2 June 2019.
———. Annex 78. Report from Commanding Officer SARV-003 Philippine Coast Guard to Commander, Coast Guard District, Northwestern Luzon, Philippine Coast Guard (28 April 2012). Vol. IV, 147–58, https://files.pca-cpa.org/pcadocs/The%20Philippines%27%20Memorial%20-%20Volume%20IV%20%28Annexes%2061-102%29.pdf, accessed 2 June 2019.
———. Annex 80. Report from Relly B. Garcia et al., FRPLEU/QRT [Fishery Resource Protection and Law Enforcement/Quick Response Team] Officers,

Bureau of Fisheries and Aquatic Resources, Republic of the Philippines (2 May 2012). Vol. IV, 163–95, https://files.pca-cpa.org/pcadocs/The%20Philippines%27%20Memorial%20-%20Volume%20IV%20%28Annexes%2061-102%29.pdf, accessed 2 June 2019.
———. Annex 82. Report from Angelito A. Arunco et al., FRPLEU-QRT Officers, Bureau of Fisheries and Aquatic Resources, Republic of the Philippines, to Director, Bureau of Fisheries and Aquatic Resources, Republic of the Philippines (28 May 2012). Vol. IV, 201–08, https://files.pca-cpa.org/pcadocs/The%20Philippines%27%20Memorial%20-%20Volume%20IV%20%28Annexes%2061-102%29.pdf, accessed 2 June 2019.
———. Annex 111. People's Republic of China, Ministry of Agriculture, "More Powerful Equipment Added to Enforce Rights and Protect Fisheries" (9 March 2010). Vol. V, 77, https://files.pca-cpa.org/pcadocs/The%20Philippines%27%20Memorial%20-%20Volume%20V%20%28Annexes%20103-157%29.pdf, accessed 2 June 2019.
———. Annex 209. Note Verbale from the Department of Foreign Affairs of the Philippines to the Embassy of the People's Republic of China in Manila, No. 12–1222 (30 April 2012). Vol. VI, 393–96, https://files.pca-cpa.org/pcadocs/The%20Philippines%27%20Memorial%20-%20Volume%20VI%20%28Annexes%20158-221%29.pdf, accessed 2 June 2019.
———. Annex 211. Note Verbale from the Embassy of the People's Republic of China in Manila to the Department of Foreign Affairs of the Republic of the Philippines, No. (12) PG-239 (25 May 2012). Vol. VI, 401–04, https://files.pca-cpa.org/pcadocs/The%20Philippines%27%20Memorial%20-%20Volume%20VI%20%28Annexes%20158-221%29.pdf, accessed 16 June 2019.
———. Annex 315. "China Marine Surveillance 84 Boat Out into the South China Sea", Xinhua (8 May 2011). Vol. X, 103, https://files.pca-cpa.org/pcadocs/The%20Philippines%27%20Memorial%20-%20Volume%20X%20%28Annexes%20307-343%29.pdf, accessed 2 June 2019.
———. Annex 317. Liang Ganghua, "China's First Large Fishery Law Enforcement Vessel Permanently Stationed at the Xisha Islands Is Officially Placed into Service", Xinhua (2 September 2011). Vol. X, 115, https://files.pca-cpa.org/pcadocs/The%20Philippines%27%20Memorial%20-%20Volume%20X%20%28Annexes%20307-343%29.pdf, accessed 2 June 2019.
———. *The Philippines' Annexes cited during Merits Hearing (Annexes 820–859)* (30 November 2015). Annex 821. China State Oceanic Administration, "Construction Work at Nansha Reefs Will Not Harm Oceanic Ecosystems" (18 June 2015), 13–14, https://files.pca-cpa.org/pcadocs/The%20Philipp

ines'%20Annexes%20cited%20during%20Merits%20Hearing%20(Annexes%20820-859).pdf, accessed 2 June 2019.

———. *The Philippines' Written Responses* (11 March 2016). Annex 872. China State Oceanic Administration, "Construction Activities at Nansha Reefs Did Not Affect the Coral Reef Ecosystem" (10 June 2015), 207–08, https://files.pca-cpa.org/pcadocs/The%20Philippines%27%20Written%20Responses%20%2811%20March%202016%29%20%28Annexes%20864-892%29.pdf, accessed 2 June 2019.

United Nations Convention on the Law of the Sea, concluded at Montego Bay on 10 December 1982. Entered into force 16 November 1994, http://www.un.org/Depts/los/convention_agreements/texts/unclos/closindx.htm, accessed 21 March 2019.

United States. *Code of Federal Regulations*. Volume 2. Title 46—Shipping, Section 69.53—Definitions. Washington, DC: Government Printing Office, 2010, https://www.gpo.gov/fdsys/pkg/CFR-2010-title46-vol2/xml/CFR-2010-title46-vol2-sec69-53.xml, accessed 9 November 2018.

———. Congress. Senate. Committee on Foreign Relations. *Maritime Issues and Sovereignty Disputes in East Asia*. Senate Hearing 111–135. 111th Cong., 1st session, 2009, https://www.gpo.gov/fdsys/pkg/CHRG-111shrg53022/html/CHRG-111shrg53022.htm, accessed 11 November 2018.

———. Navy. "Image 090308-N-0000X-003.jpg. Two Chinese Trawlers Stop Directly in Front of the Military Sealift Command Ocean Surveillance Ship USNS Impeccable (T-AGOS-23), Forcing the Ship to Conduct an Emergency 'All Stop' in order to Avoid Collision," http://www.navy.mil/management/photodb/photos/090308-N-0000X-003.jpg, or http://www.navy.mil/view_single.asp?id=69478, accessed 2 June 2019.

———. "Image 090308-N-0000X-004.jpg. A Crewmember on a Chinese Trawler Uses a Grapple Hook in an Apparent Attempt to Snag the Towed Acoustic Array of the Military Sealift Command Ocean Surveillance Ship USNS Impeccable (T-AGOS-23)," http://www.navy.mil/management/photodb/photos/090308-N-0000X-004.jpg, or https://commons.wikimedia.org/wiki/File:USNS_Impeccable_090308-N-0000X-004.jpg, accessed 2 June 2019.

Walker, George K. *Definitions for the Law of the Sea: Terms Not Defined by the Convention*. Leiden: Martinus Nijhoff Publishers, 2012.

CHAPTER 3

The COLREGS, Mariners, and States

The Convention on the International Regulations for Preventing Collisions at Sea 1972 ("COLREGS 1972") is one of several international conventions that aim to secure the safety of maritime navigation and the safety of life at sea.[1] Unlike the International Convention for the Safety of Life at Sea 1974 ("SOLAS 1974"),[2] the International Convention on Standards of Training, Certification and Watchkeeping for Seafarers,

[1] *Convention on the International Regulations for Preventing Collisions at Sea*, adopted 20 October 1972, entered into force 15 July 1977, consolidated text as amended in 1981, 1987, 1989, 1993, 2001, and 2007, http://www.ecolregs.com/index.php?option=com_k2&view=itemlist&layout=category&Itemid=505&lang=en, accessed 31 May 2019.

[2] Adopted at London, 1 November 1974, entered into force 25 May 1980, https://www.refworld.org/docid/46920bf32.html, accessed 3 June 2019. For information on SOLAS 1974, see International Maritime Organization ("IMO"), *International Convention for the Safety of Life at Sea (SOLAS), 1974* (London: IMO, 2019), http://www.imo.org/en/About/Conventions/ListOfConventions/Pages/International-Convention-for-the-Safety-of-Life-at-Sea-(SOLAS),-1974.aspx, accessed 3 June 2019. For the status of SOLAS 1974, see IMO, *Status of Conventions, Status of IMO Treaties. Comprehensive Information on the Status of Multilateral Conventions and Instruments in Respect of Which the International Maritime Organization or Its Secretary-General Performs Depositary or Other Functions* (London: IMO, 2019), 12–88, http://www.imo.org/en/About/Conventions/StatusOfConventions/Documents/Status%20-%202019.pdf, accessed 3 June 2019.

A. C. Robles Jr., *Vessel Collisions in the Law of the Sea*,
https://doi.org/10.1007/978-981-16-9793-7_3

as amended 1978/1995 ("STCW 1978/1995"),[3] and the International Convention on Maritime Search and Rescue 1979 ("SAR 1979"),[4] the COLREGS 1972 "form a single, simple, anti-collision regulatory regime for all international maritime navigation rights."[5] The COLREGS also differ from these other conventions in that they achieved general acceptance as early as the second half of the nineteenth century, when they were more widely known as the "Rules of the Road" or the "International Regulations." They were thus being applied by vessels and States much earlier than even the first version of SOLAS, which had been adopted in 1914 in response to the *Titanic* disaster but entered into force only in 1933.[6]

The Convention itself, signed on 20 October 1972 and entering into force on 15 July 1977, is quite brief, containing nine articles. It is the annexed International Regulations that lay down forty-one rules divided into six parts: A (General), B (Steering and Sailing rules), C (Lights and

[3] Adopted at London, 7 July 1978, entered into force on 28 April 1984, *United Nations Treaty Series*, vol. 1361 (New York: United Nations, 1993), 190–298 ("*UNTS*"), https://treaties.un.org/doc/Publication/UNTS/Volume%201361/volume-1361-I-23001-English.pdf, accessed 3 June 2019. For information on STCW 1978/1995, see IMO, *International Convention on Standards of Training, Certification and Watchkeeping for Seafarers (STCW)* (London: IMO, 2019), http://www.imo.org/en/About/Conventions/ListOfConventions/Pages/International-Convention-on-Standards-of-Training,-Certification-and-Watchkeeping-for-Seafarers-(STCW).aspx, accessed 3 June 2019. For the status of STCW 1978/1995, see IMO, *Status of Conventions*, 397–417.

[4] Adopted at Hamburg, 27 April 1979, entered into force 22 June 1985, *UNTS*, vol. 1405 (New York: United Nations, 1995), 119–33, https://treaties.un.org/doc/Publication/UNTS/Volume%201405/volume-1405-I-23489-English.pdf, accessed 3 June 2019. For information on SAR 1979, see IMO, *International Convention on Maritime Search and Rescue (SAR)* (London: IMO, 2019), http://www.imo.org/en/About/conventions/listofconventions/pages/international-convention-on-maritime-search-and-rescue-(sar).aspx, accessed 3 June 2019. For the status of SAR 1979, see IMO, *Status of Conventions*, 418–28.

[5] Glen Plant, "The Collision Avoidance Regulations as a Regulator of International Navigation Rights; Underlying Principles and Their Adequacy for the Twenty-first Century," *Journal of Navigation* 88 (1996): 382 ("*JON*").

[6] *International Conference on Safety of Life at Sea, Text of the Convention for the Safety of Life at Sea* (London: H.M. Stationery Office, Harrison and Sons, Printers England, 1914), http://ia802605.us.archive.org/5/items/textofconvention00inte/textofconvention00inte.pdf, accessed 3 June 2019; Intermaritime Certification Services (ICS Class), *History of SOLAS* (Panama: ICS Class, 2012), https://icsclass.org/history-of-solas/, accessed 12 November 2018.

Shapes), D (Sound and Light Signals), E (Exemptions), and F (Verification of Compliance with the Provisions of the Convention). There are also four annexes containing technical requirements concerning lights and shapes and their positioning; sound signaling appliances; additional signals for fishing vessels fishing in close proximity; and international distress signals. At the core of the International Regulations are the Steering and Sailing Rules (Part B). In a process beginning in the nineteenth century, they were generally accepted by mariners, largely because they conformed to their established practices, and by States, who realized that national regulation of collisions in the age of steamships and expanding trade was likely to be inadequate.

I. The COLREGS and Mariners

Mariners themselves believe that COLREGS, if respected, could prevent any collision.[7] The COLREGS offer them two advantages. First, historically, they were derived from mariners' practice, and second, they are characterized by their relative simplicity.

A. The COLREGS and the Practice of Mariners

The practice of mariners did not generate general rules for the prevention of collisions until the late eighteenth century. The reason is that prior to the nineteenth century, the risk of collision among vessels was negligible.[8] For thousands of years, mariners ensured the safe conduct of ships through coastal navigation, proceeding in sight of the coastline, having land on one side and the open sea on the other.[9] Ships were small, slow, and easy to repair. Any collisions that did occur were limited to harbors.[10] Technological innovations between the fifteenth and eighteenth centuries, including the magnetic compass, navigational charts,

[7] Søren Thirslund, "Collision Avoidance at Sea in the Mid-20th Century: Thoughts from Denmark," *JON* 65 (2012): 201.

[8] Edward W. Anderson, "Navigation—Technology," *Encyclopædia Britannica* (2019), https://www.britannica.com/technology/navigation-technology, accessed 4 June 2019.

[9] Peter Kemp (ed.), *Oxford Companion to Ships and the Sea* (Oxford: Oxford University Press, 1988), 576–79.

[10] David R. Owen, "The Origins and Development of Marine Collision Law," *Tulane Law Review* 51 (1977): 759–64.

astrolabes, and quadrants, began to facilitate ocean navigation.[11] Nevertheless, collisions remained infrequent. In these circumstances, rules to prevent collisions failed to develop. The rules that did develop related to the division of losses resulting from collisions.[12]

Among British naval vessels, the convention to avoid collisions mandated that ships of junior rank should give way to ships of senior rank. This convention was feasible for ships that were part of a fleet but would have been difficult to apply between merchant ships and between vessels of different States. In 1776, Lord Richard Howe, commander of a British fleet off the northeast coast of the US, issued a signal book that contained the earliest reference to a rule of the road at sea. The rule was based on the principle that only one of the two vessels should be given the responsibility for taking action. Vessels on the port tack (with the wind on their port, or left, side) should give way to vessels on the starboard tack so that a port-to-port passing could be achieved. Lord Howe's rule of the road has survived virtually unaltered to the present day.[13]

Lord Howe's approach, which has been called "a single ship responsibility" or "right of way" approach,[14] was more widely adopted in the nineteenth century, when the expansion of trade and the development of the steam engine resulted in the increasing frequency and severity of collisions. Lord Howe's rule was the basis for a steering and sailing rule for sailing ships (ships without steam engines) adopted in 1840 by Trinity House, a charity incorporated in 1514 to regulate pilotage on the River Thames and provide for aged mariners.[15] The rule was formulated in response to the realization that collisions often arose from the absence of a universal understanding of the "Rules of the Road": in some ports, meeting vessels had to pass to port (to the left), while in others, they had to pass to starboard (to the right).[16] Trinity House also proposed a

[11] Kemp, *Oxford Companion*, 577–78.

[12] Owen, "The Origins," 759–64.

[13] John F. Kemp, "Two Hundred Years of the Collision Regulations," *JON* 29 (1976): 341–42 ("Two Hundred Years").

[14] Plant, "The Collision Avoidance Regulations," 379.

[15] Trinity House, *About Us* (London: Trinity House, 2016), https://www.trinityhouse.co.uk/about-us, accessed 3 June 2019. Trinity House describes itself as a charity dedicated to safeguarding shipping and seafarers. It provides educational support and welfare to the seafaring community and acts as General Lighthouse Authority.

[16] Owen, "The Origins," 760, 768, 783.

steering and sailing rule for steamships, known as the "larboard [port] helm rule," which required that each party to any encounter should avoid collision by altering course to starboard. This "dual responsibility" rule conformed to the keep right view that applied in the local river of Trinity House, the River Thames; the convention followed by mariners on the Clyde, Mersey, and Humber Rivers followed a keep left convention.[17] In 1846, the British Parliament passed the first statutory Rules of the Road, under which steamships should pass port-to-port, without necessarily altering course to starboard. Further Acts in 1851 and 1854 reverted to the Trinity House rule for steamships (the "larboard helm" rule) and applied it to sailing ships.[18]

The "larboard helm" rule was heavily criticized by mariners, for being "unmindful as to differences of opinion" between vessels. As a Captain Drew put it before a Select Committee of the British House of Commons in 1860:

> one may think that if each continues his course there is no danger, the other, to be on the safe side, ports his helm (i.e. alters course for starboard) and causes the collision, and the collision then becomes a justification for concluding that there was danger.[19]

In a move that was welcomed by mariners, the "larboard helm" rule for steamships was repealed in 1861.

A steering and sailing rule that was applicable to steamships and that was very similar to Lord Howe's rule was incorporated into an agreement on the Rules of the Road between the UK and France in 1861. In a situation of crossing involving steamships, the vessel with the other on its starboard (right) side was required to take the avoiding action.[20] The "larboard helm" rule that was applied to sailing ships meeting end-on was repealed in 1884; it remained applicable only for steam vessels meeting head-on.[21] Since that time, the rule that the ship on the port tack should

[17] Kemp, "Two Hundred Years," 343–44.

[18] *Ibid.*, 344.

[19] Evidence of Captain Drew before a Select Committee of the House of Commons in 1860, quoted in *ibid.*

[20] Kemp, "Two Hundred Years," 345.

[21] *Ibid.*, 346.

alter course to starboard has formed the basis for the entire system of rules for preventing collisions between ships.[22]

As the Rules of the Road were being codified, they were integrated into the practice of mariners. At the time, many mariners were illiterate. Hence, Thomas Gray, a member of the British Board of Trade that had drafted the Rules in 1863, turned them into a series of verses that they could, and still can, easily remember, and published them in a pamphlet in 1867.[23] The verses had an enduring influence on mariners, as they were translated into many languages and a quarter of a million copies were printed, despite criticism that Gray put an interpretation on the rules that "could not safely be anticipated by an officer of the B0T [Board of Trade]."[24] By the first half of the twentieth century, a knowledge of the Rules of the Road was an indispensable part of the training of mariners. A British merchant ship captain recalled that in the oral examination for Second Mate (third in command of a merchant ship), verbatim knowledge of the Regulations was required.[25] A Danish ship master reported that when he began his studies at the navigation school in Copenhagen in 1941, he and his colleagues were warned that if they were not able to repeat the Regulations by heart, they would be dismissed.[26] Interestingly, he recalled that even in the mid-twentieth century, young mariners on board ship were still taught the old rhyme taken from Gray's verses—"Both in safety and in doubt – always keep a good look-out," bad look-out being a frequent cause of collisions.[27] At present, the Rules of the Road are so well-integrated into the practice of mariners that the requirement of compliance with them, together with other rules and regulations, is considered self-evident.[28]

22 *Ibid.*, 341.

23 Andrew Craig-Bennett in The WoodenBoat Forum > Misc. Boat Related > When Both Lights You See Ahead...and Other Rhymes of the Sea... 08-02-2010, 09:15 AM, http://forum.woodenboat.com/archive/index.php/t-118056.html, accessed 2 June 2019. For the text of the verses, see Annex 3.1.

24 Thirslund, "Collision Avoidance," 201, note 5.

25 Mike Bechley, "Collision Avoidance at Sea in the Mid-20th Century: Collision Avoidance in the 1960s," *JON* 65 (2012): 194.

26 Thirslund, "Collision Avoidance," 201.

27 *Ibid.*

28 Zdisław Kopacz et al., "An Attempt of [sic] the Specification of the Ship's Navigation Process," *Annual of Navigation* 3 (2001): 201.

Mariners also had a decisive, though less well-known, role in the international acceptance of the Rules of the Road. In the early 1860s, as France was preparing a new draft of its collision regulations, the French Admiralty Council expressed the view that regulations intended to prevent collisions had to be adopted by all States and that before undertaking any reforms, it was indispensable that France reach an agreement with the main maritime powers. As we shall see in the next section, the French government responded to this opinion by submitting a new draft of collision regulations to the UK, accompanied by proposals either to convene an international conference or to transmit the draft to other States for their acceptance.[29]

Until the mid-twentieth century, the technical means available to mariners to assist them in preventing collisions were "rudimentary," as a British merchant ship captain described them,[30] yet compliance with the Rules of the Road was deemed sufficient to prevent collisions. The COLREGS 1960 took account of the increasing use of radar as a collision avoidance aid, by incorporating recommendations on the use of radar information into an annex; the annex was incorporated into the body of COLREGS in 1972.[31] Despite these amendments, the COLREGS offer the advantage of simplicity to mariners.

[29] France, Ministère de la Marine et des Colonies [Ministry of the Navy and of the Colonies], *Abordages. Décrets des 25 octobre 1862 et 26 mai 1869. Questionnaire réglementaire sur les signaux de brume, les feux que doivent porter les bâtiments et les règles à suivre pour la navigation tant à la voile qu'à la vapeur* [Collisions. Decrees of 25 October 1862 and 26 May 1869. Regulatory Questionnaire on the Fog Signals, the Lights That Vessels Should Carry and the Rules to Be Followed for Sail-Powered as Well as by Steam Navigation] (Paris: Imprimerie Administrative de Paul Dupont, 1869), 6, https://babel.hathitrust.org/cgi/pt?id=njp.32101058626910;view=plaintext;page=root;size=100;seq=12;num=6, accessed 3 June 2019.

[30] Bechley, "Collision Avoidance," 197.

[31] The COLREGS 1960 were not published in the *United Nations Treaty Series*. Extracts, including Appendix 2, The Radar Annexe 2, can be found at *Ancient Mariner*, 26 November 2006, http://rsyms.blogspot.com/2006/11/colregs-1960.html, accessed 3 June 2019. The entire text was published in Italian translation when it was promulgated as a law in Italy. See *Legge 5 maggio 1966* [Law of 5 May 1966], *n. 276*, *Norme per prevenire gli abbordi in mare [Rules to Prevent Collisions at Sea]. (GU Serie Generale [Official Gazette General Series] n.120 del 17-05-1966)*, https://www.gazzettaufficiale.it/eli/id/1966/05/17/066U0276/sg, accessed 3 June 2019. Kemp, "Two Hundred Years," 347.

B. The Simplicity of the COLREGS

The simplicity of the COLREGS is manifested in several ways, as persuasively argued by Glen Plant.[32] In the first place, their aim is limited to collision avoidance. They are concerned with safety, rather than the efficiency, of navigation.[33] They do not even attempt to regulate comprehensively stranding, another type of disaster that could befall a vessel.[34] They do require that all efforts be devoted to the avoidance of collisions altogether.[35]

Second, the COLREGS cater for all levels of shipping technology. As a Captain Syms pointed out in 1980, they were conceived in such a way that all the rules could be carried out without resorting to technical aids.[36] Plant adds that all a ship strictly needs in order to comply with them is a visual look-out (required by Rule 5), a means of propulsion, a steering mechanism, and the appropriate lights, shapes, and sound signaling devices (required by Rules 20–37).[37]

Third, the COLREGS entail minimum interference to navigation consistent with safety. Action under the steering and sailing rules is required only when there is a degree of proximity, usually involving risk of collision. They leave the ship's master free to decide whether to alter the vessel's course or speed or both, although they do emphasize course changes. No distance to be kept from other ships is specified, nor are speed limits imposed.[38]

Next, the interference by COLREGS with other uses of the sea, particularly fishing, naval exercises and maneuvers, and marine sports activities, is reduced to a minimum.[39] Finally, even the drafting of the COLREGS 1972 is intended to make the rules readily comprehensible. A non-native English speaker observed that during his naval training in the 1940s, the late nineteenth-century language of the Regulations had not yet been

[32] Plant, "The Collision Avoidance Regulations," 382–83.

[33] *Ibid.*, 377.

[34] *Ibid.*, 391.

[35] *Ibid.*, 382.

[36] Captain Syms, letter to *Seaways*, May 1980, quoted in *ibid.*

[37] Plant, "The Collision Avoidance Regulations," 382.

[38] *Ibid.*, 383.

[39] *Ibid.*

updated.[40] In the COLREGS 1972, the imperative character of the rules was stressed with the more frequent use of the word "shall" in the text.[41] The Regulations themselves were completely reorganized, so that the steering and sailing rules, which in all previous versions followed the rules on lights and shapes as well as those on sound signals, now precede them. In addition, the rules were given titles that summarize their content.

The COLREGS 1972 have not escaped criticism. The following are said to present significant challenges to the COLREGS: nuclear-powered ships, large passenger vessels and large bulk carriers; the maneuvering differences of deep-draft vessels; multi-ship encounters; naval vessels singly or in "shadowing" operation or in formation; encounters between merchant vessels and formations of warships; close encounters between Greenpeace-style protest vessels and their target ships; rapidly increasing vessel speed differentials; confined or crowded waters; fast vessels like aircraft carriers; and non-displacement craft.[42] Clearly, none of the scenarios that the COLREGS 1972 are allegedly ill-equipped to deal with corresponds to the situations in which the Chinese and Philippine vessels found themselves on 28 April and 26 May 2012. Consequently, it is not necessary to determine whether any alleged shortcomings of the COLREGS made it inappropriate to apply them to the two incidents that were the object of Philippine Submission No. 13.[43]

[40] Thirslund, "Collision Avoidance," 201.

[41] Plant, "The Collision Avoidance Regulations," 388.

[42] *Ibid.*, 383–85.

[43] Those interested in the debate on the revision of the COLREGS may fruitfully consult Craig H. Allen, "Whatever Became of the Change to COLREGS Rule 8," *Professionalmariner.com*, 2 May 2008, http://www.professionalmariner.com/May-2008/Whatever-became-of-the-change-to-COLREGS-Rule-8/, accessed 3 June 2019 (Allen was the author of the expert opinion submitted by the Philippines on the incidents of 28 April and 26 May 2012); Kirk Greiner, "COLREG Amendments," *The Expert* 6 (1990), http://www.maritimeconsultant.com/macnewsletters/spring90/colreg_amendments.htm, accessed 2 June 2019; Dag Pike, "Collision Rules for High-Speed Craft," *JON* 58 (2005): 159–63; Carlos F. Salinas, "Collision Regulations Discussions," *JON* 55 (2002): 501–5; I. P. A. Stitt, "The COLREGS—Time for a Rewrite?" *JON* 55 (2002): 419–30; Rolf Johannes Undrum, "Definition of a Fast and Manoeuverable Craft and Amendments to the Collision Regulations," *JON* 58 (2005): 154–59; Hanno Weber, "Clarification of the Steering and Sailing Rules of the COLREGS," *JON* 48 (1995): 289–92; and Karen Williams, "Collision Regulation: Not to Impede," *JON* 55 (2002): 500–1.

General acceptance by mariners of the COLREGS has been accompanied by general acceptance on the part of States of these "Rules of the Road" since the second half of the nineteenth century.

II. The COLREGS and States

Very early on, States realized that for collision regulations to be effective, they must be accepted by as many States as possible. Once a State has accepted the Rules of the Road, it is their duty to give effect to them.

A. International Acceptance of the COLREGS

In the nineteenth century, the influence of the UK as the leading naval and trading power led other States to adopt the British collision avoidance rules as the "common law of the sea," as Plant calls them.[44] Nevertheless, even as British influence diminished, international acceptance of the International Regulations was by no means adversely affected.

The Rules of the Road passed by the British Parliament in 1846 and 1848 applied to British ships everywhere, to foreign ships within British jurisdiction, and to British ships out of British jurisdiction, but they did not apply to foreign ships on the high seas or in foreign waters.[45] The Merchant Shipping Act 1862, which adopted a new set of regulations for preventing collisions, gave the British Crown the power to direct by Order in Council that the Regulations be applied by British Courts to ships of foreign States that had adopted them.[46] The Regulations, which

[44] Plant, "The Collision Avoidance Regulations," 378.

[45] Reginald Godfrey Marsden, *A Treatise on the Law of Collisions at Sea, with an Appendix Containing Extracts from the Merchant Shipping Acts, the International Regulations (of 1863 and 1880) for Preventing Collisions at Sea and Local Rules for the Same Purpose in Force in the Thames, The Mersey and Elsewhere* (London: Stevens and Sons, 1880), 135, https://ia800205.us.archive.org/26/items/cu31924022403897/cu31924022403897.pdf, accessed 3 June 2019. The text of the International Regulations for Preventing Collisions at Sea 1863 and 1880 may be found at 247–58.

[46] *Ibid.*, 135. An order in council is an order by the sovereign with the advice of the privy council. The privy council is the chief council of the sovereign, called, by preeminence, "the Council," composed of those whom the king appoints. By the nineteenth century, only those members of the privy council who were cabinet ministers were ordinarily summoned to advise the sovereign. The cabinet ministers were those members of the Council who actually conducted the business of the government. Orders in council were either prerogative or issued under parliamentary authority. The latter delegated either to

entered into force in 1863, were declared applicable to the ships of 24 States that had expressed the desire to be bound by the British rules. Of the 24, there were 14 from Europe, six from South America, and one each from Africa, the Caribbean, North America, and the Pacific.[47] British and American commentaries of the time do not provide the diplomatic background to the extension of the Regulations to foreign States, which they simply took for granted.[48] Perhaps this was a manifestation in itself of British preeminence. Fortunately, a French source sheds some light on the process.

France had already agreed with the UK in 1848 rules concerning lights and signals for steamships, which were then extended to sailing ships by the UK on 1 March 1852 and by France on 17 August 1852. These were further revised and supplemented by regulations adopted in the UK on 24 February 1858 and in France on 28 May 1858.[49] Subsequently, a commission consisting of commanders of French naval vessels set out to revise French regulations aimed at preventing collisions in crossing and overtaking situations. The draft revision was submitted to

the crown (the executive) or even to the minister of a department charged with carrying out an act, the power to make rules and orders under it. John Bouvier and Francis Rawle, *Bouvier's Law Dictionary and Concise Encyclopedia: Rawle's Revision*, vol. III (Kansas City, MO: Vernon Law Book Company, 1914), 2423, 2723, https://ia600201.us.archive.org/29/items/cu31924022836245/cu31924022836245.pdf, accessed 2 June 2019.

[47] The 14 European States were Austria, Belgium, Denmark, France, Germany, Greece, Italy, the Netherlands, Norway, Portugal, Russia, Spain, Sweden, and Turkey. The six South American States were Argentina, Brazil, Chile, Ecuador, Peru, and Uruguay. The four others were Morocco, Haiti, the Hawaiian Islands, and the US. In the latter, they applied to ships both at sea and on the inland waters. Marsden, *A Treatise* (1880), 135.

[48] *Ibid.*, 133–35, 236–38; see also Alexander Charles Boyd, *The Merchant Shipping Laws: Being a Consolidation of All the Merchant Shipping and Passenger Acts from 1854 to 1875, Inclusive; with Notes of All the Leading British and American Cases on the Subjects Affected by Legislation; and an Appendix Containing the New Rules Issued in October 1876, Forming a Complete Treatise on Maritime Law* (London: Stevens & Sons, 1876), 262–63, 316, https://ia800208.us.archive.org/28/items/cu31924022429298/cu31924022429298.pdf, accessed 3 June 2019; Herbert Ransom Spencer, *A Treatise on the Law of Marine Collisions* (Chicago: Callaghan and Company, 1895), 37–38, http://www.minnesotalegalhistoryproject.org/assets/Spencer%20on%20Marine%20Collisions.pdf, accessed 3 June 2019.

[49] Louis Thiébaut, *Traité théorique et pratique de l'abordage maritime. Études pratiques de droit maritime* [A Theoretical and Practical Treatise on Maritime Collisions. Practical Studies on Maritime Law] (Paris: Librairie de la Société du Recueil Général des Lois et des Arrêts, 1903), 46–47, https://ia800305.us.archive.org/16/items/traitthoriqueet01thigoog/traitthoriqueet01thigoog.pdf, accessed 3 June 2019.

the French Council of the Admiralty, which expressed the view that regulations intended to prevent collisions had to be adopted by all States and that before undertaking any reforms, it was indispensable to reach an agreement with the main maritime powers. The French Minister of the Navy and of the Colonies then explained to Emperor Napoleon III (r. 1852–1870) that while collisions may have been attributable to the absence on board of the required signals, collisions were most often the result of a diversity of rules adopted by different States concerning the action to be taken in situations where vessels were overtaking or crossing each other. The Ministry had thus proposed to the Ministry of Foreign Affairs that France submit to the UK the draft regulations, accompanied by a proposal either to convene an international conference or to request adherence of the different powers to an eventual Anglo-French agreement. In spite of the reference to the "main maritime powers," it seems that the French draft was submitted only to the UK. Since the French draft regulations had been accepted by the British, with some modifications, and adopted in their modified form by the British Parliament, the two States believed that it was preferable and simpler to submit simultaneously to the other maritime powers an identical note with the text of the new regulations and to request their adhesion to it.[50] These were the Regulations that entered into force in 1863 and were adopted by 20 States.

It is not clear if France had a role in the modifications to the British regulations introduced in 1880, whereby whistle signals were allowed to be given to indicate the action taken by steamships to avoid collision, and in 1884, which specified the signals to be used by vessels in distress.[51] By means of several Orders in Council, the 1880 Regulations were declared applicable to 17 States (13 in Europe, two in South America, and one each from North America and the Pacific), five territories in India, one territory in the Middle East, and one territory in Africa.[52] The application

[50] France, Ministère de la Marine et des Colonies, 6.

[51] Anthony Norman Cockcroft and J. N. F. Lameijer, *Guide to the Collision Avoidance Rules—International Regulations for Preventing Collisions at Sea Incorporating the 1981, 1987, 1989, 1993, 2001 and 2007 Amendments* (7th ed.; Amsterdam: Elsevier, 2012), xi–xii.

[52] The 13 European States, apart from Great Britain itself, were the States listed in note 45 except for Turkey. The others were Chile, Ecuador, the United States, and the Hawaiian Islands. Marsden, *A Treatise* (1880), 135. The five territories in India

of the Regulations 1884 was extended to 10 States (eight in Europe and two in South America).[53] The numbers of States accepting the Rules of the Road, which might seem to be relatively low to modern eyes, did not prevent the US Supreme Court from declaring as early as 1871 that they were general "laws of the sea."

> The rules of navigation established in the British orders in council, of January 9, 1863 (prescribing the sorts of lights to be used on British vessels), and in our act of Congress of 1861, having, before the close of the year 1864, been accepted as obligatory by more than thirty of the principal commercial states of the world, including almost all which have any shipping on the Atlantic Ocean, were in April, 1867, to be regarded, so far as relates to the vessels of these states, as laws of the sea. And of the historical fact that by common consent of mankind, they have been acquiesced in as of general obligation, courts may take judicial notice.[54]

Marsden, writing in 1880, believed that the US Supreme Court declared in this judgment that the International Regulations were of universal application and a part of international or general maritime law.[55]

In 1889, though, the manner of drafting the International Regulations underwent a major change, one that would be more in conformity with contemporary methods of drafting multilateral treaties. In that year, the

were Cochin, Khattyawar, Khelat, Kutch, and Travancore; the territory in the Middle East was Muscat; and the territory in Africa was Zanzibar. The Regulations 1884 were declared applicable to Brazil, Chile, Denmark, France, Greece, Italy, Norway, Portugal, Sweden, and Turkey. Reginald Godfrey Marsden, Edward Stanley Roscoe, and Helenus Macaulay Robertson, *A Treatise on the Law of Collisions at Sea* (6th ed.; London: Stevens and Sons, Limited, 1910), 316, https://ia600207.us.archive.org/26/items/cu31924022403921/cu31924022403921.pdf, accessed 3 June 2019.

[53] The eight European States were Denmark, France, Greece, Italy, Norway, Portugal, Sweden, and Turkey. The South American States were Chile and Brazil. Reginald Godfrey Marsden, *A Treatise on the Law of Collisions at Sea with an Appendix Containing the International Regulations for Preventing Collisions at Sea, and Local Rules for the Same Purpose in Force in the Thames, Mersey, and Elsewhere, also the Regulations Approved at the Washington International Maritime Conference* (London: Stevens and Sons, Limited, 1891), 340, https://ia800205.us.archive.org/6/items/treatiseonsealaw00mars/treatiseonsealaw00mars.pdf, accessed 3 June 2019. The text of the International Regulations 1884 may be found at 537–71.

[54] *The Scotia*, 81 U.S. 14 Wall. 170 (1871), para. 5, https://supreme.justia.com/cases/federal/us/81/170/, accessed 3 June 2019.

[55] Marsden, *A Treatise* (1880), 135.

US convened an International Maritime Conference, held in Washington, D.C., with the aim, among others, of revising the International Regulations. To justify the need for revision, the US highlighted the greater risk of collision arising from the greater number and speed of steamships. The UK was skeptical about the necessity for such a conference, believing that if one were to be held, it had to take place in London. The UK was also concerned that in any such conference, the UK, whose shipping tonnage was equal to that of all other powers combined, might be outvoted by "minor maritime powers." The UK finally agreed to attend the Conference subject to certain conditions on its participation.[56]

The Conference was attended by 26 States (13 European, four Central American, four South American, two North American, two Asian, and one Pacific).[57] On its ambitious agenda were thirteen points, but all items except one were either rejected, or reserved to national governments to negotiate, or made the subject of mere recommendations.[58] The exception was the International Regulations, which entered into force in 1897. It was agreed that the stand-on vessel (the vessel that maintains its course and speed) should keep her speed as well as its course; that the giving-way vessel should avoid crossing ahead of the other vessel; and that steamships should be permitted to carry a second white masthead light. These International Regulations were extended by means of a British Order in Council to 26 States (13 in Europe, five in South America, three in Asia, two each in North America and Central America, and one in Africa).[59]

[56] Sarah Palmer, "Leaders and Followers: The Development of International Maritime Policy in the Nineteenth Century," *International Journal of Maritime History* 17 (2005): 302–3.

[57] See "Final Act of the International Marine Conference Held at Washington, October 16 to December 31, 1889," *American Journal of International Law* 5, *Supplement: Official Documents* (1911): 42–73. The 13 European States were Austria-Hungary, Belgium, Denmark, France, Great Britain, Italy, the Netherlands, Norway, Portugal, Russia, Spain, Sweden, and Turkey. The four Central American States were Costa Rica, Guatemala, Honduras, and Nicaragua. The four South American States were Brazil, Chile, Uruguay, and Venezuela. The two North American States were Mexico and the US. The two Asian States were China and Japan. The Pacific State was Hawaii.

[58] Palmer, "Leaders," 305.

[59] The 13 European States were Austria-Hungary, Belgium, Denmark, France, Germany, Greece, Italy, the Netherlands, Norway, Portugal, Russia, Spain, and Sweden. The five South American States were Argentina, Brazil, Chile, Ecuador, and Peru. The three Asian States were China, Japan, and Siam. The two North American States were

In France, a draft law was submitted to the French Parliament incorporating the resolution of Division 5 of the Conference, under the terms of which the master of a vessel that had collided with another vessel was obliged to stay by the other vessel until it had been determined that the latter had no further need for assistance and to render assistance to the master, the vessel, and its passengers. On this occasion, the need for international cooperation in order to prevent collisions was explained once more.[60] The numerous factors that increased greatly the risk of collisions were enumerated as follows: the progress of navigation; the substitution of steam for sails; the stimulus of international competition; the ever greater speeds that could be achieved; the increase in the size of the merchant fleets of all countries; and the sophistication of nautical instruments, making it possible for vessels to travel in a straight line and for the wake of a vessel to become the common, mathematical, and precise path to be taken by vessels that followed it.[61]

In the years following the Washington Conference, smaller States, like Belgium, and private associations, such as the *Comité Maritime International* (International Maritime Committee), established by a Belgian lawyer with the support of the Belgian government, took over the initiative from the UK of formulating proposals and convening conferences on maritime issues. It was Belgium that convened an International Maritime Conference, held in Brussels in 1910, which again revised the International Regulations.[62] The "Right of Way" system continued to underlie the International Regulations, except in cases of those situations where it was impossible to allocate responsibility to one or other of the vessels,

Mexico and the US. The two Central American States were Costa Rica and Guatemala. The African State was Egypt. Marsden, Roscoe, and Robertson, *A Treatise*, 315.

60 "Final Act of the International Marine Conference, 1889," 59–60.

61 "France: Loi sur les accidents et collisions en mer, du 10 mars 1891, *Journal officiel du 12 mars 1891* [France: Law on Accidents and Collisions at Sea of 10 March 1891, Official Journal of 12 March 1891]," in Felix Stoerk (ed.), *Nouveau recueil général de traités et autres actes relatifs aux rapports de droit international. Continuation du Grand Recueil de G. F. de Martens*, Deuxième Série, Tome XIII, Première Livraison [New General Collection of Treaties and Other Acts concerning Relations under International Law. Continuation of the Great Collection of G.F. de Martens, Second Series, Vol. XIII, First Issue] (Gottingue: Librairie Dieterich, 1893), 83, https://ia601401.us.archive.org/15/items/recueildetraits18martuoft/recueildetraits18martuoft.pdf, accessed 3 June 2019.

62 Palmer, "Leaders," 306–7.

as in "meeting" situations, or where experience had shown dual responsibility to be more suitable.[63] In 1929, a recommendation made at a Conference on the Safety of Life at Sea that helm and steering orders should be given in the direct sense, so that "right rudder" or "starboard" meant "put the vessel's rudder to starboard," was accepted and came into force in 1933.[64]

In 1948, a Conference on the Safety of Life at Sea attended by 30 States and 4 observer States revised the International Regulations, which were subsequently attached as Annex B to the Final Act of the Conference.[65] No major changes were made to the steering and sailing rules; the significant changes made referred to masthead lights, stem lights, and wake-up signals.[66] The International Regulations, which entered into force in 1954, were accepted by 43 States.[67] Further minor changes were introduced at a Conference held in 1960.[68]

The decline in British influence did not impair the international consensus on the need for International Regulations. It also seems that even if the manner of drafting the International Regulations had drastically changed, the UK continued to administer them, in the sense that a British Order in Council was still the instrument used to extend their application to the ships of States that had accepted them. Marsden reports that by Order in Council of 13 October 1910, the International Regulations 1910 were applied to the ships of 30 States (16 from Europe, six from South America, three from Asia, two each from North America and Central America, and one from Africa).[69]

[63] Plant, "The Collison Avoidance Regulations," 378.

[64] Cockcroft and Lameijer, *Guide*, xii.

[65] "Final Act of the International Conference on Safety of Life at Sea, 1948, Signed at London, on 10 June 1948, and International Regulations for Preventing Collisions at Sea, 1948. Approved by the International Conference on Safety of Life at Sea, on 10 June, 1948, and Annexed to the Above-Mentioned Final Act," *United Nations Treaty Series*, vol. 191 (New York: United Nations, 1954), 3–58 ("*UNTS*"), https://treaties.un.org/doc/Publication/UNTS/Volume%20191/v191.pdf, accessed 4 June 2019.

[66] Cockcroft and Lameijer, *Guide*, xii.

[67] One should recall that the UN had 51 founding members.

[68] As pointed out in note 29, the COLREGS 1960 were not published in the *UNTS*.

[69] The 16 European States were Austria-Hungary, Belgium, Bulgaria, Denmark, France, Germany, Greece, Italy, the Netherlands, Norway, Portugal, Rumania, Russia, Spain, Sweden, and Turkey. The six South American States were Argentina, Brazil, Chile,

In the early post-war period, the UK's role in administering the International Regulations was still central. The Conference that revised the International Regulations in 1948 was organized under British auspices. For the entry into force of the International Regulations, the Conference requested the UK:

> when substantial unanimity [sic] has been reached as to the acceptance of the International Regulations for Preventing Collisions at Sea, 1948, to fix the date on and after which the International Regulations for Preventing Collisions at Sea, 1948, shall be applied by the Governments which have agreed to accept them.[70]

The 1960 Conference was the first to be held under the auspices of the Intergovernmental Maritime Consultative Organization ("IMCO," now International Maritime Organization, "IMO"), rather than those of the UK. The exact role of the UK in the entry into force of the International Regulations 1960 cannot be determined, as they were not published in the *UNTS*.

By the time the International Regulations 1960 came into force in 1965, States and other actors had realized that a more thorough revision was necessary to take account of changes such as the widespread acceptance and the use of radar, the introduction of traffic separation schemes, and the increase in size and speed of many ships.[71] An International Conference on Revision of the International Regulations for Preventing Collisions at Sea was organized in London under the auspices of the IMCO from 4 to 20 October 1972. It was attended by 46 States and five Observer States.

Among other substantial changes, States decided to attach the text of the International Regulations as an annex to a proper international treaty, the Convention on the International Regulations for Preventing Collisions at Sea, instead of attaching them to the final act of the conference.

Ecuador, Peru, and Venezuela. The three Asian States were China, Japan, and Siam. The two Central American States were Costa Rica and Guatemala. The North American States were Mexico and the United States. The African State was Egypt. Reginald Godfrey Marsden and Marcus Warre Slade, *A Treatise on the Law of Collisions at Sea* (London: Stevens and Sons, 1919), 298, https://ia800200.us.archive.org/7/items/cu31924022403970/cu31924022403970.pdf, accessed 4 June 2019.

[70] "Final Act of the International Conference on Safety of Life at Sea, 1948," 8.

[71] Cockcroft and Lameijer, *Guide*, vii.

The Convention proper is quite brief, containing provisions on general obligations (Article I), territorial application (Article III), procedures for revision and amendments (Articles V and VI, respectively), languages (Article IX), and the final provisions (Signature, Ratification, Acceptance, Approval and Accession, Article II; Entry into Force, Article IV; Denunciation, Article VII; and Deposit and Registration, Article VIII). The Convention 1972 entered into force in August 1977, twelve months after the date on which 45 States, whose merchant fleets constituted at least 65 percent by number or by tonnage of the world fleet of vessels of 100 gross tons and over, became Parties to it, as stipulated in its Article 1 V.1(a). By the time of the Award on the merits in the *South China Sea Arbitration*, 156 States representing 98.52 percent of world tonnage were parties to the COLREGS.[72] As the Arbitral Tribunal aptly put it, it is one of the most widely adopted multilateral conventions in force.[73]

The COLREGS 1972 make explicit what was assumed for over a century: that while the COLREGS are addressed to vessels, States parties accept the duty to "give effect" to them.

B. The Duty of States Parties to Give Effect to the COLREGS

Two provisions will help us to analyze the duties of States to give effect to the COLREGS. Article I of the COLREGS 1972 stipulates that States parties "undertake to give effect to the Rules and other Annexes constituting the International Regulations for Preventing Collisions at Sea." Rule 1(a) makes clear that States will "give effect" to the Regulations with respect to all types of vessels: "These Rules shall apply to all vessels upon the high seas and in all waters connected therewith navigable by seagoing vessels."

The flag State's obligation to give effect to the COLREGS is one of due diligence. The Philippines explained during the Hearing on the Merits the nature of a due diligence obligation by quoting from an advisory opinion of the International Tribunal for the Law of the Sea

[72] *South China Sea Arbitration*, Independent Expert Report, Report of the International Navigational Safety Expert Appointed by the Permanent Court of Arbitration [sic], The Hague, The Netherlands, by Captain Gupreet S. Singhota, 15 April 2016, 2, para. 2, https://pcacases.com/web/sendAttach/1810, accessed 4 June 2019.

[73] *South China Sea Arbitration*, Award of 12 July 2016, 428, para. 1081, https://pcacases.com/web/sendAttach/2086, accessed 4 June 2019.

("ITLOS"). A due diligence obligation requires a State on which it is incumbent "to deploy adequate means, to exercise the best possible efforts and to do the utmost to obtain this result."[74] Concretely, a State party to the COLREGS should ensure that it has adopted legislation and has established administrative and judicial mechanisms and procedures requiring and enabling vessels to comply with the COLREGS.[75]

At the time of the adoption of the International Regulations in 1863, collision law was already emerging on the basis of judicial decisions in both the UK and the US.[76] There was no doubt in the minds of commentators that once the International Regulations were adopted or modified, it was the duty of States parties to adopt laws that would punish infractions against these obligations.[77] Following the adoption of the International Regulations and the extension of their application to States that accepted them, they were incorporated into the domestic law of several States. The US did so through an Act of Congress of 29 April 1864. In France, which as we saw above was already undertaking a reform of its regulations before it approached the UK, they were incorporated into domestic law by the Decrees of 25 October 1862, 26 May 1869, and 28 October 1873.[78] In the German Empire, the International Regulations 1863 were incorporated into the Criminal Code 1871.[79] Since

[74] *South China Sea Arbitration*, Hearing on the Merits and Remaining Issues of Jurisdiction and Admissibility. Final Transcript, Day 3 (26 November 2015), 71 ("Hearing on the Merits, Final Transcript, Day 3"), https://pcacases.com/web/sendAttach/1549, accessed 4 June 2019. The Philippines was quoting from *Responsibilities and Obligations of States Sponsoring Persons and Entities with Respect to Activities in the Area (Request for Advisory Opinion Submitted to the Seabed Disputes Chamber), Advisory Opinion of 1 February 2011, ITLOS Reports 2011*, 41, para. 110, https://www.itlos.org/fileadmin/itlos/documents/cases/case_no_17/17_adv_op_010211_en.pdf, accessed 4 June 2019.

[75] Plant, "The Collision Avoidance Regulations," 387, note 5.

[76] Owen, "The Origins," 767–76.

[77] See, for example, Jules Charet, *Notions de droit maritime international* [Concepts of International Maritime Law] (Paris: Berger-Levrault et Cie, Éditeurs, 1907), 34, https://ia801408.us.archive.org/33/items/notionsdedroitm00chargoog/notionsdedroitm00chargoog.pdf, accessed 4 June 2019.

[78] For the first two decrees, see France, Ministère de la Marine et des Colonies, 7–12, 14–15, 27.

[79] Karl Lueder, *Das Strafgesetzbuch für das Deutsche Reich vom 15. Mai 1871 nach der Novelle von 26 Februar 1876, nebst Einführungs-und Abänderungs-Gesetz* [The Criminal Code for the German Empire of 15 May 1871 Following the Amendment of 26 February 1876, Together with the Introductory and Amending Law] (Erlangen: Verlag

that time, States have also incorporated into domestic law the successive revisions of the International Regulations. As we have seen above, when the International Regulations were modified in 1889, the French government introduced legislation in parliament that would incorporate them into French law.[80] In the twentieth century, the COLREGS 1972 were adopted as law by the US.[81] In the UK, the COLREGS 1972 were incorporated into domestic law by the Merchant Shipping Act of 1995, while they were published by decree in France in 1977.[82]

The consistent practice of China in this respect, as summarized by Captain Yuelin Zhao, is quite interesting, in view of the changes of political regime that occurred in the country in the twentieth century.[83] China attended the International Maritime Conference held in Washington, D.C. in 1889, at a time when the Qing dynasty still ruled the country. In 1896, China adopted the International Regulations agreed upon in 1889, with the reservation that they would apply only to "ships of foreign type," i.e., power-driven vessels.[84] It is not clear whether China attended the 1910 Conference that amended the International Regulations 1889, but since the Empire was overthrown in 1912, it was the Republic that adopted the International Regulations 1910. In 1948, Taiwan attended the Safety of Life at Sea ("SOLAS") Conference,

von Andreas Deichert, 1876), 55–56, https://ia800206.us.archive.org/13/items/dasstrafgesetzb00germgoog/dasstrafgesetzb00germgoog.pdf, accessed 4 June 2019.

[80] "France: Loi sur les accidents et collisions en mer, du 10 mars, 1891 [France: Law on Accidents and Collisions at Sea]," in Stoerk, *Nouveau recueil général*, 83.

[81] Title 33, US Code (USC), Sections 101 to 1606 (33 USC 1601 and 1606), U.S. Navy, U.S. Marine Corps, U.S. Coast Guard, *The Commander's Handbook on the Law of Naval Operations*, Doc. No. NWP 1-14M/MCWP 5-12.1/COMDTPUB P5800.7A NWP ([Washington, DC:] Department of the Navy, Office of the Chief of Naval Operations and Headquarters, U.S. Marine Corps, Department of Homeland Security, and U.S. Coast Guard, 2007), 2–15 ("*The Commander's Handbook*"), http://www.jag.navy.mil/documents/NWP_1-14M_Commanders_Handbook.pdf, accessed 4 June 2019.

[82] Leslie Monteil, "L'application des conventions internationales de droit maritime en droit français [The Application of International Conventions on Maritime Law in French Law]," unpublished doctoral dissertation in law, Université Panthéon-Sorbonne - Paris I (2018), 60, 333, https://tel.archives-ouvertes.fr/tel-01785786/document, accessed 4 June 2019.

[83] Yuelin Zhao, "The Regulations for Preventing Collisions at Sea and Liability Apportionment in China," *The Asian Business Lawyer* 8 (Fall 2011): 101, asianbusinesslawyer.korea.ac.kr/xe/?module=file&act…file_srl=436, accessed 4 June 2019.

[84] Marsden and Slade, *A Treatise*, 297.

which revised the Regulations 1910. The People's Republic of China having been established in October 1949, it was the 88th Conference of the National People's Congress Standing Committee of the PRC which accepted the COLREGS 1948 on 23 December 1957, with the same reservation on power-driven vessels. It was Taiwan that was invited to the SOLAS Conference in 1960 that revised the COLREGS, but the Peoples' Republic of China formally accepted them, with the same reservation, on 6 June 1975. In 1972, neither Taiwan nor the People's Republic of China were invited to the International Conference on Revision of the International Regulations for Preventing Collisions at Sea,[85] but on 1 January 1980, the latter acceded to the COLREGS 1972 and formally enacted them into law on 10 April 1980.[86]

The duty of a State party to the COLREGS to give effect to them goes beyond due diligence as regards official vessels, including warships. As the Philippines observed during the Hearing on the Merits, official vessels are under the command and control of the flag State, which is by definition in a position to exercise operational control over them. It can give instructions to them and determine their operational rules.[87] Consequently, the duty of the State party to the COLREGS is to ensure that its official vessels comply with the COLREGS.

That the COLREGS also apply to official vessels, including warships, may be deduced from the text of the COLREGS itself. The Philippines took great pains to stress this point during the Merits Hearing. It cited the definition of "vessel" in Rule 3(a), which includes "every description of water craft…used or capable of being used as a means of transportation on water."[88] The inclusion of government vessels in the scope of the COLREGS is confirmed by the inclusion of special rules relating to signal lights or whistle signals for ships of war (Rule 1(c)), to vessels engaged in launching or recovery of aircraft (Rule 3(g)(iv)), and to vessels engaged

[85] "Final Act of the International Conference on Revision of the International Regulations for Preventing Collisions at Sea, 1972," *UNTS*, vol. 1050 (New York: United Nations, 1993), 151, https://treaties.un.org/doc/Publication/UNTS/Volume%201050/volume-1050-I-15824-English.pdf, accessed 4 June 2019.

[86] Yuelin Zhao, "The Regulations," 101. China has also accepted all six amendments to the COLREGS 1972.

[87] Hearing on the Merits, Final Transcript, Day 3, 71.

[88] *Ibid.*, 60.

in mine sweeping operations (Rule 3(g)(v)). These vessels would typically be government or military vessels.[89] As the Philippines observed, if official or military vessels had been excluded from the scope of the COLREGS, there would have been specific provisions to this effect. This is the approach adopted by treaties that recognize that special rules may have to apply to government ships.[90]

State practice confirms that the COLREGS are applicable to official vessels, including warships. It is worthwhile to refer here briefly to the regulations in force in the US, since the CSIL's rationalization of China's conduct, as we shall see later, singled out US regulations for justifying the allegedly unlimited use of force in law enforcement operations, even in violation of the COLREGS. The *Commander's Handbook on the Law of Naval Operations* reminds the reader that "US Navy Regulations, 1990 Article 1139 'directs that all persons in the naval service responsible for the operation of naval ships and craft 'shall diligently observe'" the COLREGS 1972.[91]

The conduct during the Cold War of the two superpowers provides further evidence that the COLREGS are applicable to official vessels. An initial examination might seem to yield evidence that supports the contrary conclusion. Between the late 1950s and the 1960s, a number of incidents at sea seemed to indicate that the official vessels of both States neglected to take the precautions required by the ordinary practice of seamen, as stipulated in Rule 2 of the COLREGS. The result of such neglect was a number of collisions. Details of the incidents were not always made public, but the information that is publicly available does prove that failure to comply with the COLREGS was the major cause of the collisions. For example, in March 1964, a Soviet Auxiliary, General, Intelligence ("AGI") vessel closed to within 150 yards of the USS *Daniel A. Joy*, 450 miles east of New York, and ended up colliding with it.[92]

[89] *Ibid.*

[90] The Philippines cited SOLAS 1974, Chapter V, Regulation 1, and the International Convention for the Prevention of Pollution from Ships, 1973 as modified by the Protocol of 1978, adopted at London, on 2 November 1973, entered into force on 2 October 1983 ("MARPOL 1973"), http://www.mar.ist.utl.pt/mventura/Projecto-Navios-I/IMO-Conventions%20%28copies%29/MARPOL.pdf, accessed 16 June 2019, in *ibid.*, 60–61.

[91] *The Commander's Handbook*, 2–15.

[92] David F. Winkler, "The Evolution and Significance of the 1972 Incidents at Sea Agreement," *Journal of Strategic* Studies 28 (2005): 373, note 10.

In May 1967, a US carrier was involved in two separate incidents with two Soviet destroyers in the Sea of Japan. In the first incident, the Soviet warships came within 100 yards of the US vessel on 14 occasions, until the two vessels rubbed up against each other for almost a minute. In the second incident, the Soviet and American warships collided with each other.[93] A US State Department survey for 1966 attributed a quarter of the 36 incidents that had occurred in the previous 12 months to violations of the COLREGS by Soviet merchant vessels.[94] These vessels could be considered official vessels by virtue of the State monopoly of foreign trade in the Soviet Union.

Some of the incidents may have resulted from excessive zeal or incompetence.[95] A Soviet naval official admitted in 1971 that the expansion of the Soviet navy had led to a decision to promote many young and inexperienced officers to command new cruisers and destroyers, rather than retraining more senior officers, who had achieved rank in coastal defense-oriented force.[96] Yet it is probably fair to say that most of these incidents were almost inevitable consequences of official policy on both sides. The USSR was said to be motivated by a desire to demonstrate to the US Navy that Soviet ships could deny to the US the freedom of action that the US had traditionally enjoyed on the high seas; to convey Soviet resentment over US naval operations in waters that the USSR considered to be home waters (the Black Sea, the Baltic Sea, and the Sea of Japan); and to achieve tactical purposes (e.g., to obtain information on US responses to Soviet actions). The US aims were to impede the operational effectiveness of Soviet ships, to counter surveillance of US naval forces and operations, and to minimize Soviet ships' ability to launch a surprise attack.[97]

Realizing that incidents at sea, which also involved aircraft, could endanger lives and vessels, increase tensions, and heighten the risk of war, the US and the USSR concluded in May 1972 the *Agreement on the Prevention of Incidents On and Over the High Seas*, more widely

[93] *Ibid.*, 365.

[94] *Ibid.*, 375.

[95] Sean M. Lynn-Jones, "The Incidents at Sea Agreement," in Alexander A. George et al. (eds.), *U.S.-Soviet Security Cooperation: Achievements, Failures, Lessons* (New York: Oxford University Press, 1988), 484.

[96] Winkler, "The Evolution," 368.

[97] Lynn-Jones, "The Incidents at Sea Agreement," 484–86.

known as the "Incidents at Sea Agreement." The Agreement, among other provisions, reaffirmed the applicability of the COLREGS to their naval ships. Under Article II of the Agreement, the two Parties undertook to "take measures to instruct the commanding officers of their respective ships to observe strictly the letter and spirit of the International Regulations for Preventing Collisions at Sea, hereinafter referred to as the Rules of the Road."[98] The Incidents at Sea Agreement, which is considered an example of successful security cooperation between the US and the USSR,[99] takes on added significance because it became the model for similar bilateral agreements between the USSR and other Western States (the UK, France, the Federal Republic of Germany, Spain, and Italy).[100] It was also the model for an agreement between two NATO member States, Greece and Turkey.[101]

Having established that the duties of the flag State consist in ensuring the existence of legislative and judicial mechanisms for the enforcement of the COLREGS as well as compliance by official vessels with the COLREGS, one might ask whether the flag State has the further duty of subjecting to criminal or disciplinary proceedings a mariner alleged to be responsible for a breach of the COLREGS. While this is theoretically possible, Plant remarks that such prosecution is rare.[102] In practice, it is the private parties involved who engage in litigation with the aim of determining liability for collisions and obtaining compensation for damage. They may do so in the courts of any State whose law permits this in respect of the collision in question.[103] Nevertheless, such prosecution, though rare, is still possible. As regards official vessels, it would be the

[98] U.S. Department of State, Bureau of International Security and Nonproliferation, *Agreement Between the Government of The United States of America and the Government of The Union of Soviet Socialist Republics on the Prevention of Incidents On and Over the High Seas*, signed at Moscow May 25, 1972, entered into force May 25, 1972, https://2009-2017.state.gov/t/isn/4791.htm, accessed 4 June 2019.

[99] Lynn-Jones, "The Incidents at Sea Agreement," 482.

[100] Fabio Caffio, "Lo Stretto di Hormuz e la minaccia al regime internazionale di transito [The Strait of Hormuz and the Threat to the International Transit Regime]," in Norman A. Martínez Gutiérrez (ed.), *Serving the Rule of Maritime Law: Essays in Honour of Professor David Joseph Attard* (London: Routledge, 2010), 215, note 27.

[101] Winkler, "The Evolution," 372.

[102] Plant, "The Collision Avoidance Regulations," 378.

[103] *Ibid.*, 387.

duty of the flag State, as the Philippines indicated in its *Note Verbale* to China, to instruct them to comply with the COLREGS.[104] During the Hearing on the Merits, the Philippines also alluded to remedies, which presumably would cover investigation by the flag State of the violations committed by official vessels, followed by the appropriate action.[105]

What would be the recourse of a State if one of the vessels involved in a collision is a foreign vessel? A rare instance of a State complaining against a breach by a vessel of the COLREGS was cited by the Philippines during the Hearing on the Merits. It was not by chance that the Philippines did so, for the State concerned was China. On 3 March 1971, a Soviet ship, the *Ernst Thaelmann*, collided with a Chinese fishing vessel, which sank on the high seas, about 60 nautical miles southwest of Shenyu port of Hainan Island in Kwangtung Province. At the time of the incident, both the USSR and China were bound by the COLREGS 1948. China specifically invoked them, claiming that the accident was entirely caused by the fact that the Soviet ship had failed to observe the COLREGS and did not make way for the Chinese fishing vessel.[106] Unfortunately, no further information is available about the consequences of the Chinese complaint. The fact remains that China relied on the COLREGS in its diplomatic practice.[107]

[104] *South China Sea Arbitration, Memorial of the Philippines* (30 March 2014), Annex 209, Note Verbale from the Department of Foreign Affairs of the Philippines to the Embassy of the People's Republic of China in Manila, No. 12–1222 (30 April 2012), vol. VI, 393–96, http://www.pcacases.com/pcadocs/The%20Philippines%27%20Memorial%20-%20Volume%20VI%20%28Annexes%20158-221%29.pdf, accessed 4 June 2019.

[105] Hearing on the Merits, Final Transcript, Day 3, 72–73. One American author believes that China should have investigated the conduct of Chinese vessels during the *Impeccable* incident. Jonathan G. Odom, "The True 'Lies' of the Impeccable Incident: What Really Happened, Who Disregarded International Law, and Why Every Nation (Outside of China) Should Be Concerned," *Michigan State University College of Law Journal of International Law* 18 (2010): 431, https://digitalcommons.law.msu.edu/cgi/viewcontent.cgi?article=1025&context=ilr, accessed 4 June 2019. This article was republished under the title "The Case of USNS Impeccable versus 5 Chinese Ships: A Close Examination of the Facts, the Evidence and the Law," in Jon M. Van Dyke, Sherry Broder, Seokwoo Lee, and Jin-Hyun Paik (eds.), *Governing Ocean Resources: New Challenges and Emerging Regimes: A Tribute to Judge Choon-Ho Park* (Leiden: Martinus Nijhoff Publishers, 2013), 307–43.

[106] Jeanette Greenfield, *China's Practice in the Law of the Sea* (Oxford: Clarendon Press, 1992), 113–14.

[107] Hearing on the Merits, Final Transcript, Day 3, 62–63.

May a State bring a claim against another State alleging a breach of the COLREGS? Plant expressed the view over 20 years ago that it was theoretically possible but unlikely in practice.[108] What is significant in his observation is the idea that it is theoretically possible. Arguably, this scenario is most relevant when government vessels are involved. As the Philippines pointed out during the Hearing on the Merits, a flag State's power over government vessels is not limited to legislative and enforcement jurisdiction. A flag State can give government vessels instructions and operating rules, putting it in a position to ensure that its vessels fully comply with the COLREGS. From the point of view of State responsibility, the actions of government vessels, owned and controlled by a government agency, are directly attributable to the State.[109] The attribution of the acts of a State organ to the State itself is a well-established principle of international law, reflected in Articles 4 and 5 of the International Law Commission's Draft Articles on Responsibility of States for Internationally Wrongful Acts 2001.[110]

[108] Plant, "The Collision Avoidance Regulations," 378, note 5.

[109] Hearing on the Merits, Final Transcript, Day 3, 71–72.

[110] The text of Article 4 (Conduct of organs of a State) is as follows:

1. The conduct of any State organ shall be considered an act of that State under international law, whether the organ exercises legislative, executive, judicial, or any other functions, whatever position it holds in the organization of the State, and whatever its character as an organ of the central government or of a territorial unit of the State.
2. An organ includes any person or entity which has that status in accordance with the internal law of the State.

The text of Article 5 (Conduct of persons or entities exercising elements of governmental authority) is as follows:

> The conduct of a person or entity which is not an organ of the State under article 4 but which is empowered by the law of that State to exercise elements of the governmental authority shall be considered an act of the State under international law, provided the person or entity is acting in that capacity in the particular instance.

United Nations International Law Commission, Draft Articles on Responsibility of States for Internationally Wrongful Acts, with Commentaries (2001), in *Report of the International Law Commission on the Work of Its Fifty-Third Session, 23 April–1 June and 2 July–10 August 2001, Official Records of the General Assembly, Fifty-Sixth Session*, Supplement No. 10, UN Doc. A/56/10, in *Yearbook of the International Law Commission 2001*, Vol. II, Part 2, *Report of the Commission to the General Assembly on the Work of Its Fifty-Third Session*, UN Doc. A/CN.4/SER.A/2001/Add.1 (Part 2) (New York: United

In 2009, the US had grounds to bring a claim against China, for several of the vessels that harassed the USNS *Impeccable* were official vessels. Nevertheless, the US preferred to engage in a dialogue with China on the freedom of navigation, the result of which was a Memorandum of Understanding between the US Department of Defense and China's Ministry of Defense regarding the rules of behavior for the safety of air and maritime encounters, signed on 9 and 10 November 2014, five and a half years after the *Impeccable* incident. Section I of Annex II on Rules of Behavior for the safety of Surface-to-Surface Encounters affirms that "military vessels that encounter each other at sea are to abide by the *Convention on the International Regulations for Preventing Collisions at Sea, 1972 and the Collision Regulations (COLREGs)* contained therein..." Sections III, IV (General Navigation Safety Rules), and V (Rules for Specially Designated Areas) contain specific references to Rules 2, 3, 8, 18, 27, and 35 of the COLREGS. The MOU is not intended to be binding under international law nor to affect the rights or obligations of either China or the US under relevant agreements or customary law.[111] These caveats cannot affect the binding force of the COLREGS, since both China and the US are already bound by them as parties.

After examining the process by which the COLREGS became generally accepted by States, we must now turn to the question of the way in which the concept of "generally accepted international regulations" was integrated into the Arbitral Tribunal's reasoning concerning its jurisdiction over Philippine Submission No. 13.

Annex 3.1: Aids to Memory in Four Verses by Thomas Gray, 14 October 1867

1. Two Steam Ships meeting:
When both side lights you see ahead—
Port your helm, and show your RED.

Nations, 2007), 40, 42, http://legal.un.org/docs/?path=../ilc/publications/yearbooks/english/ilc_2001_v2_p2.pdf&lang=EFSRAC, accessed 4 June 2019.

[111] U.S. Department of Defense, *Annual Report to Congress: Military and Security Developments Involving the People's Republic of China 2016* (Washington, DC: Department of Defense, 2016), 117–19, https://dod.defense.gov/Portals/1/Documents/pubs/2016%20China%20Military%20Power%20Report.pdf, accessed 4 June 2019.

2. Two Steam Ships passing:
GREEN to GREEN—or RED to RED—
Perfect safety—Go ahead!

3. Two Steam Ships Crossing:
Note: This is the position of greatest danger: there is nothing for it but good
look-out, caution, and judgment.
If to Starboard RED appear,
It is your duty to keep clear;
To act as judgment says is proper:—
To Port or Starboard—Back—or, Stop her!
But when, upon your Port is seen
A Steamer's Starboard light of GREEN,
There's not so much for you to do,
For GREEN to Port keeps clear of you.

4. All ships must keep a good look-out and Steamships must stop and go astern, if necessary:
Both in safety and in doubt,
Always keep a good lookout;
In danger with no room to turn,
Ease her!—Stop her!—Go astern!

Source John F. Kemp, "Two Hundred Years of the Collision Regulations," *Journal of Navigation*, 29 (1976): 348–49.

References

Allen, Craig H. "Whatever Became of the Change to COLREGS Rule 8." *Professionalmariner.com*, 2 May 2008, http://www.professionalmariner.com/May-2008/Whatever-became-of-the-change-to-COLREGS-Rule-8/, accessed 3 June 2019.

Anderson, Edward W. "Navigation—Technology." *Encyclopædia Britannica* (2019), https://www.britannica.com/technology/navigation-technology, accessed 4 June 2019.

Bechley, Mike. "Collision Avoidance at Sea in the Mid-20th Century: Collision Avoidance in the 1960s." *Journal of Navigation* 65 (2012): 194–97.

Bouvier, John, and Francis Rawle. *Bouvier's Law Dictionary and Concise Encyclopedia: Rawle's Revision*, Vol. III. Kansas City, MO: Vernon Law Book Company, 1914, https://ia600201.us.archive.org/29/items/cu31924022836245/cu31924022836245.pdf, accessed 2 June 2019.

Boyd, Alexander Charles. *The Merchant Shipping Laws: Being a Consolidation of All the Merchant Shipping and Passenger Acts from 1854 to 1875, Inclusive; with Notes of All the Leading British and American Cases on the Subjects Affected by Legislation; and an Appendix Containing the New Rules Issued in October 1876, Forming a Complete Treatise on Maritime Law*. London: Stevens & Sons, 1876, https://ia800208.us.archive.org/28/items/cu31924022429298/cu31924022429298.pdf, accessed 3 June 2019.

Caffio, Fabio. "Lo Stretto di Hormuz e la minaccia al regime internazionale di transito [The Strait of Hormuz and the Threat to the International Transit Regime]." *Serving the Rule of Maritime Law: Essays in Honour of Professor David Joseph Attard*, 203–15. Ed. Norman A. Martínez Gutiérrez. London: Routledge, 2010.

Charet, Jules. *Notions de droit maritime international* [Concepts of International Maritime Law]. Paris: Berger-Levrault et Cie, 1907, https://ia801408.us.archive.org/33/items/notionsdedroitm00chargoog/notionsdedroitm00chargoog.pdf, accessed 4 June 2019.

Cockcroft, Anthony Norman, and J. N. F. Lameijer. *Guide to the Collision Avoidance Rules—International Regulations for Preventing Collisions at Sea Incorporating the 1981, 1987, 1989, 1993, 2001 and 2007 Amendments*, 7th ed. Amsterdam: Elsevier, 2012.

"COLREGS 1960 (Extracts)." *Ancient Mariner*, 26 November 2006, http://rsyms.blogspot.com/2006/11/colregs-1960.html, accessed 3 June 2019.

Convention on the International Regulations for Preventing Collisions at Sea. Adopted 20 October 1972. Entered into force 15 July 1977. Consolidated text as Amended in 1981, 1987, 1989, 1993, 2001 and 2007, http://www.ecolregs.com/index.php?option=com_k2&view=itemlist&layout=category&Itemid=505&lang=en, accessed 31 May 2019.

Craig-Bennett, Andrew. The WoodenBoat Forum > Misc. Boat Related > When Both Lights You See Ahead...and Other Rhymes of the Sea... 08-02-2010, 09:15 AM, http://forum.woodenboat.com/archive/index.php/t-118056.html, accessed 2 June 2019.

"Final Act of the International Conference on Revision of the International Regulations for Preventing Collisions at Sea, 1972." *United Nations Treaty* Series, Vol. 1050, 151–53. New York: United Nations, 1993, https://treaties.un.org/doc/Publication/UNTS/Volume%201050/volume-1050-I-15824-English.pdf, accessed 4 June 2019.

"Final Act of the International Conference on Safety of Life at Sea, 1948. Signed at London, on 10 June 1948 and International Regulations for Preventing Collisions at Sea, 1948. Approved by the International Conference on Safety of Life at Sea, on 10 June 1948, and Annexed to the Above-Mentioned Final Act." *United Nations Treaty Series*, Vol. 191, 3–58.

New York: United Nations, 1954, https://treaties.un.org/doc/Publication/UNTS/Volume%20191/v191.pdf, accessed 4 June 2019.

"Final Act of the International Marine Conference Held at Washington, October 16 to December 31, 1889." *American Journal of International Law* 5, *Supplement: Official Documents* (1911): 42–73.

"France: Loi sur les accidents et collisions en mer, du 10 mars 1891. *Journal official du 12 mars 1891* [France: Law on Accidents and Collisions at Sea of 10 March 1891. Official Journal of 12 March 1891]." *Nouveau recueil général de traités et autres actes relatifs aux rapports de droit international. Continuation du Grand Recueil de G. F. de Martens. Deuxième Série. Tome XIII. Première Livraison* [New General Collection of Treaties and Other Acts Concerning Relations Under International Law. Continuation of the Great Collection of G.F. de Martens. Second Series. Vol. XIII. First Issue], 79–99. Ed. Felix Stoerk. Gottingue: Librairie Dieterich, 1893, https://ia601401.us.archive.org/15/items/recueildetraits18martuoft/recueildetraits18martuoft.pdf, accessed 3 June 2019.

France. Ministère de la Marine et des Colonies [Ministry of the Navy and of the Colonies]. *Abordages. Décrets des 25 octobre 1862 et 26 mai 1869. Questionnaire réglementaire sur les signaux de brume, les feux que doivent porter les bâtiments et les règles à suivre pour la navigation tant à la voile qu'à la vapeur* [Collisions. Decrees of 25 October 1862 and 26 May 1869. Regulatory Questionnaire on the Fog Signals, the Lights That Vessels Should Carry and the Rules to Be Followed for Sail-Powered as Well as by Steam Navigation]. Paris: Imprimerie Administrative de Paul Dupont, 1869, https://babel.hathitrust.org/cgi/pt?id=njp.32101058626910;view=plaintext;page=root;size=100;seq=12;num=6, accessed 3 June 2019.

Greenfield, Jeanette. *China's Practice in the Law of the Sea*. Oxford: Clarendon Press, 1992.

Greiner, Kirk. "COLREG Amendments." *The Expert* 6 (1990), http://www.maritimeconsultant.com/macnewsletters/spring90/colreg_amendments.htm, accessed 2 June 2019.

Intermaritime Certification Services (ICS Class). *History of SOLAS*. Panama: ICS Class, 2012, https://icsclass.org/history-of-solas/, accessed 12 November 2018.

International Conference on Safety of Life at Sea: Text of the Convention for the Safety of Life at Sea. London: H.M. Stationery Office, Harrison and Sons, Printers England, 1914, http://ia802605.us.archive.org/5/items/textofconvention00inte/textofconvention00inte.pdf, accessed 3 June 2019.

International Convention for the Safety of Life at Sea (SOLAS 1974). Adopted at London, 1 November 1974. Entered into Force 25 May 1980, https://www.refworld.org/docid/46920bf32.html, accessed 3 June 2019.

International Convention on Maritime Search and Rescue (SAR 1979). Adopted at Hamburg, 27 April 1979. Entered into Force 22 June 1985. *United Nations Treaty Series*, Vol. 1405, 119–33. New York: United Nations, 1995, https://treaties.un.org/doc/Publication/UNTS/Volume%201405/volume-1405-I-23489-English.pdf, accessed 3 June 2019.

International Convention on Standards of Training, Certification and Watchkeeping for Seafarers, as Amended (STCW 1978/1995). Adopted at London, 7 July 1978. Entered into Force on 28 April 1984. *United Nations Treaty Series*, Vol. 1361, 190–298. New York: United Nations, 1993, https://treaties.un.org/doc/Publication/UNTS/Volume%201361/volume-1361-I-23001-English.pdf, accessed 3 June 2019.

International Maritime Organization (IMO). *International Convention for the Safety of Life at Sea (SOLAS), 1974*. London: IMO, 2019, http://www.imo.org/en/About/Conventions/ListOfConventions/Pages/International-Convention-for-the-Safety-of-Life-at-Sea-(SOLAS),-1974.aspx, accessed 3 June 2019.

———. *International Convention on Maritime Search and Rescue (SAR)*. London: IMO, 2019, http://www.imo.org/en/About/conventions/listofconventions/pages/international-convention-on-maritime-search-and-rescue-(sar).aspx, accessed 3 June 2019.

———. *International Convention on Standards of Training, Certification and Watchkeeping for Seafarers (STCW)*. London: IMO, 2019, http://www.imo.org/en/About/Conventions/ListOfConventions/Pages/International-Convention-on-Standards-of-Training,-Certification-and-Watchkeeping-for-Seafarers-(STCW).aspx, accessed 3 June 2019.

———. *Status of Conventions, Status of IMO Treaties. Comprehensive Information on the Status of Multilateral Conventions and Instruments in Respect of Which the International Maritime Organization or Its Secretary-General Performs Depositary or Other Functions*. London: IMO, 2019, http://www.imo.org/en/About/Conventions/StatusOfConventions/Documents/Status%20-%202019.pdf, accessed 3 June 2019.

International Tribunal for the Law of the Sea. *Responsibilities and Obligations of States Sponsoring Persons and Entities with Respect to Activities in the Area (Request for Advisory Opinion Submitted to the Seabed Disputes Chamber). Advisory Opinion of 1 February 2011. ITLOS Reports 2011*, 10–78, https://www.itlos.org/fileadmin/itlos/documents/cases/case_no_17/17_adv_op_010211_en.pdf, accessed 4 June 2019.

Kemp, John F. "Two Hundred Years of the Collision Regulations." *Journal of Navigation* 29 (1976): 341–49.

Kemp, Peter (ed.). *Oxford Companion to Ships and the Sea*. Oxford: Oxford University Press, 1988.

Kopacz, Zdisław et al. "An Attempt of [sic] the Specification of the Ship's Navigation Process." *Annual of Navigation* 3 (2001): 91–101.

Legge 5 maggio 1966 [Law of 5 May 1966], *n. 276. Norme per prevenire gli abbordi in mare* [Rules to Prevent Collisions at Sea]. (*GU Serie Generale* [Official Gazette General Series] n.120 del 17-05-1966), http://www.gazzettaufficiale.it/eli/id/1966/05/17/066U0276/sg;jsessionid=tlY54quTSf62HLWeAoOHmA__.ntc-as2-guri2a, accessed 3 June 2019.

Lueder, Karl. *Das Strafgesetzbuch für das Deutsche Reich vom 15. Mai 1871 nach der Novelle von 26 Februar 1876, nebst Einführungs-und Abänderungs-Gesetz* [The Criminal Code for the German Empire of 15 May 1871 Following the Amendment of 26 February 1876, Together with the Introductory and Amending Law]. Erlangen: Verlag von Andreas Deichert, 1876, https://ia800206.us.archive.org/13/items/dasstrafgesetzb00germgoog/dasstrafgesetzb00germgoog.pdf, accessed 4 June 2019.

Lynn-Jones, Sean M. "The Incidents at Sea Agreement." *U.S.-Soviet Security Cooperation: Achievements, Failures, Lessons*, 482–509. Eds. Alexander A. George et al. New York: Oxford University Press, 1988.

Marsden, Reginald Godfrey. *A Treatise on the Law of Collisions at Sea, with an Appendix Containing Extracts from the Merchant Shipping Acts, the International Regulations (of 1863 and 1880) for Preventing Collisions at Sea and Local Rules for the Same Purpose in Force in the Thames, The Mersey and Elsewhere*. London: Stevens and Sons, 1880, https://ia800205.us.archive.org/26/items/cu31924022403897/cu31924022403897.pdf, accessed 3 June 2019.

———. *A Treatise on the Law of Collisions at Sea with an Appendix Containing the International Regulations for Preventing Collisions at Sea, and Local Rules for the Same Purpose in Force in the Thames, Mersey, and Elsewhere, also the Regulations Approved at the Washington International Maritime Conference*. London: Stevens and Sons, Limited, 1891, https://ia800205.us.archive.org/6/items/treatiseonsealaw00mars/treatiseonsealaw00mars.pdf, accessed 3 June 2019.

Marsden, Reginald Godfrey, and Marcus Warre Slade. *A Treatise on the Law of Collisions at Sea*. London: Stevens and Sons, 1919, https://ia800200.us.archive.org/7/items/cu31924022403970/cu31924022403970.pdf, accessed 4 June 2019.

Marsden, Reginald Godfrey; Edward Stanley Roscoe; and Helenus Macaulay Robertson. *A Treatise on the Law of Collisions at Sea*, 6th ed. London: Stevens and Sons, Limited, 1910, https://ia600207.us.archive.org/26/items/cu31924022403921/cu31924022403921.pdf, accessed 3 June 2019.

Monteil, Leslie. "L'application des conventions internationales de droit maritime en droit français [The Application of International Conventions on Maritime

Law in French Law].” Unpublished doctoral dissertation in law, Université Panthéon-Sorbonne - Paris I (2018), https://tel.archives-ouvertes.fr/tel-01785786/document, accessed 4 June 2019.

Odom, Jonathan G. “The Case of USNS Impeccable versus 5 Chinese Ships: A Close Examination of the Facts, the Evidence and the Law.” *Governing Ocean Resources: New Challenges and Emerging Regimes: A Tribute to Judge Choon-Ho Park*, 307–43. Eds. Jon M. Van Dyke et al. Leiden: Martinus Nijhoff Publishers, 2013.

———. “The True ‘Lies’ of the Impeccable Incident: What Really Happened, Who Disregarded International Law, and Why Every Nation (Outside of China) Should Be Concerned.” *Michigan State University College of Law Journal of International Law* 18 (2010): 411–52, https://digitalcommons.law.msu.edu/cgi/viewcontent.cgi?article=1025&context=ilr, accessed 4 June 2019.

Owen, David R. “The Origins and Development of Marine Collision Law.” *Tulane Law Review* 51 (1977): 759–819.

Palmer, Sarah. “Leaders and Followers: The Development of International Maritime Policy in the Nineteenth Century.” *International Journal of Maritime History* 17 (2005): 299–309.

Pike, Dag. “Collision Rules for High-Speed Craft.” *Journal of Navigation* 58 (2005): 159–63.

Plant, Glen. “The Collision Avoidance Regulations as a Regulator of International Navigation Rights: Underlying Principles and Their Adequacy for the Twenty-first Century.” *Journal of Navigation* 88 (1996): 377–93.

Salinas, Carlos F. “Collision Regulations Discussions.” *Journal of Navigation* 55 (2002): 501–05.

South China Sea Arbitration. Award of 12 July 2016, https://pcacases.com/web/sendAttach/2086, accessed 4 June 2019.

———. Hearing on the Merits and Remaining Issues of Jurisdiction and Admissibility. Final Transcript, Day 3 (26 November 2015), https://pcacases.com/web/sendAttach/1549, accessed 4 June 2019.

———. Independent Expert Report. Report of the International Navigational Safety Expert Appointed by the Permanent Court of Arbitration [sic], The Hague, The Netherlands, by Captain Gupreet S. Singhota, 15 April 2016, https://pcacases.com/web/sendAttach/1810, accessed 4 June 2019.

———. *Memorial of the Philippines* (30 March 2014). Annex 209. Note Verbale from the Department of Foreign Affairs of the Philippines to the Embassy of the People’s Republic of China in Manila, No. 12–1222 (30 April 2012). Vol. VI, 393–96, http://www.pcacases.com/pcadocs/The%20Philippines%27%20Memorial%20-%20Volume%20VI%20%28Annexes%20158-221%29.pdf, accessed 4 June 2019.

Spencer, Herbert Ransom. *A Treatise on the Law of Marine Collisions*. Chicago: Callaghan and Company, 1895, http://www.minnesotalegalhistoryproject.org/assets/Spencer%20on%20Marine%20Collisions.pdf, accessed 3 June 2019.

Stitt, I. P. A. "The COLREGS—Time for a Rewrite?" *Journal of Navigation* 55 (2002): 419–30.

Stoerk, Felix (ed.). *Nouveau recueil général de traités et autres actes relatifs aux rapports de droit international. Continuation du Grand Recueil de G. F. de Martens*. Deuxième Série. Tome XIII. Première Livraison [New General Collection of Treaties and Other Acts Concerning Relations Under International Law. Continuation of the Great Collection of G.F. de Martens. Second Series. Vol. XIII. First Issue]. Gottingue: Librairie Dieterich, 1893, https://ia601401.us.archive.org/15/items/recueildetraits18martuoft/recueildetraits18martuoft.pdf, accessed 3 June 2019.

Thiébaut, Louis. *Traité théorique et pratique de l'abordage maritime. Études pratiques de droit maritime* [A Theoretical and Practical Treatise on Maritime Collisions. Practical Studies on Maritime Law]. Paris: Librairie de la Société du Recueil Général des Lois et des Arrêts, 1903, https://ia800305.us.archive.org/16/items/traitthoriqueet01thigoog/traitthoriqueet01thigoog.pdf, accessed 3 June 2019.

Thirslund, Søren. "Collision Avoidance at Sea in the Mid-20th Century. Thoughts from Denmark." *Journal of Navigation* 65 (2012): 201–3.

Trinity House. *About Us*. London: Trinity House, 2016, https://www.trinityhouse.co.uk/about-us, accessed 3 June 2019.

Undrum, Rolf Johannes. "Definition of a Fast and Manoeuverable Craft and Amendments to the Collision Regulations." *Journal of Navigation* 58 (2005): 154–59.

United Nations. International Law Commission. Draft Articles on Responsibility of States for Internationally Wrongful Acts, with Commentaries (2001). *Report of the International Law Commission on the Work of Its Fifty-Third Session, 23 April–1 June and 2 July–10 August 2001. Official Records of the General Assembly, Fifty-Sixth Session, Supplement No. 10*. UN Doc. A/56/10. *Yearbook of the International Law Commission 2001*. Vol. II, Part 2. *Report of the Commission to the General Assembly on the Work of Its Fifty-Third Session*. UN Doc. A/CN.4/SER.A/2001/Add.1 (Part 2), 26–143. New York: United Nations, 2007, http://legal.un.org/docs/?path=../ilc/publications/yearbooks/english/ilc_2001_v2_p2.pdf&lang=EFSRAC, accessed 4 June 2019.

United States. Department of Defense. *Annual Report to Congress: Military and Security Developments Involving the People's Republic of China 2016*. Washington, DC: Department of Defense, 2016, https://dod.defense.gov/

Portals/1/Documents/pubs/2016%20China%20Military%20Power%20Report.pdf, accessed 4 June 2019.

———. Department of State. Bureau of International Security and Nonproliferation. *Agreement Between the Government of The United States of America and the Government of The Union of Soviet Socialist Republics on the Prevention of Incidents On and Over the High Seas*. Signed at Moscow May 25, 1972. Entered into Force May 25, 1972, https://2009-2017.state.gov/t/isn/4791.htm, accessed 4 June 2019.

———. Navy; U.S. Marine Corps; and U.S. Coast Guard. *Commander's Handbook on the Law of Naval Operations Edition July 2007*. Doc. NWP1-14M/MCWP 5-12.1/COMDTPUB P5800.7A. [Washington, DC]: Department of the Navy, Office of the Chief of Naval Operations and Headquarters, US Marine Corps, Department of Homeland Security and US Coast Guard, 2007, http://www.jag.navy.mil/documents/NWP_1-14M_Commanders_Handbook.pdf, accessed 4 June 2019.

———. Supreme Court. *The Scotia*. 81 U.S. 14 Wall. 170 (1871), https://supreme.justia.com/cases/federal/us/81/170/, accessed 3 June 2019.

Weber, Hanno. "Clarification of the Steering and Sailing Rules of the COLREGS." *Journal of Navigation* 48 (1995): 289–92.

Williams, Karen. "Collision Regulation: Not to Impede." *Journal of Navigation* 55 (2002): 500–1.

Winkler, David F. "The Evolution and Significance of the 1972 Incidents at Sea Agreement." *Journal of Strategic Studies* 28 (2005): 361–77.

Zhao, Yuelin. "The Regulations for Preventing Collisions at Sea and Liability Apportionment in China." *The Asian Business Lawyer* 8 (Fall 2011): 100–15, asianbusinesslawyer.korea.ac.kr/xe/?module=file&act...file_srl=436, accessed 4 June 2019.

CHAPTER 4

The COLREGS and the Arbitral Tribunal's Jurisdiction

The Philippines' Submission No. 13 raised the question of the relations between the United Nations Convention on the Law of the Sea ("the Convention") and other international agreements, in this case the Convention on the International Regulations for Preventing Collisions at Sea 1972 ("COLREGS").[1] One provision of the Convention that sheds light on this relationship is Article 293(1), which authorizes any court or tribunal having jurisdiction under the Convention to apply the latter together with other rules of international law that are not incompatible with the Convention.[2] This provision was not invoked by the Philippines, since there were other provisions of the Convention that expressly or implicitly referred to the COLREGS.

In its *Memorial* the Philippines invoked first Article 94 of the Convention, followed by the COLREGS, as the law applicable to its Submission

[1] *United Nations Convention on the Law of the Sea*, concluded at Montego Bay on 10 December 1982, entered into force 16 November 1994, http://www.un.org/depts/los/convention_agreements/texts/unclos/unclos_e.pdf, accessed 6 June 2019; *Convention on the International Regulations for Preventing Collisions at Sea*, adopted 20 October 1972, entered into force 15 July 1977; consolidated text as amended in 1981, 1987, 1989, 1993, 2001 and 2007, http://www.ecolregs.com/index.php?option=com_k2&view=itemlist&layout=category&Itemid=505&lang=en, accessed 31 May 2019.

[2] Article 293(1), Applicable Law, reads as follows: "1. A court or tribunal having jurisdiction under this section shall apply this Convention and other rules of international law not incompatible with this Convention."

A. C. Robles Jr., *Vessel Collisions in the Law of the Sea*,
https://doi.org/10.1007/978-981-16-9793-7_4

No. 13. Article 94(3)(Duties of the Flag State) requires each State party to the Convention to take "such measures for ships flying its flag as are necessary to ensure safety at sea with regard, *inter alia*, to:...(c) the use of signals, the maintenance of communications and the prevention of collisions." Article 94(5) stipulates that "[in] taking the measures called for in paragraph 3...each State is required to conform to generally accepted international regulations, procedures and practices and to take any steps which may be necessary to secure their observance."[3] The Philippines argued that the reference to "generally accepted international regulations" was understood to include the COLREGS and cited the International Maritime Organization ("IMO") as its authority for this interpretation.[4]

The Philippines was at this stage proceeding on the assumption that it was a party to the COLREGS as at April and May 2012, when the near-collisions occurred at Scarborough Shoal. The recourse by a State party to the COLREGS to the Convention's dispute settlement mechanism would have made sense, simply because the COLREGS lack a dispute settlement mechanism. An amendment to Part F of the COLREGS, which entered into force in January 2016, now makes possible verification of compliance with their provisions through an audit. This mechanism would not have been applicable to any alleged violation of the COLREGS occurring before 2016. In any event, the audit provided for in the amendment is not equivalent to a dispute settlement mechanism.[5]

[3] *South China Sea Arbitration, Memorial of the Philippines* (30 March 2014), vol. I, 207–8, paras. 6.128–6.130 ("*MP*"), http://www.pcacases.com/pcadocs/Memorial%20of%20the%20Philippines%20Volume%20I.pdf, accessed 5 June 2019. International regulations relating to the prevention of collisions are expressly or implicitly referred to in Article 39(2)(1), relating to the duties of ships and aircraft during transit passage in straits that are used for international navigation; in Article 54, on the duties of ships and aircraft exercising archipelagic sea lanes passage, which applies, among others, Article 39 to archipelagic sea lanes passage; and in Article 58(2), on the rights and duties of other States in the EEZ, which applies, among others, Article 94, to the EEZ.

[4] *MP*, vol. I, 208, para. 6.130.

[5] *COLREG Convention on the International Regulations for Preventing Collisions at Sea, 1972. Consolidated Edition, 2003. Supplement January 2016*, http://www.imo.org/en/Publications/Documents/Supplements%20and%20CDs/English/QB904E_012016.pdf, accessed 5 June 2019; Framework and Procedures for the IMO Member State Audit Scheme (resolution A.1067(28)), IMO Doc. A 28/Res.1067 (5 December 2013), http://www.imo.org/en/OurWork/TechnicalCooperation/Documents/A%2028-Res%201067.pdf, accessed 5 June 2019; "IMO Assembly Adopts Mandatory Audit Scheme,"

In the absence of a dispute settlement mechanism, a State party to the COLREGS that alleges violation of one or more of its provisions by another State party would have to resort to the means of dispute settlement available to them under general international law or any other relevant international agreement in force between them. The Convention would be one such agreement, by virtue of the concept of "generally accepted international regulations" in Article 94(5), for States that are parties to both the Convention and the COLREGS. The concept assumed greater importance in the proceedings than perhaps the Philippines had anticipated when it turned out that the Philippines was not a party to the COLREGS at the time of the incidents in April and May 2012. The status of the Philippines as a third State with respect to the COLREGS as at April and May 2012 confronted the Tribunal with the problem whether a State party to the Convention could avail itself of the latter's dispute settlement provisions on the basis that the COLREGS, to which that State was not a party, were "generally accepted international regulations" within the meaning of Article 94(5) of the Convention.[6]

The Arbitral Tribunal had no difficulty in determining that the COLREGS were indeed "generally accepted international regulations" within the meaning of Article 94(5) of the Convention, and were consequently binding on the Philippines, although it was not a party to the COLREGS at the time of the incidents of April and May 2012. As a party to the COLREGS, the Philippines would be subject to the obligations that they imposed. Conversely, the Philippines would enjoy the rights conferred on all States parties by the COLREGS. The Philippines would be able to invoke them in case of a breach of an obligation under the COLREGS committed by another State party to the COLREGS. There is practically no discussion at all in the Award of 12 July 2016 of the concept of "generally accepted international regulations." As this appears to be the first time that an international tribunal has established jurisdiction on the basis of this concept, an examination of the nature of such

World Maritime News, 5 December 2013, https://worldmaritimenews.com/archives/99206/imo-assembly-adopts-mandatory-audit-scheme/, accessed 5 June 2019.

[6] The Vienna Convention on the Law of Treaties defines a "third State" as" a State not a party to the treaty." *Vienna Convention on the Law of Treaties (with annex)*, concluded at Vienna on 23 May 1969, entered into force on 27 January 1980, Article 2(1)(h), *United Nations Treaty Series*, vol. 1155 (New York: United Nations, 1980), 333, https://treaties.un.org/doc/publication/unts/volume%201155/volume-1155-i-18232-english.pdf, accessed 5 June 2019.

regulations is imperative.[7] The discussion in the first part of this chapter will show that the COLREGS are the paradigmatic "generally accepted international regulations."

The Tribunal's acceptance of the COLREGS as "generally accepted international regulations" did not resolve all issues concerning its jurisdiction to hear Philippine Submission No. 13. Despite the fact that China's Position Paper did not raise any objection to jurisdiction in this respect, the Tribunal had to examine whether one optional limitation to jurisdiction set out in Part XV, Section 3 of the Convention, the "law enforcement activities" exception, barred it from exercising jurisdiction with respect to Submission No. 13. The post-arbitration critique of the Tribunal's decision formulated by the Chinese Society of International Law ("CSIL") contended that the Tribunal lacked jurisdiction, due to the alleged absence of an enabling provision that made possible the application of the COLREGS to the territorial sea of Scarborough Shoal, over which China allegedly had sovereignty.[8] The "law enforcement activities" exception and the absence of an enabling provision will be examined together as possible limits to the Tribunal's jurisdiction in Part II of this Chapter.

I. The COLREGS as "Generally Accepted International Regulations"

The Philippine argument in the *Memorial* assumed that the Philippines was a party to the COLREGS on 28 April and 26 May 2012. According to the Philippines, it had acceded on 15 December 1981 to the COLREGS 1972, which had allegedly entered into force for it on 15 March 1982.[9] In reality, the Philippines acceded to the COLREGS 1972 only on 10 June 2013, nearly six months after the initiation of the

[7] A recent commentary on Article 94 contains no reference to international caselaw. Douglas Guilfoyle, "Article 94. Duties of the flag State," in Alexander Proelss et al. (eds.), *United Nations Convention on the Law of the Sea. A Commentary* (München: Verlag C.H. Beck oHG, 2017), 707–14.

[8] Chinese Society of International Law ("CSIL"), "The South China Sea Arbitration Awards: A Critical Study," *Chinese Journal of International Law* 17 (2018): 594–607.

[9] *MP*, vol. I, 208, para. 6.132.

proceedings (22 January 2013).[10] The treaty to which the Philippines had acceded in 1980 was the International Convention for the Safety of Life at Sea 1974 (SOLAS 1974),[11] which the Philippines had inexplicably confused with the COLREGS in the *Memorial*.

Presumably by the time of the Hearing on the Merits in November 2015, the Philippines had discovered this error, which would explain why at the Hearing, the Philippines did not reiterate its claim, put forward in the *Memorial*, that it was a party to the COLREGS.[12] Instead, the Philippines stressed that the principal legal basis of Submission No. 13 was Article 94 of the Convention and that there was "little doubt that the 1972 Convention [on the International Regulations for Preventing Collisions at Sea] and its regulations are generally accepted for purposes of Article 94 [of the United Nations Convention on the Law of the Sea]."[13] It was the expert appointed by the Tribunal, Captain Singhota,

[10] IMO, *Status of IMO Treaties. Comprehensive Information on the Status of Multilateral Conventions and Instruments in respect of which the International Maritime Organization or Its Secretary-General Performs Depositary or Other Functions* (London: IMO, 2019), 95, http://www.imo.org/en/About/Conventions/StatusOfConventions/Documents/Status%20-%202019.pdf, accessed 3 June 2019. There are no publicly available records of proceedings of the Philippine Senate in the course of which the Senate would have given its concurrence to ratification of the COLREGS. It may be assumed that the Philippine Executive treated the COLREGS as an executive agreement, for which the concurrence of the Philippine Senate was not necessary, and on this basis acceded to the COLREGS. For the distinction between treaties and international agreements, see Republic of the Philippines, Executive Order No. 459, providing for the Guidelines in the Negotiation of International Agreements and Its [sic] Ratification (25 November 1997), https://www.gppb.gov.ph/laws/laws/EO_459-1997.pdf, accessed 15 July 2021.

[11] *International Convention for the Safety of Life at Sea* (SOLAS 1974), done at London, 1 November 1974, entered into force 25 May 1980, https://www.refworld.org/docid/46920bf32.html, accessed 3 June 2019.

[12] If one examines the chronology, one may assume that the Philippines discovered its error sometime between 22 January 2013, the date of initiation of the *Arbitration*, and 10 June 2013, when it finally acceded to the COLREGS. Under Article IV (3) of the COLREGS, they enter into force for the acceding State on the date of deposit of the instrument of accession. But then one is hard put to explain why the *Memorial*, which was submitted to the Tribunal on 30 March 2014, reproduced the error. Perhaps this error is the result of miscommunication between the Philippines and the foreign lawyers who drafted the *Memorial*.

[13] *South China Sea Arbitration*, Hearing on the Merits and Remaining Issues of Jurisdiction and Admissibility, Final Transcript, Day 3 (26 November 2015), 59–60 ("Hearing on the Merits"), https://pcacases.com/web/sendAttach/1549, accessed 5 June 2019.

who provided the correct date.[14] The Arbitral Tribunal, observing that "the Philippines did not become party to the COLREGS until 2013," nonetheless decided that the COLREGS "bound both States relating to the conduct of their vessels by virtue of Article 94."[15] Interestingly enough, neither China nor the Chinese Society of International Law ("CSIL") raised at any time any objection to the Tribunal's jurisdiction based on the status of the Philippines as a third State in relation to the COLREGS in 2012.

That said, it is worthwhile examining the notion of "generally accepted international regulations," without which the Philippines would not have been considered bound by the COLREGS prior to 2013. By virtue of the principle of "non-retroactivity of treaties," a treaty's provisions "do not bind a party in relation to any act or fact which took place or any situation which ceased to exist before the date of entry into force of the treaty with respect to that party."[16] As we shall see, while there is some debate among scholars about the meaning of "generally accepted international regulations" in the Convention, we can have no doubt as regards the applicability of the notion to the COLREGS once we have examined the *travaux préparatoires* of the Geneva Convention on the High Seas 1958.[17]

A. The Scholarly Debate on the Concept of "Generally Accepted International Regulations" in the Convention

There are two interrelated aspects of the scholarly debate: the legal consequences of the application of "generally accepted international regulations" and the criterion (or criteria) for general acceptance of the international regulations concerned.

[14] *South China Sea Arbitration*, Independent Expert Report, Report of the International Navigational Safety Expert Appointed by the Permanent Court of Arbitration [sic], The Hague, The Netherlands, 15 April 2016, by Captain Gupreet S. Singhota, 2, para. 3, https://pcacases.com/web/sendAttach/1810, accessed 6 June 2019.

[15] *South China Sea Arbitration*, Award of 12 July 2016, 428, para. 1082, https://pcacases.com/web/sendAttach/2086, accessed 5 June 2019.

[16] *Vienna Convention on the Law of Treaties*, Article 28, Non-Retroactivity of Treaties.

[17] The term "*travaux préparatoires*" refers to the preparatory work (in American parlance, the legislative history) of a treaty, as used as a means of interpretation. John P. Grant and J. Craig Barker, *Parry & Grant Encyclopedic Dictionary of International Law* (3rd ed. Oxford: Oxford University Press, 2009), 613.

The degree of consensus on the first point is somewhat greater than on the second point. Bernard Oxman, who was a member of the US Delegation to the Third United Nations Conference on the Law of the Sea ("UNCLOS III") and who has written an authoritative paper on the need to respect internationally agreed international standards, declared succinctly that the effect of the duty is "to impose legal obligations on States to respect a standard which it would not otherwise be legally bound to respect."[18] Daniel Vignes, a noted legal scholar who attended UNCLOS III as coordinator on behalf of the European Commission of the positions of Member States of the then European Community (EC), explains that the "generally accepted international rules" will be binding for the flag State or the coastal State, even if it has not accepted them, because it has ratified the Convention. To put it differently, a State that has not participated in the formulation of the rules will be bound by them.[19] The exception to the consensual basis of international law that has been inserted in this manner in the Convention is justified by the nature of the Convention as a legal framework. While it might appear to be incongruous to describe a treaty with 320 articles and nine annexes as a legal framework, the fact is that it was impossible for the Convention to lay down all the detailed provisions that were required for its application.[20] Even as the Convention was being drafted, it was already anticipated that a secondary law would have to be developed outside the Convention framework due to the technical nature of the secondary

[18] Bernard Oxman, "The Duty to Respect Generally Accepted International Standards," *New York University Journal of International Law and Politics* 24 (1991): 144, https://repository.law.miami.edu/cgi/viewcontent.cgi?article=1403&context=fac_articles, accessed 5 June 2019. Oxman was one of the members of the Philippine legal team in the *Arbitration*. United Nations Office of Legal Affairs, Codification Division, *United Nations Diplomatic Conferences. Third United Nations Conference on the Law of the Sea, 1973–1982*, 2019, http://legal.un.org/diplomaticconferences/1973_los/, accessed 4 April 2019.

[19] Daniel Vignes, "La valeur juridique de certaines règles, normes ou pratiques, mentionnées au TNCO [Texte de négociation composite et officieux] comme 'généralement acceptées' [The Binding Force of Certain Rules, Norms or Practices Mentioned in the ICNT (Informal Composite Negotiating Text] as "Generally Accepted"]," *Annuaire Français de Droit International* [French Yearbook of International Law] 25 (1979): 716 ("*AFDI*"), https://www.persee.fr/doc/afdi_0066-3085_1979_num_25_1_2182, accessed 5 June 2019.

[20] *Ibid.*, 712.

law.[21] In the course of time, the legal framework offered by the Convention would be "filled in, rounded out and complemented by additional international agreements and customary law."[22]

The Tribunal determined that Article 94 of the Convention incorporated the COLREGS into the Convention, which are thus binding on China.[23] It was perhaps not strictly necessary to declare that the COLREGS are binding on China, given that China had acceded to the COLREGS in January 1980. It is of greater interest to examine the implications of the notion of "generally accepted international regulations" for a State party to the Convention like the Philippines, who may not have ratified a particular convention or regulation relating to the use of signals, the maintenance of communications, and the prevention of collisions, as well as to all other matters enumerated in Article 94(3). For such States, it is essential to be able to identify the regulations. Such an undertaking is complicated by the fact that the Convention did not define the notion of "generally accepted." In its *Memorial* the Philippines cited the IMO as the authority for its interpretation of the concept.

> The basic obligations imposed upon the flag State are contained in article 94 of UNCLOS which requires flag States to take measures to ensure safety at sea which conform to "generally accepted international regulations, procedures and practices" (article 94 (3), (4) and (5)). The following IMO conventions may, on account of their world-wide acceptance, be deemed to fulfill the requirement of general acceptance:. . .Convention on the International Regulations for Preventing Collisions at Sea, 1972. (COLREG 1972)[24]

The Arbitral Tribunal refrained from expressing a view on the authority of the IMO to interpret the Convention and confined itself to the observation that the COLREGS, to which 156 States representing over 98

[21] *Ibid.*

[22] Craig H. Allen, "Revisiting the Thames Formula: The Evolving Role of the International Maritime Organization and Its Member States in Implementing the 1982 Law of the Sea Convention," *San Diego International Law Journal* 10 (2009): 274, https://digitalcommons.law.uw.edu/faculty-articles/86/, accessed 5 June 2019. Allen was the author of the expert opinion on the incidents of April and May 2012 that was submitted by the Philippines to the Arbitral Tribunal.

[23] Award of 12 July 2016, 429, para. 1083.

[24] *MP*, vol. I, 208, para. 6.130.

percent of world tonnage were parties, was one of the most widely adopted multilateral conventions in force.[25]

The Italian scholar Tullio Treves, who was also a delegate to UNCLOS III and who later became a member of the International Tribunal for the Law of the Sea ("ITLOS"), confirmed that most of the conventions referred to in Article 94 are conventions on safety at sea concluded within the IMO framework. These conventions "distilled the experiences gained over decades." He explained that the drafters of the Convention did not wish to impose, through the Convention, the application of obligations that had not yet acquired any solid foundation in the international community. Yet the drafters could not have had in mind instruments that were already in force for the States concerned, as it would have been pointless to prescribe that States should apply instruments that they already had a duty to apply. In his view, the conventions or regulations in question, while including customary rules, also referred to those that may be less generally accepted than customary rules. It goes without saying for Treves that the degree of acceptance had to be very high, but it was difficult to say how many States had to be parties to a convention for one to be able to describe it as "generally accepted."[26]

One unique feature of IMO Conventions is that they go beyond the usual requirement in multilateral treaties that a minimum number of States should ratify the treaty concerned before it can enter into force. To take an obvious example, the UN Convention on the Law of the Sea stipulated only that it would enter into force 12 months after sixty States, without further qualification, had ratified or acceded to the Convention.[27] Conventions concluded under IMO auspices, in addition to requiring that a minimum number of States ratify the Convention concerned before it can enter into force, also require a minimum tonnage, so that they enter into force only if the States that ratify or accede to them represent at the same time a major portion of world shipping. Again, to take another obvious example, Article IV(1)(a) of the COLREGS provided that it would enter into force 12 months after the date on which at least 15 States, whose merchant fleets constituted at least 65 percent by number

[25] *South China Sea Arbitration*, Award of 12 July 2016, 428, para. 1081.

[26] Tullio Treves, "La navigation [Navigation]," in René-Jean Dupuy and Daniel Vignes (eds.), *Traité du Nouveau droit de la mer* [Treatise on the New Law of the Sea] (Paris: Éditions Économica, 1985), 722–23.

[27] Article 308(1).

or by tonnage of the world fleet of vessels of 100 gross tons and over, became parties to it. Treves was of the view that given these requirements, one could assume that the entry into force of a convention was a very important indicator that it was "generally accepted." The presumption would be stronger if the number of States parties to the convention was appreciably higher than the required minimum.[28] As already mentioned, the COLREGS 1972, which entered into force after 45 States representing the required tonnage had become parties to it, now has 156 States parties, representing 98.52 percent of world tonnage.[29]

Guilfoyle objects to the view that a regulation that requires a substantial number of States and States representing most of the world's shipping tonnage is generally accepted when it enters into force, on the grounds that there exists in practice a great variety of provisions relating to entry into force. He also rejects the view that a regulation is generally accepted when it meets the criteria for the acceptance of a rule as a rule of customary international law, as this criterion would obviate the need to impose a duty to comply with generally accepted international standards. He points out that a third approach admits that precise formulation is impossible and that a combination of quantitative and qualitative criteria must be taken into account. Guilfoyle's preferred approach seems to combine the percentage of the world shipping fleet and agreement on the part of commentators.[30]

It is not necessary to provide here a definitive response to the question of what constitutes "general acceptance." A survey of the *travaux préparatoires* of the Geneva Convention on the High Seas 1958 should suffice to convince us that the COLREGS are the paradigmatic "generally accepted international regulations."

B. The Travaux Préparatoires *of the Geneva Convention on the High Seas 1958*

Article 94(3) of the Convention, which imposes a duty on flag States to take the necessary measures to ensure safety at sea with regard to, among others, the prevention of collisions, and Article 94(5), which requires that

28 Treves, 723.

29 *South China Sea Arbitration*, Award of 12 July 2016, 428, para. 1081.

30 Guilfoyle, "Article 94," 712–13.

in taking such measures, flag States must conform to generally accepted international regulations, procedures, and practices, are adapted from Article 10(1) and Article 10(2), respectively, of the Geneva Convention on the High Seas 1958.[31] Bernard Oxman demonstrated convincingly that the duty was mainly articulated during discussions within the United Nations International Law Commission ("ILC"), the purpose being to require uniform rules of the road and safety practices; it was UNCLOS III that substantially expanded the range of situations in which it applied. Oxman traced the origin of the duty to comply with generally accepted international standards to the need for universal observance of the maritime rules of the road—in other words, the COLREGS.

Our analysis shows that in the course of the ILC discussions, two issues had to be settled. The first was the need for provisions on collisions in the future convention on the law of the sea. Once a compromise had been reached on a formula that required States to take measures to prevent collisions in conformity with "generally accepted international regulations," the degree of acceptance of the international regulations had to be specified.

At the outset, there was no agreement on the need to incorporate provisions regarding collisions in a future convention. The ILC Special Rapporteur's initial report, citing the two main conventions in this area, the SOLAS 1912[32] and the International Regulations for Preventing Collisions at Sea 1948,[33] and the responsibility of the Intergovernmental

[31] Myron H. Nordquist et al. (eds.), *United Nations Convention on the Law of the Sea 1982 Commentary*, vol. II, *Second Committee: Territorial Sea, Innocent Passage, Straits Used for International Navigation, Archipelagic States, the Exclusive Economic Zone, and the Continental Shelf* (Leiden: Martinus Nijhoff Publishers, 1993), 137. *Geneva Convention on the High Seas*, done at Geneva on 29 April 1958, entered into force 30 September 1962, *United Nations Treaty Series*, vol. 450 (New York: United Nations, 1964), 82–102 ("*UNTS*"), https://treaties.un.org/doc/Publication/UNTS/Volume%20450/volume-450-I-6465-English.pdf, accessed 5 June 2019.

[32] *International Conference on Safety of Life at Sea. Text of the Convention for the Safety of Life at Sea* (London: H.M. Stationery Office, Harrison and Sons, Printers England, 1914), http://ia802605.us.archive.org/5/items/textofconvention00inte/textofconvention00inte.pdf, accessed 5 June 2019.

[33] The International Regulations 1948 were attached as Annex B to the "Final Act of the International Conference on Safety of Life at Sea, 1948. Signed at London, on 10 June 1948," *UNTS*, vol. 191 (New York: United Nations, 1954), 3–58, https://treaties.un.org/doc/Publication/UNTS/Volume%20191/v191.pdf, accessed 5 June 2019.

Maritime Consultative Organization ("IMCO") for promoting the adoption of practical methods concerning maritime safety, believed that the subject of safety of human life did not lend itself to codification.[34] Unlike the Special Rapporteur, the UN Secretariat believed that it was essential that on some points, such as sailing routes, navigation lights, and signals between ships, there should be strict uniformity in the regulations adopted by States. The problem, in the Secretariat's view, was that even if a subject matter were already covered by international regulations, the latter did not always require that national regulations should be absolutely uniform. Yet it was precisely in such matters that uniformity was desirable.[35]

At the ILC session in 1950, Manley Hudson, recalling that the maritime Rules of the Road had been in existence since 1863, observed that their international application was not compulsory. They had been adopted by States in their municipal laws, but uniformity alone could not guarantee the safety of navigation. What was needed were compulsory international regulations of general application.[36] Hudson's observations might at first glance seem surprising, given the widespread view among

[34] United Nations International Law Commission ("ILC"), *Régime of the High Seas. Rapport de J. P. A. François, rapporteur spécial* [Report of J.P.A. François, Special Rapporteur], UN Doc. A/CN.4/17 (17 March 1950), in *Yearbook of the International Law Commission 1950*, vol. II, *Documents of the second session including the report of the Commission to the General Assembly*, UN Doc. A/CN.4/SER.A/1950/Add. 1 (New York: United Nations, 1957), 39, para. 2, http://legal.un.org/docs/?path=../ilc/publications/yearbooks/english/ilc_1950_v2.pdf&lang=E, accessed 5 June 2019. The Report is available in the original French version only. From 1949 to 1955, reports to the ILC were published in the original language only. Translations were distributed in mimeographed form to the ILC members. The Special Rapporteur was J.P.A. François, a national of the Netherlands.

[35] ILC, *Mémorandum présenté par le Secrétariat* [Memorandum Submitted by the Secretariat], UN Doc. A/CN.4/32 (14 July 1950), in *Yearbook of the International Law Commission 1950*, vol. II, *Documents of the second session including the report of the Commission to the General Assembly*, UN Doc. A/CN.4/SER.A/1950/Add. 1 (New York: United Nations, 1957), 75, para. 53, http://legal.un.org/docs/?path=../ilc/publications/yearbooks/english/ilc_1950_v2.pdf&lang=E, accessed 5 June 2019. The Mémorandum is available in the original French version only.

[36] ILC, *Summary Record of the 64th Meeting* (10 July 1950), UN Doc. A/CN.4/SR.64, in *Yearbook of the International Law Commission 1950*, vol. I, *Summary records of the second session*, UN Doc. A/CN.4/SER.A/1950 (New York: United Nations, 1958), 193, para. 86, http://legal.un.org/docs/?path=../ilc/publications/yearbooks/english/ilc_1950_v1.pdf&lang=E, accessed 5 June 2019. Manley O. Hudson, a US national, was a judge at the Permanent Court of International Justice ("PCIJ"), the predecessor of

commentators and judicial authorities, including the US Supreme Court, as early as the nineteenth century that the International Regulations were binding on States, whether they had accepted them or not. Perhaps Hudson had in mind the fact that in 1950 the COLREGS 1948 had not yet entered into force. In response to Hudson's view that the future convention should contain provisions that were similar to those of the Rules of the Road and that could be ratified by all States, the ILC requested that the Special Rapporteur endeavor to establish a general principle.[37]

Under the Special Rapporteur's first proposal, whenever two vessels approached each other so as to involve risk of collision, the internationally recognized steering and sailing rules to prevent collisions had to be observed.[38] Hudson proposed that the principle derived by the Rapporteur should be introduced by a phrase to the effect that "Each state is bound to provide by its legislation that…."[39] Several ILC members raised objections to the inclusion of a provision of this type in a codification convention. Jean Spiropoulos contended that regulations for the prevention of collisions were instructions addressed to masters and did not specify the rights or duties of States.[40] Jesús María Yepes believed

the International Court of Justice ("ICJ"), from 1936 to 1946. In the following discussion, ILC members are identified individually, as they sit in the Commission in their individual capacity, and not as representatives of governments.

[37] ILC, *Summary Record of the 66th Meeting* (12 July 1950), UN Doc. A/CN.4/SR.66, in *Yearbook of the International Law Commission 1950*, vol. I, 208, para. 3, http://legal.un.org/docs/?path=../ilc/publications/yearbooks/english/ilc_1950_v1.pdf&lang=E, accessed 5 June 2019.

[38] ILC, *Régime of the High Seas. Deuxième rapport de M. J. P. A. François, rapporteur spécial* [Second Report of Mr. J. P. A. François, Special Rapporteur], UN Doc. A/CN.4/42 (10 April 1951), in *Yearbook of the International Law Commission 1951*, vol. II, *Documents of the second session including the report of the Commission to the General Assembly*, UN Doc. A/CN.4/SER.A/1951/Add. 1 (New York: United Nations, 1957), 81, http://legal.un.org/docs/?path=../ilc/publications/yearbooks/english/ilc_1951_v2.pdf&lang=E, accessed 5 June 2019. The Report is available in the original French version only.

[39] ILC, *Summary Record of the 123rd Meeting* (12 July 1951), UN Doc. A/CN.4/SR.123, in *Yearbook of the International Law Commission 1951*, vol. I, *Summary records of the third session, 16 May–27 July 1951*, UN Doc. A/CN.4/SER.A/1951 (New York: United Nations, 1957), 346, para. 10, http://legal.un.org/docs/?path=../ilc/publications/yearbooks/english/ilc_1951_v1.pdf&lang=E, accessed 5 June 2019.

[40] *Ibid.*, 346, para. 14. See also ILC, *Summary Record of the 122nd Meeting* (11 July 1951), UN. Doc. A/CN.4/SR.122, in *Yearbook of the International Law Commission*

that shipping regulations did not come under international law and that including them in a convention would be comparable to incorporating rules concerning road signs and signals in a civil code.[41] Roberto Córdova responded that the high seas regime should include navigation rules, since the high seas were mainly used for navigation.[42] A compromise formula, proposed by Ricardo J. Alfaro and accepted by the ILC, would bind States to enact legislation to ensure the safety of life at sea, with the minimum provisions that such legislation should contain to be specified.[43] Hudson did not go so far as to advocate the codification of the International Regulations but thought that a recommendation to States to refrain from issuing regulations that conflicted with the regulations jointly agreed by other maritime States could be considered as part of codification.[44]

The debate now shifted to the manner of determining the degree of conformity of national regulations with regulations "jointly agreed by other maritime states." The danger implicit in Hudson's suggestion was identified by Georges Scelle: the main maritime powers might set themselves up as shipping controllers.[45] Subsequent discussions attempted to reconcile the need to require States to refrain from issuing regulations contrary to those agreed to by other maritime States and the desire to avoid attributing to the principal maritime powers any exclusive right to regulate the policing of shipping and consequently to oblige other States to adopt the regulations thus laid down.[46] In 1951, the Special Rapporteur referred to regulations on the safety of life at sea

1951, vol. I, 345, para. 120, http://legal.un.org/docs/?path=../ilc/publications/yearbooks/english/ilc_1951_v1.pdf&lang=E, accessed 5 June 2019. Spiropoulous was a national of Greece.

41 ILC, *Summary Record of the 123rd Meeting*, 347, para. 22. Yepes was a national of Colombia.

42 *Ibid.*, 347, para. 23. Córdova was a national of Mexico.

43 *Ibid.*, 348, para. 38. Alfaro was a national of Panama.

44 *Ibid.*, 349, para. 54.

45 *Ibid.*, 348, para. 48. Scelle was a national of France.

46 *Ibid.*, *Summary Record of the 285th Meeting* (5 May 1955), *Yearbook of the International Law Commission 1955*, vol. I, *Summary records of the seventh session 2 May–8 July 1955*, UN Doc. A/CN.4/SER.A/1955 (New York: United Nations, 1960), 15, para. 8, http://legal.un.org/docs/?path=../ilc/publications/yearbooks/english/ilc_1955_v1.pdf&lang=E, accessed 25 July 2018.

"jointly agreed with the majority of maritime States."[47] In 1954, his draft distinguished between regulations on the safety of life at sea, which could not be "inconsistent with those established by common agreement with the majority of maritime States," and the use of signals, in relation to which States should prescribe those used by the majority of seagoing vessels.[48] In Georges Scelle's view, the reference to "the majority of maritime States" was unacceptable, since it gave equal weight to all maritime powers and because it gave the impression that a special agreement between States was necessary to establish the regulations.[49] The Special Rapporteur then presented a consolidated text, according to which States should issue "regulations concerning both signals and the prevention of collisions and that such regulations should not be inconsistent with those fixed by international agreement and applying to the majority of sea-going vessels."[50] A.E.F. Sandström, dissatisfied with a purely quantitative criterion, proposed to replace the expression "the

[47] "Les Etats sont tenus de s'abstenir d'édicter des règles en contradiction avec celles qui ont été établies de concert par la plupart des autres Etats maritimes, dans la mesure où une telle contradiction pourrait compromettre la sauvegarde de la vie humaine en mer." ILC, *Régime of the High Seas. Troisième rapport par J. P. A. François, rapporteur spécial* [Third Report of J. P. A. François, Special Rapporteur], UN Doc. A/CN.4/51 (28 February 1952), in *Yearbook of the International Law Commission 1952*, vol. II, *Documents of the second session including the report of the Commission to the General Assembly*, UN Doc. A/CN.4/SER.A/1952/Add. 1 (New York: United Nations, 1958), 46, http://legal.un.org/docs/?path=../ilc/publications/yearbooks/english/ilc_1952_v2.pdf&lang=E, accessed 5 June 2018. The Report is available in the original French version only.

[48] "Ne peuvent être édictées par aucun Etat des règles qui seront en contradiction avec celles établies d'un commun accord par la majorité des Etats maritimes, au cas où une telle contradiction compromettrait la sauvegarde de la vie humaine en mer." ILC, *Régime of the High Seas. Sixième rapport de J. P. A. François, rapporteur spécial* [Sixth Report of J. P. A. François, Special Rapporteur], UN Doc. A/CN.4/79 (1 March 1954), in *Yearbook of the International Law Commission 1954*, vol. II, *Documents of the second session including the report of the Commission to the General Assembly*, UN Doc. A/CN.4/SER.A/1954/Add. 1 (New York: United Nations, 1960), 11, http://legal.un.org/docs/?path=../ilc/publications/yearbooks/english/ilc_1954_v2.pdf&lang=E, accessed 5 June 2019. The Report is available in the original French version only.

[49] ILC, *Summary Record of the 285th Meeting*, 16, para. 24.

[50] *Ibid., Summary Record of the 294th Meeting* (18 May 1955), UN Doc. A/CN.4/SR.294, in *Yearbook of the International Law Commission 1955*, vol. I, *Summary records of the seventh session 2 May–8 July 1955*, UN Doc. A/CN.4/SER.A/1955 (New York: United Nations, 1960), 66, para. 78, http://legal.un.org/docs/?path=../ilc/publications/yearbooks/english/ilc_1955_v1.pdf&lang=E, accessed 25 July 2018.

majority of seagoing vessels" by "the greater part of the tonnage of sea-going vessels."[51] Jaroslav Zourek proposed to return to the formulation "majority of maritime States," since a rule inconsistent with that followed by the majority of States, even if applied by one with a small merchant fleet, would be just as dangerous.[52] As a compromise, Gerald Fitzmaurice proposed to substitute "generally accepted internationally and applicable" for "fixed by international agreement and applying," in order to take into account the fact that in some fields certain rules had come to be generally accepted and applied even if no definite agreements existed. The purpose was to oblige States to conform to generally accepted rules that were not necessarily accepted by all States.[53] This was the first proposal that used the key words "generally applicable."

Fitzmaurice's formulation was reflected in the 1955 provisional articles on the regime of the high seas, which required States to issue for their ships regulations concerning the use of signals and the prevention of collisions on the high seas that were not inconsistent with those concerning the safety of life at sea "internationally accepted for vessels forming the greater part of the tonnage of sea-going vessels."[54] Debate continued on the criterion of tonnage. Zourek declared the criterion to be unsatisfactory, in that it introduced the concept of size, based on economic or political power. That concept was alien to international law, which was based on equality of States.[55] The resistance of Fitzmaurice, who asserted that States with large fleets had already been forced to give serious consideration to the best means for ensuring maximum safety at sea, was not sufficient to prevent the requirement of tonnage from

[51] *Ibid.* Sandström was a national of Sweden.

[52] *Ibid.*, 236, para. 90. Jaroslav Zourek was a national of Czechoslovakia.

[53] ILC, *Summary Record of the 294th Meeting*, 68, para. 101.

[54] ILC, *Report of the International Law Commission covering the work of its seventh session, 2 May–8 July 1955*, UN Doc. A/2934, in *Yearbook of the International Law Commission 1955*, vol. II, *Documents of the seventh session including the report of the Commission to the General Assembly*, A/CN.4/SER.A/1955/Add. 1 (New York: United Nations, 1960), 23, http://legal.un.org/docs/?path=../ilc/publications/yearbooks/english/ilc_1955_v2.pdf&lang=E, accessed 5 June 2019.

[55] ILC, *Summary Record of the 342nd Meeting* (8 May 1956), UN Doc. A/CN.4/SR.342, in *Yearbook of the International Law Commission 1956*, vol. I, *Summary records of the eighth session 23 April–4 July 1956*, UN Doc. 1956. V. 3, Vol. I (New York: United Nations, 1956), 44, para. 79, http://legal.un.org/docs/?path=../ilc/publications/yearbooks/english/ilc_1956_v1.pdf&lang=EFS, accessed 5 June 2019.

being removed.[56] There remained only the requirement that the regulations should conform to generally accepted standards, the scope of which had been broadened to include the crew as well as the construction, equipment, and seaworthiness of ships.[57]

At the United Nations Conference on the Law of the Sea ("UNCLOS") in 1958, the UK proposed to delete the article on the safety of navigation, arguing that it would be difficult for States parties to existing agreements to accept new obligations.[58] Several States opposed the UK proposal. The Netherlands believed that the codification convention would be incomplete without a provision ensuring that the flag state exercised effective jurisdiction over its ships on the high seas.[59] Yugoslavia observed that even if certain matters referred to in the article were already regulated by treaties, the latter had not been generally ratified. Therefore, the convention should embody general rules binding on all States.[60] Interestingly enough, it was the USSR that pointed to the fact that "a certain number of recently-constituted States were participating in the conference" as the reason for including provisions on the

[56] *Ibid.*, 44, paras. 82, 83.

[57] ILC, *Report of the International Law Commission covering the work of its eighth session, 23 April–4 July 1956*, UN Doc. A/3159, in *Yearbook of the International Law Commission 1956*, vol. II, *Documents of the eighth session including the report of the Commission to the General* Assembly, UN Doc. A/CN.4/SER.A/1956/Add. 1 (New York; United Nations, 1957), 280, http://legal.un.org/docs/?path=../ilc/publications/yearbooks/english/ilc_1956_v2.pdf&lang=EFS, accessed 5 June 2019.

[58] United Nations Conference on the Law of the Sea ("UNCLOS"), *United Kingdom of Great Britain and Northern Ireland: Proposal*, UN Doc. A/CONF.13/C.2/L.49 (21 March 1958), in *United Nations Conference on the Law of the Sea, Official Records*, vol. IV, *Second Committee (High Seas: General Regime), Summary records of meetings and Annexes, Geneva, 24 February–27 April 1958*, UN Doc. A/CONF.13/40 (New York: United Nations, 1958), 129, http://legal.un.org/docs/?path=../diplomaticconferences/1958_los/docs/english/vol_4.pdf&lang=E, accessed 5 June 2019. United Nations Codification Division Publications, *United Nations Conference on the Law of the Sea (Geneva, 24 February–27 April 1958)* (New York: United Nations Codification Division, Office of Legal Affairs, 2019), http://legal.un.org/diplomaticconferences/1958_los/, accessed 5 June 2019.

[59] UNCLOS, *Summary Record of the 19th Meeting* (28 March 1958), UN Doc. A/CONF.13/C.2/SR.19, in *United Nations Conference on the Law of the Sea, Official Records*, vol. IV, 51, para. 18.

[60] *Ibid.*, 50, para. 4.

safety of navigation in the convention.[61] The USSR's remark seemed to assume that these new States may not (yet) have ratified conventions on the safety of navigation by the time of UNCLOS; however, if they became parties to the convention on the law of the sea that was being negotiated, they would be bound by those of its provisions relating to the safety of navigation. The only amendment to the ILC draft that was accepted at UNCLOS was that put forward by Israel, which replaced "regulations" with "measures," so that States would be free to employ whatever means they considered appropriate, whether legislation, collective agreements, arbitral awards, or other forms of action.[62]

The absence of agreement within the ILC on the criterion for general acceptance of international regulations should not prevent us from observing that the COLREGS were considered the "generally accepted international regulations" par excellence and that the scope of the latter was broadened only in the later phase of the preparation of the draft convention submitted to UNCLOS. The COLREGS 1972, by requiring a minimum of 15 States representing 65 percent by number or by tonnage of the world fleet of vessels of 100 gross tons and over for their entry into force, adopted a combination of the number of States and tonnage that States represented.

The implication of Article 10 of the Geneva Convention on the High Seas 1958 was that as soon as a State became party to the latter, the International Regulations 1948 would become binding on them, even if they had not accepted them. The International Regulations had not set a minimum number of States that should accept them before they entered into force. The Conference on the Safety of Life at Sea 1948 had simply requested that the UK set the date for its application by States that accepted them "when substantial unanimity [sic] has been reached as to the acceptance of the International Regulations for Preventing Collisions at Sea, 1948."[63]

[61] UNCLOS, *Summary Record of the 22nd Meeting* (31 March 1958), UN Doc. A/CONF.13/C.2/SR.22, in *United Nations Conference on the Law of the Sea, Official records*, vol. IV, 57, para. 2.

[62] UNCLOS, *Summary Record of the 23rd Meeting* (1 April 1958), UN Doc. A/CONF.13/C.2/SR.23, in *United Nations Conference on the Law of the Sea, Official records*, vol. IV, 60, para. 3.

[63] "Final Act of the International Conference on Safety of Life at Sea, 1948," 8.

The Philippines, which never became a party to the Geneva Convention on the High Seas, would in any case have been bound by the International Regulations 1948, for the simple reason that it reportedly accepted them.[64] No list of States that accepted the International Regulations 1960 is available online, making it impossible to determine if the Philippines had ever accepted them. It is certain, though, that the Philippines did not accede to COLREGS 1972. It did ratify the Convention on 8 May 1984. Consequently, when the latter entered into force on 16 November 1994, the Philippines was *ipso facto* bound by the COLREGS 1972 by virtue of Article 94, whether or not it was aware of the fact. It was only in the course of the arbitral proceedings that the legal consequences of Article 94(5), adapted from Article 10(2) of the Convention on the High Seas, became manifest for the Philippines, which had not acceded to the COLREGS until six months after the initiation of the *Arbitration*.

Since the COLREGS were incorporated into the Convention, it logically followed that disputes concerning the COLREGS would be subject to the system of automatic limitations and optional exceptions to the Convention's compulsory dispute settlement system. These limits could bar the Arbitral Tribunal from exercising its jurisdiction with respect to Submission No. 13 of the Philippines. To these limitations and exceptions, the CSIL added, in its post-arbitration critique of the Award on Jurisdiction and Admissibility, the inapplicability of the COLREGS in the territorial sea.

II. The COLREGS and the Limits of the Convention's Compulsory Dispute Settlement System

The expression "limits" used here is to be understood broadly. It covers the provisions in Section 3 of Part XV setting forth automatic limitations and optional exceptions to jurisdiction of procedures under Section 2 of Part XV, although only one of the optional exceptions was examined in relation to Submission No. 13 during the proceedings. The preconditions to jurisdiction, set out in Part 1 of Section XV of the Convention, will not be examined here, as the Arbitral Tribunal found that the dispute

[64] *Ibid.*, 20.

reflected in the Submission was not barred from its consideration by any requirement of Section 1 of Part XV.[65] The expression "limits" also refers to the CSIL's post-arbitration rationalization of China's conduct, which contended that the lack of an enabling clause in the Convention deprived the Tribunal of jurisdiction with respect to Submission No. 13.

A. The COLREGS and the Inapplicability of the "Law Enforcement Activities" Exception

The "law enforcement activities" exception in Article 298(1)(b) is one of the three optional exceptions to jurisdiction that are identified in Article 298, which may be activated by a State party to the Convention through a declaration. The other two optional exceptions concern disputes involving sea boundary delimitations or involving historic bays or titles (Article 298(1)(a)) and disputes in respect of which the UN Security Council is exercising its functions (Article 298(1)(c)). These last two categories are not relevant to the present discussion, as the Tribunal also found that the dispute was not a dispute regarding sovereignty or maritime boundary delimitation.[66] To understand the inapplicability of the "law enforcement activities" exception, it is essential to explore the linkage between Article 298(1)(b), on the one hand, and Article 297(2) and (3), on the other. Prior to the Hearing on Jurisdiction and Admissibility, the Tribunal posed written questions to the Philippines in its Request for Further Written Argument on the applicability of the "law enforcement activities" exception specifically to Submission No. 13. In response to the Philippine explanations in the *Supplemental Written Submission* and during the Hearing on Jurisdiction, the Award on Jurisdiction and Admissibility only noted that "Article 298(1)(b) has no application in the territorial sea,"[67] without further explanation. The complexity of the linkage between the two sets of provisions prompts one to ask why the Tribunal did not devote more time to discussing the inapplicability of the "law enforcement activities" exception.

[65] *South China Sea Arbitration*, Award on Jurisdiction, 29 October 2015, 146, para. 410, https://pcacases.com/web/sendAttach/2579, accessed 5 June 2019.

[66] *Ibid.*

[67] *Ibid.*

The optional exceptions to jurisdiction had been activated in 2006 by a Chinese Declaration.[68] Interestingly, China did not raise the "law enforcement activities" exception in its Position Paper, published in December 2014.[69] As part of its efforts to ensure that its decisions were well founded in fact and law, the Tribunal asked the Philippines whether Article 298(1)(b) applied to the Philippine submissions regarding China's activities, including Submission No. 13.[70] The Philippines had no trouble in admitting that attempting to drive Philippine vessels away from Scarborough Shoal by exposing them to the danger of collision was indeed a law enforcement activity, carried out by vessels of China Marine Surveillance ("CMS") and Fisheries Law Enforcement Command ("FLEC").[71] In the view of the Philippines, the "law enforcement activities" exception did not apply, for two reasons. To begin with, the law enforcement activities in April and May 2012 took place in the territorial sea of Scarborough Shoal, where the "law enforcement activities" exception did not apply.[72] It was this conclusion that was incorporated in the Award on Jurisdiction and Admissibility.

[68] On 25 August 2006, China made the following *Declaration under article 298:*

> The Government of the People's Republic of China does not accept any of the procedures provided for in Section 2 of Part XV of the Convention with respect to all the categories of disputes referred to in paragraph 1 (a) (b) and (c) of Article 298 of the Convention.

United Nations, Office of Legal Affairs, Treaty Section, *United Nations Treaty Collection, XXI6., Law of the Sea,* 11, https://treaties.un.org/doc/Publication/MTDSG/Volume%20II/Chapter%20XXI/XXI-6.en.pdf, accessed 5 June 2019.

[69] *South China Sea Arbitration, Supplemental Written Submissions of the Philippines* (16 March 2015), Annex 467, People's Republic of China, Position Paper of the Government of the People's Republic of China on the Matter of Jurisdiction in the South China Sea Arbitration Initiated by the Republic of the Philippines (7 December 2014), vol. VIII, 21 ("*SWSP*"), https://files.pca-cpa.org/pcadocs/The%20Philippines%27%20Supplemental%20Written%20Submission%20-%20Volume%20VIII%20%28Annexes%20466-499%29.pdf, accessed 5 June 2019.

[70] *SWSP*, vol. I, 43–50, https://files.pca-cpa.org/pcadocs/Supplemental%20Written%20Submission%20Volume%20I.pdf, accessed 5 June 2019; *South China Sea Arbitration,* Hearing on Jurisdiction and Admissibility, Final Transcript, Day 2 (8 July 2015), 77 ("Hearing on Jurisdiction, Final Transcript - Day 2"), https://pcacases.com/web/sendAttach/1400, accessed 5 June 2019.

[71] Hearing on Jurisdiction, Final Transcript, Day 2, 89.

[72] *SWSP,* vol. I, 47–48, paras. 9.21–9.22.

The absence of explicit reference to the territorial sea in Article 298(1)(b), on the one hand, and Article 297(2) and (3), on the other, might make this conclusion puzzling. Analysis of the content of the exception reveals that the exception applies in a coastal State's Exclusive Economic Zone ("EEZ"). This brings us to the second reason adduced by the Philippines for the inapplicability of the "law enforcement activities" exception: "the law enforcement activities involved in this case do not come within the scope of the exception in Article 298(1)(b) because they fall outside the scope of the referenced exclusions in Article 297."[73] These last are automatic limitations to jurisdiction.

The law enforcement activities exception in Article 298(1)(b) is not a blanket exception for all disputes over law enforcement activities of the coastal State. Rather the disputes must concern "law enforcement activities in regard to the exercise of sovereign rights or jurisdiction excluded from the jurisdiction of a court or tribunal under article 297, paragraph 2 or 3." Article 297(2)(a), in turn, refers us to Article 246 (Marine Scientific Research in the Exclusive Economic Zone and on the Continental Shelf) and Article 253 (Suspension or Cessation of Marine Scientific Research Activities). Although Article 297(3)(a) does not specify any article(s) in particular, one may deduce from a close reading that it refers to Article 62 (Utilization of the Living Resources of the EEZ), Article 69 (Right of Land-Locked States in the EEZ), and Article 70 (Right of Geographically Disadvantaged States).

Under Article 246(3), coastal States shall, in normal circumstances, grant consent for marine scientific research projects to be carried out by other States or by international organizations in their EEZ or on their continental shelf. That said, according to Article 246(5), coastal States have the discretion to refuse consent if the project is of direct significance for the exploration and exploitation of living or non-living natural resources; involves drilling into the continental shelf, the use of explosives or the introduction of harmful substances into the marine environment; involves the construction, operation, or use of artificial islands, installations, and structures; contains inaccurate information submitted to the coastal State; or if the researching State or international organization has outstanding obligations to the coastal State from a prior research project.

[73] Hearing on Jurisdiction, Final Transcript, Day 2, 78.

Under Article 253, a coastal State has the right to suspend a marine scientific research project if the research is not carried out in accordance with the project submitted to it, or if the project is substantially modified, or if the coastal State's rights (such as the right to participate in the project) are not respected. In the event of a dispute arising between the coastal State and the researching State or international organization over the coastal State's exercise of its discretionary powers under Articles 246 and 253, these disputes may not, under Article 297(2), be submitted to a compulsory procedure entailing binding decisions (i.e., to a procedure under Section 2 of Part XV). This limitation to jurisdiction is automatic. No declaration on the part of the coastal State is necessary to activate it.

Now it cannot be excluded that in the event of disputes concerning the coastal State's exercise of its powers in the area of marine scientific research, the coastal State will carry out law enforcement activities. A coastal State who wishes to prevent disputes over these law enforcement activities from being submitted to compulsory dispute settlement may make a declaration excluding the law enforcement activities from compulsory dispute settlement, under Article 298(1)(b). In this manner, it is not just the disputes concerning the exercise of its discretionary powers in the area of marine scientific research that will be excluded from compulsory dispute settlement. Disputes concerning law enforcement activities related to the exercise of these discretionary powers will also be excluded from compulsory dispute settlement.

Article 62 lists the sovereign rights of the coastal State in fisheries (living resources) in its EEZ. It has the right to determine its capacity to harvest the fish in the EEZ; if it does not have the capacity to harvest the entire allowable catch, it shall give other States access to the surplus of the allowable catch (Article 62(2)). The coastal State may establish laws and regulations on such matters as the licensing of fishermen, fishing vessels and equipment, determining the species which may be caught, and fixing quotas of catch, regulating seasons and areas of fishing, the types, sizes, and amount of gear, and the types, sizes, and number of fishing vessels that may be used; and fixing the age and size of fish and other species that may be caught (Article 62(4)). Article 69 lays down the principle that land-locked States have the right to participate in fishing of part of the surplus of the living resources of the EEZs of coastal States of the same subregion or region. Article 70 grants geographically disadvantaged States the same right. If a dispute arises between a coastal State and another State over its sovereign rights in the EEZ, that dispute may not be submitted to compulsory settlement entailing binding decisions, under Article 297(3)(a); instead, the dispute may be submitted by either State to conciliation, the outcome of which is not binding (Article 297(3)(b). As in matters involving marine scientific research, it is possible that in the course of a dispute over the coastal State's exercise of its sovereign rights with respect to fisheries in the EEZ, the coastal State will undertake law enforcement activities. If it wishes to prevent disputes over these law enforcement activities from being submitted to compulsory dispute settlement, it may make a declaration under Article 298(1)(b) excluding disputes over enforcement activities from compulsory dispute settlement. In this manner, it is not just the disputes concerning the exercise of sovereign rights over fisheries in the EEZ that will be excluded from compulsory dispute settlement. Disputes concerning law enforcement activities related to the exercise of sovereign rights will also be excluded from compulsory dispute settlement.

In the Award on Jurisdiction, the Tribunal did not discuss at length the scope of the "law enforcement activities" exception. There may be two reasons for this. First, the scope of the "law enforcement activities" exception had long been understood. From authoritative commentaries of Articles 297 and 298, one can deduce that a coastal State's law enforcement activities cannot be excluded from compulsory dispute settlement if they relate to activities in the EEZ that could be submitted to compulsory dispute settlement, such as the freedoms and rights of navigation, overflight or the laying of submarine cables and pipelines, or other internationally lawful uses of the sea (Article 298(1)(a)).[74] Disputes relating to the coastal State's exercise of discretion in the area of marine scientific research in the EEZ (Article 297(2)(a)(i) and (2)(a)(ii)) or its exercise of sovereign rights over fisheries in the EEZ are excluded from compulsory dispute settlement (Article 297(3)(a)), but the law enforcement activities that are related to such matters are not automatically excluded from compulsory dispute settlement. However, the coastal State has the option of excluding law enforcement activities related to these matters from compulsory dispute settlement.[75]

[74] Myron H. Nordquist et al. (eds.), *United Nations Convention on the Law of the Sea 1982 Commentary*, vol. V, *Settlement of Disputes, General and Final Provisions and related Annexes and resolutions* (Leiden: Martinus Nijhoff Publishers, 1989), 137.

[75] *Ibid.*, 100, 105, 136; Bernard Oxman, "The Regime of Warships Under the United Nations Convention on the Law of the Sea," *Virginia Journal of International Law*

The second reason for the lack of discussion in the Award on Jurisdiction of the scope of the "law enforcement activities" exception is probably the fact that this interpretation of the exception had been confirmed, by the time the Hearing on Jurisdiction and Admissibility was held in July 2015, by the International Tribunal for the Law of the Sea ("ITLOS") and an arbitral tribunal, also constituted under Annex VII of the Convention, in the "*Arctic Sunrise*" case, as the Philippines pointed out.[76] The *Arctic Sunrise* was an icebreaker flying the flag of the Netherlands and chartered and operated by Greenpeace International, which used it to stage a protest action on 18 September 2013 at a Russian offshore platform located in the Barents Sea, in the EEZ of the Russian Federation. After the failure of two campaigners to scale the platform, the Russian authorities pursued the *Arctic Sunrise* on 19 September and boarded it, took control of it, and detained it at Murmansk, without the consent of the flag State. The crew members were arrested and detained; judicial proceedings were initiated against them. On 28 September the Russian authorities once again boarded the vessel to investigate it, again without the consent of the Netherlands. The latter, as the flag State of the *Arctic Sunrise*, repeatedly requested the immediate release of the vessel and crew. In view of Russia's refusal to comply with its requests, the Netherlands initiated arbitration under Annex VII of the Convention and requested provisional measures with a view to the release of the vessel and its crew as well as the suspension of all administrative and judicial proceedings against them.[77]

Russia refused to accept arbitration and to appear before the ITLOS, invoking a declaration it had made upon ratification of the Convention to the effect that "it does not accept procedures provided for in Section 2

24 (1984): 823–24, https://repository.law.miami.edu/cgi/viewcontent.cgi?article=1401&context=fac_articles, accessed 5 June 2019. The latter article was first published in French as "Le régime des navires de guerre dans le cadre de la Convention des Nations Unies sur le droit de la mer [The Regime of Warships Under the United Nations Convention on the Law of the Sea]," *AFDI* 28 (1982): 811–50, https://www.persee.fr/docAsPDF/afdi_0066-3085_1982_num_28_1_2519.pdf, accessed 5 June 2019.

[76] Hearing on Jurisdiction and Admissibility, Final Transcript, Day 2, 78.

[77] Permanent Court of Arbitration, *The Arctic Sunrise Arbitration (Netherlands v. Russian Federation), Arbitral Tribunal Renders Award on the Merits*, Press Release of 24 August 2015, 2, https://pcacases.com/web/sendAttach/1444, accessed 5 June 2019; *Statement of the Claim and Grounds on Which It Is Based*, dated 4 October 2013, 2, paras. 1–5, https://pcacases.com/web/sendAttach/1314, accessed 5 June 2019.

of Part XV of the Convention, entailing binding decisions with respect to disputes [...] concerning law-enforcement activities in regard to the exercise of sovereign rights or jurisdiction."[78] The ITLOS, in acceding to the Netherlands request for provisional measures, observed that

> the declaration made by the Russian Federation with respect to law enforcement activities under article 298, paragraph 1(b), of the Convention prima facie applies only to disputes excluded from the jurisdiction of a court or tribunal under article 297, paragraph 2 or 3, of the Convention.[79]

In a joint individual opinion, two judges pointed out that a "convincing reasoning" to justify this observation was called for but was missing.[80]

The reasoning was provided in the Award on Jurisdiction issued on 26 November 2014 by the Annex VII Tribunal that was established upon the request of the Netherlands. In the Tribunal's view, Russia's Declaration could not exclude from the jurisdiction of procedures in Section 2 every dispute that concerns "law enforcement activities in regard to the exercise of sovereign rights or jurisdiction." Rather it could only exclude

> disputes "concerning law enforcement activities in regard to the exercise of sovereign rights or jurisdiction" which are also "excluded from the jurisdiction of a court or tribunal under article 297, paragraph 2 or 3." Accordingly, the Declaration cannot and does not exclude from the jurisdiction of the procedures in Section 2 of Part XV of the Convention any dispute that concerns "law-enforcement activities in regard to the exercise of sovereign rights or jurisdiction" unless the dispute is also excluded from the jurisdiction of a court or tribunal under paragraph 2 or 3 of article 297.[81]

[78] Note verbale dated 22 October 2013, quoted in *"Arctic Sunrise" (Kingdom of the Netherlands v. Russian Federation), Provisional Measures, Order of 22 November 2013, ITLOS Reports 2013*, 232–33, https://www.itlos.org/fileadmin/itlos/documents/cases/case_no.22/published/C22_Order_221113.pdf, accessed 5 June 2019.

[79] *"Arctic Sunrise," Provisional Measures, Order*, 241, para. 45.

[80] *Ibid.*, Joint Separate Opinion of Judge Wolfrum and Judge Kelly, 259, para. 9, https://www.itlos.org/fileadmin/itlos/documents/cases/case_no.22/published/C22_Wolfrum_Kelly_221113.pdf, accessed 5 June 2019. Judge Wolfrum was one of the five members of the Tribunal in the *South China Sea Arbitration.*

[81] *"Arctic Sunrise" (Kingdom of the Netherlands v. Russian Federation)*, Award on Jurisdiction, 26 November 2014, 13, para. 69, https://pcacases.com/web/sendAttach/1325, accessed 5 June 2019. It should be noted that Judge Mensah and Professor Soons were

The Tribunal noted that Russia's Declaration left out the words "excluded from the jurisdiction of a court or tribunal under article 297, paragraph 2 or 3," which appear in Article 298(1)(b). Yet Russia's Declaration could not create an exclusion that was wider in scope than what was permitted by Article 298(1)(b).[82] Accepting such a declaration would be tantamount to accepting reservations to the Convention, which are prohibited by Article 309 of the Convention itself.[83]

The applicability of automatic limitations and optional exceptions with respect to Submission No. 13 was not taken up by the CSIL in its post-arbitration critique of the Tribunal's Award on Jurisdiction. Instead, it attempted to demonstrate that the COLREGS did not apply in the territorial sea without an enabling clause.

B. The CSIL's Post-Arbitration Critique of the Award on Jurisdiction: The Alleged Inapplicability of the COLREGS in the Territorial Sea

The CSIL asserts that the Convention does not require a coastal State to apply the COLREGS in its territorial sea, and that without an enabling clause in the Convention, it could not apply to the territorial sea. The response to these arguments is twofold: they misunderstand the Tribunal's reasoning, and they are contradicted by the COLREGS.

In the CSIL's opinion, the Tribunal erred in applying the COLREGS through Article 94 of the Convention.[84] Article 94, as explained above, requires flag States to take the necessary measures to ensure safety at sea with regard to, *inter alia*, the prevention of collisions; in taking such measures, they should conform to generally accepted regulations, standards, and procedures. According to the CSIL, Article 86 of the Convention, which like Article 94, is found in Part VII of the Convention, limits the application of Article 94 to the high seas.[85] It allegedly follows that Article 94 would not apply, on its own, to other parts of the

both members of the *Arctic Sunrise* and the *South China Sea Arbitration* tribunals. Judge Mensah was president of both Tribunals.

[82] *Ibid.*, 14, para. 72.

[83] *Ibid.*, 13, para. 70. Article 309 (Reservations and exceptions) reads as follows: "No reservations or exceptions may be made to this Convention unless expressly permitted by other articles of this Convention.".

[84] CSIL, "The South China Sea Arbitration Awards," 597, para. 835.

[85] Article 86 (Application of the provisions of this Part) reads as follows:

sea, unless there were another provision that enabled such application. The CSIL cites as an example the fact that the Convention has extended the application of certain provisions on the high seas to the EEZ, through Article 58(2).[86] In the CSIL's view, if Article 94 of the Convention also incorporated the COLREGS into the regime of the territorial sea, Article 58(2) would become meaningless.[87] From these considerations the CSIL concludes that without resting on an enabling provision, Article 94 does not apply to the territorial sea.[88]

The CSIL believes that in order for the COLREGS to apply to the territorial sea the Tribunal should have looked for a provision similar to Article 58(2), but that the Tribunal failed to do so.[89] It thinks that the Philippines did attempt to find such a provision, which was said to be Article 21(4). Through this provision, all generally accepted international regulations relating to the prevention of collisions at sea are incorporated into the rules that apply to foreign ships in a coastal State's territorial sea.[90] The Tribunal allegedly failed to make use of this provision. If we

> The provisions of this Part apply to all parts of the sea that are not included in the exclusive economic zone, in the territorial sea or in the internal waters of a State, or in the archipelagic waters of an archipelagic State. This article does not entail any abridgement of the freedoms enjoyed by all States in the exclusive economic zone in accordance with article 5.

[86] The first two paragraphs of Article 58 (Rights and duties of other States in the exclusive economic zone) read as follows:

> 1. In the exclusive economic zone, all States, whether coastal or land-locked, enjoy, subject to the relevant provisions of this Convention, the freedoms referred to in article 87 of navigation and overflight and of the laying of submarine cables and pipelines, and other internationally lawful uses of the sea related to these freedoms, such as those associated with the operation of ships, aircraft and submarine cables and pipelines, and compatible with the other provisions of this Convention.
> 2. Articles 88 to 115 and other pertinent rules of international law apply to the exclusive economic zone in so far as they are not incompatible with this Part.

[87] CSIL, "The South China Sea Arbitration Awards," 599, para. 837.

[88] *Ibid.*, 597–99, paras. 836–38.

[89] *Ibid.*, 599, para. 838.

[90] Paragraph 4 of Article 21 (Laws and regulations of the coastal State relating to innocent passage) reads as follows: "4. Foreign ships exercising the right of innocent passage through the territorial sea shall comply with all such laws and regulations and all generally accepted international regulations relating to the prevention of collisions at sea."

are to believe the CSIL, the Tribunal's problems would not have ended there: if it had followed the Philippine view, it would have had to determine which ships of which State were "foreign ships" and to determine sovereignty.[91] In this manner, the CSIL reprised the theme of China's Position Paper: that "the essence of the subject-matter of the arbitration" was territorial sovereignty over several maritime features in the South China Sea, "which is beyond the scope of the Convention and does not concern the interpretation or application of the Convention."[92]

Similarly, the CSIL believes that the Tribunal should have attempted to find a provision in the Convention that enables Article 94 to apply to internal waters.[93] The justification for this requirement was that China, which in the CSIL's view has sovereignty over Scarborough Shoal, had not yet announced the base points and baselines for Scarborough Shoal's territorial sea, leaving unclear the line between internal waters and the territorial sea.[94]

The first response to these arguments is that they misunderstand the reasoning of the Tribunal. The latter emphasized that the obligations under Article 94 are imposed on flag States.[95] It follows that the Tribunal's conclusion does not depend on and does not involve any finding of sovereignty over Scarborough Shoal and its waters.[96] It would not matter which State had sovereignty, because both the Philippines and China were flag States. As such, both were bound by Article 94 of the Convention. The Tribunal's reasoning relied on an Advisory Opinion of the ITLOS, cited by the Philippines during the Hearing on the Merits. In the opinion of the ITLOS, "[t]he Convention contains provisions concerning general obligations which are to be met by the flag state in all marine areas regulated by the Convention," and that "[t]hese general obligations are set out in articles 91, 92 and 94 of the Convention."[97]

[91] CSIL, "The South China Sea Arbitration Awards," 599, para. 838.

[92] *MP*, Annex 467, 21, para. 3.

[93] CSIL, "The South China Sea Arbitration Awards," 599, para. 839.

[94] *Ibid.*, 597, para. 833.

[95] Award of 12 July 2016, 428, para. 1082.

[96] *Ibid.*, 435, para. 1108.

[97] *Request for Advisory Opinion submitted by the Sub-Regional Fisheries Commission, Advisory Opinion, 2 April 2015, ITLOS Reports 2015*, 34, para. 111, https://www.itlos.org/fileadmin/itlos/documents/cases/case_no.21/advisory_opinion_published/2015_21-advop-E.pdf, accessed 6 June 2019; quoted in Hearing on the Merits, Final Transcript, Day 3, 56–57.

The implication was that China had obligations under the Convention when its own vessels were operated in the territorial sea of Scarborough Shoal or anywhere else. It was irrelevant which State had sovereignty over that territorial sea.[98] In the Award, the Tribunal at no point used the expression "coastal State." The CSIL may also have been misled by the Tribunal's conclusion in the Award on Jurisdiction and Admissibility that "Article 298(1)(b) has no application in the territorial sea."[99] In this phrase, the Tribunal was merely excluding the application of the "law enforcement activities" exception to Submission No. 13. The phrase was not a finding that required the Tribunal to determine who had sovereignty over the territorial sea of Scarborough Shoal.

One might add that the CSIL also misunderstood the position of the Philippines. As counsel for the Philippines emphasized during the Hearing on the Merits, Article 21 of the Convention, which authorizes the coastal State to adopt laws and regulations relating to innocent passage in the territorial sea in a number of matters, is irrelevant: "the Philippines is not alleging a violation of Article 21."[100] The CSIL may have been misled by the Philippines' use of the term "coastal State" in its *Memorial*, usage of which would seem to require a prior determination of the identity of the coastal State. The Philippines had cited Article 21(4) in its *Memorial* in two contexts. First, it identified "the international regulations relating to the prevention of collisions at sea," referred to in Article 21(4) of the Convention as the COLREGS.[101] Second, it argued that while Article 21(4) literally applied only to foreign ships in innocent passage, in fact the coastal State was also bound to comply with the COLREGS.[102] However, during the Hearing on the Merits, the Philippines refrained from using the expression "coastal State" and explicitly stated that it was arguing that China had violated its obligations as a flag State. The COLREGS were applicable on that basis, regardless of the location of the ships at any point in time.[103]

[98] Hearing on the Merits, Final Transcript, Day 3, 57.

[99] *Ibid.*

[100] *Ibid.*

[101] *MP*, vol. I, 208, para. 6.131.

[102] *Ibid.*, 209, para. 6.133.

[103] Hearing on the Merits, Final Transcript, Day 3, 56.

The clarification of the Tribunal's reasoning should render superfluous, at least in theory, any rebuttal of the CSIL's claim that the COLREGS are not applicable in the territorial sea in the absence of an enabling provision comparable to Article 58(2). The CSIL's claim is so astonishing—it would result in a situation in which foreign vessels engaged in innocent passage would be bound by the COLREGS, while the vessels of the coastal State would not—that one feels obliged to respond to the CSIL's post-arbitration rationalization of China's conduct. Simply put, the CSIL's scarcely conceivable claim is contradicted by the text and the history of the COLREGS.

A rapid perusal of the text of the COLREGS should suffice to convince the reader that the CSIL's claim should be rejected. Rule 1 (a) (Application) of the COLREGS makes it clear that the Rules "shall apply to all vessels upon the high seas and in all waters connected therewith navigable by seagoing vessels." According to the authoritative interpretation provided by the IMO and quoted by the Philippines in its *Memorial*: "Within the general framework established by the provisions of UNCLOS, COLREG applies to the high seas, the EEZ, the territorial sea, archipelagic waters, straits used for international navigation and archipelagic sea lanes."[104] Under the COLREGS and consequently, under the Convention, the coastal State would have to apply the COLREGS in its territorial sea. Only this interpretation could prevent the occurrence of the incongruous situation in which foreign ships engaged in innocent passage in the territorial sea would be liable for violations of the COLREGS, while ships flying the flag of the coastal State would not.

The history of the International Regulations since the end of the nineteenth century confirms the applicability of the Regulations in the territorial sea. The first version of Rule 1(a) seems to have been incorporated in the International Regulations at the Washington Conference 1889, in almost identical terms: "These rules shall be followed by all vessels upon the high seas and in all waters connected therewith, navigable

[104] IMO, *Implications of the United Nations Convention on the Law of the Sea for the International Maritime Organization*, IMO Doc. LEG/MISC.6, 2008, in Myron H. Nordquist et al. (eds.), UNCLOS 1982 *Commentary. Supplementary Documents* (Leiden: Martinus Nijhoff Publishers, 2012), 775; quoted in *MP*, vol. I, 209, para. 6.133.

by sea-going vessels."[105] At the end of the nineteenth century, the only "waters connected therewith [i.e., with the high seas] navigable by sea-going vessels" were those of the territorial sea, international straits being by definition part of the high seas. The implication is that the COLREGS already applied to the territorial sea in the nineteenth century.

In this regard, a commentary on the International Regulations published in 1880, which discussed the implications of the phrase "at sea," is instructive. Marsden acknowledges that the International Regulations appear to be expressly binding only on ships at sea. Yet he believed that except in waters where local rules were in force, it would probably be held that vessels are required to navigate in accordance with the collision regulations even in rivers and harbors, as well as at sea. He noted that many cases had been decided on the assumption that the Collision Regulations applied in rivers. Moreover,

> [t]he words of Article 25 of the new Regulations [concerning local rules] seem to imply that, except in the cases mentioned in that article, they apply everywhere. On the sea, everywhere, except where local rules apply, they are directly applicable.[106]

Now rivers and harbors are part of internal waters, which are found landward of the baselines of the territorial sea. If the International Regulations are applicable even in internal waters—over which the coastal State enjoys

[105] "Final Act of the International Marine Conference held at Washington, October 16 to December 31, 1889," *American Journal of International Law* 5:1, *Supplement: Official Documents* (1911) 44. For the 1863 and 1880 texts of the International Regulations, see Reginald Godfrey Marsden, *A Treatise on the Law of Collisions at Sea, with an Appendix Containing Extracts from the Merchant Shipping Acts, the International Regulations (of 1863 and 1880) for Preventing Collisions at Sea and Local Rules for the Same Purpose in Force in the Thames, The Mersey and Elsewhere* (London: Stevens and Sons, 1880), 247–58, https://ia800205.us.archive.org/26/items/cu31924022403897/cu31924022403897.pdf, accessed 3 June 2019. For the 1884 text of the International Regulations, see Reginald Godfrey Marsden, *A Treatise on the Law of Collisions at Sea with an Appendix Containing the International Regulations for Preventing Collisions at Sea, and Local Rules for the Same Purpose in Force in the Thames, Mersey, and Elsewhere, also the Regulations Approved at the Washington International Maritime Conference* (London: Stevens and Sons, Limited, 1891), 537–71, https://ia800205.us.archive.org/6/items/treatiseonsealaw00mars/treatiseonsealaw00mars.pdf, accessed 3 June 2019.

[106] Marsden, *A Treatise* (1880), 134.

complete sovereignty—it stands to reason that they are also applicable in the territorial sea. A later edition of Marsden's commentary cites a case decided in 1907, *The Anselm*, concerning a collision in the Para Estuary of the Amazon River. The British Court of Appeals, having regard to the many cases in which the International Regulations had been treated as applicable to rivers and narrow waters, refused to interfere with what had become established practice. Marsden added that by 1910, it could be regarded as "settled law" that the Regulations were applicable to all waters within the preliminary paragraph of the Regulations 1891—"the high seas and all waters connected therewith, navigable by seagoing vessels."[107]

The COLREGS do take into account the possibility that national authorities may have to adopt special rules for areas that lie outside the usual limit of inland waters. According to Rule 1(b),

> Nothing in these Rules shall interfere with the operation of special rules made by an appropriate authority for roadsteads, harbours, rivers, lakes or inland waterways connected with the high seas and navigable by seagoing vessels. Such special rules shall conform as closely as possible to these Rules.

The last sentence is crucial: the special rules "shall conform as closely as possible" to the COLREGS. In the words of the authors of a standard text on the COLREGS, the purpose of consistency is to minimize "confusion, errors, and the potential for collisions."[108]

Once again, it is instructive to read Marsden's nineteenth-century commentaries. Marsden noted in 1880 that local rules were in force in the Thames, the Mersey, the Clyde, the Tees, the Tyne and at Belfast, Dublin, and Cork. In the case of the Thames and some other rivers, the local rules were almost identical with those of the International Regulations,[109] in which case no conflicts could be expected to arise. A subsequent edition added that in Scotland, notwithstanding the existence of local rules of navigation applicable to the River Clyde, a steamship was held in fault for

[107] Reginald Godfrey Marsden, Edward Stanley Roscoe, and Helenus Macaulay Robertson, *A Treatise on the Law of Collisions at Sea* (6th ed.; London: Stevens and Sons, Limited, 1910), 317, https://ia600207.us.archive.org/26/items/cu31924022403921/cu31924022403921.pdf, accessed 3 June 2019.

[108] Christopher B. Llana and George P. Wisneskey, *Handbook of the Nautical Rules of the Road: A Convenient Take-Along Guide for Sail and Power Boaters* (3rd [online] ed., 2009), 66, http://navruleshandbook.com/Rule1.html, accessed 6 June 2019.

[109] Marsden, *A Treatise* (1880), 238.

disobedience to two rules of the International Regulations 1863, which were therefore held to be applicable to rivers. He concluded from this that in Scotland, where local rules were in force, they were to be construed and applied in conjunction with the International Regulations. Marsden also noted that in Canada, the collisions were applicable over all inland and other navigable waters of Canada. Finally, he found it significant that the title of the US act that embodied the Regulations 1863 expressed the aim of the act as preventing "collisions on water."[110] These remarks indicate that in the nineteenth century, the International Regulations were applicable in internal waters and the territorial sea, and that even when local rules were in force for inland waters, they did not impair the applicability of the International Regulations.

China, as we may recall, ratified the successive versions of the International Regulations from 1889 onwards. China has also adopted special rules for roadsteads, harbors, rivers, lakes, or inland waterways, based on the specific characteristics of the vessels, traffic, and natural circumstances, notably the Shanghai Harbor Code and the Regulations for Preventing Collisions in Inland Waters of China. Captain Yuelin Zhao remarks that in China, all special rules do not exclude the applicability of the COLREGS. The special rules will prevail where they conflict with the COLREGS; when they do not conflict with the COLREGS, the latter are supplementary to the special rules. It is perhaps significant that he did not report any instance of a contradiction between the COLREGS and the inland rules.[111]

As there can be no doubt concerning the Arbitral Tribunal's jurisdiction with respect to Philippine Submission No. 13, it is now possible to reexamine the conduct of China's official vessels on 28 April and 26 May 2012 in light of the COLREGS.

References

Allen, Craig H. "Revisiting the Thames Formula: The Evolving Role of the International Maritime Organization and Its Member States in Implementing the 1982 Law of the Sea Convention." *San Diego International Law Journal* 10

[110] Marsden, *A Treatise* (1891), 343.

[111] Yuelin Zhao, "The Regulations for Preventing Collisions at Sea and Liability Apportionment in China," *The Asian Business Lawyer* 8 (2011): 102, https://asianbusinesslawyer.korea.ac.kr/xe/?module=file&act...file_srl=436, accessed 24 September 2018.

(2009): 265–333, https://digitalcommons.law.uw.edu/faculty-articles/86/, accessed 5 June 2019.

"Arctic Sunrise" Arbitration (Netherlands v. Russian Federation). Award on Jurisdiction, 26 November 2014, https://pcacases.com/web/sendAttach/1325, accessed 5 June 2019.

———. Joint Separate Opinion of Judge Wolfrum and Judge Kelly. *ITLOS Reports 2013*, 256–61, https://www.itlos.org/fileadmin/itlos/documents/cases/case_no.22/published/C22_Wolfrum_Kelly_221113.pdf, accessed 5 June 2019.

———. *Provisional Measures. Order of 22 November 2013. ITLOS Reports 2013*, 224–53, https://www.itlos.org/fileadmin/itlos/documents/cases/case_no.22/published/C22_Order_221113.pdf, accessed 5 June 2019.

———. *Statement of the Claim and Grounds on which It Is Based*, dated 4 October 2013, https://pcacases.com/web/sendAttach/1314, accessed 5 June 2019.

Chinese Society of International Law. "The South China Sea Arbitration Awards: A Critical Study." *Chinese Journal of International Law* 17 (2018): 207–748.

COLREG Convention on the International Regulations for Preventing Collisions at Sea, 1972. Consolidated Edition, 2003. Supplement January 2016, http://www.imo.org/en/Publications/Documents/Supplements%20and%20CDs/English/QB904E_012016.pdf, accessed 5 June 2019.

Convention on the International Regulations for Preventing Collisions at Sea. Adopted 20 October 1972. Entered into force 15 July 1977. Consolidated text as amended in 1981, 1987, 1989, 1993, 2001 and 2007, http://www.ecolregs.com/index.php?option=com_k2&view=itemlist&layout=category&Itemid=505&lang=en, accessed 31 May 2019.

"Final Act of the International Conference on Safety of Life at Sea, 1948. Signed at London, on 10 June 1948." *United Nations Treaty Series*. Vol. 191, 3–58. New York: United Nations, 1954, https://treaties.un.org/doc/Publication/UNTS/Volume%20191/v191.pdf, accessed 5 June 2019.

"Final Act of the International Marine Conference held at Washington, October 16 to December 31, 1889." *American Journal of International Law*, 5, *Supplement: Official Documents* (1911): 42–73.

Geneva Convention on the High Seas. Done at Geneva on 29 April 1958. Entered into force on 30 September 1962. *United Nations Treaty Series*. Vol. 450, 82–102. New York: United Nations, 1964, https://treaties.un.org/doc/Publication/UNTS/Volume%20450/volume-450-I-6465-English.pdf, accessed 5 June 2019.

Grant, John P., and J. Craig Barker. *Parry & Grant Encyclopedic Dictionary of International Law*, 3rd ed. Oxford: Oxford University Press, 2009.

Guilfoyle, Douglas. "Article 94. Duties of the flag State." *United Nations Convention on the Law of the Sea. A Commentary*, 707–14. Eds. Alexander Proelss et al. München: Verlag C.H. Beck oHG, 2017.

"IMO Assembly Adopts Mandatory Audit Scheme." *World Maritime News*, 5 December 2013, https://worldmaritimenews.com/archives/99206/imo-assembly-adopts-mandatory-audit-scheme/, accessed 5 June 2019.

International Conference on Safety of Life at Sea. Text of the Convention for the Safety of Life at Sea. London: H.M. Stationery Office, Harrison and Sons, Printers England, 1914, http://ia802605.us.archive.org/5/items/textofconvention00inte/textofconvention00inte.pdf, accessed 5 June 2019.

International Convention for the Safety of Life at Sea (SOLAS 1974). Done at London, 1 November 1974. Entered into force 25 May 1980, https://www.refworld.org/docid/46920bf32.html, accessed 3 June 2019.

International Maritime Organization (IMO). Framework and Procedures for the IMO Member State Audit Scheme (resolution A.1067(28)). IMO Doc. A 28/Res.1067 (5 December 2013), http://www.imo.org/en/OurWork/TechnicalCooperation/Documents/A%2028-Res%201067.pdf, accessed 5 June 2019.

———. *Status of IMO Treaties. Comprehensive Information on the Status of Multilateral Conventions and Instruments in Respect of Which the International Maritime Organization or Its Secretary-General Performs Depositary or Other Functions*. London: IMO, 2019, http://www.imo.org/en/About/Conventions/StatusOfConventions/Documents/Status%20-%202019.pdf, accessed 3 June 2019.

Llana, Christopher B., and George P. Wisneskey. *Handbook of the Nautical Rules of the Road: A Convenient Take-Along Guide for Sail and Power Boaters*, 3rd. [online] ed., 2009, http://navruleshandbook.com/Rule1.html, accessed 6 June 2019.

Marsden, Reginald Godfrey. *A Treatise on the Law of Collisions at Sea, with an Appendix Containing Extracts from the Merchant Shipping Acts, the International Regulations (of 1863 and 1880) for Preventing Collisions at Sea and Local Rules for the Same Purpose in Force in the Thames, The Mersey and Elsewhere*. London: Stevens and Sons, 1880, https://ia800205.us.archive.org/26/items/cu31924022403897/cu31924022403897.pdf, accessed 3 June 2019.

———. *A Treatise on the Law of Collisions at Sea with an Appendix Containing the International Regulations for Preventing Collisions at Sea, and Local Rules for the Same Purpose in Force in the Thames, Mersey, and Elsewhere, also the Regulations Approved at the Washington International Maritime Conference*. London: Stevens and Sons, Limited, 1891, https://ia800205.us.archive.org/6/items/treatiseonsealaw00mars/treatiseonsealaw00mars.pdf, accessed 3 June 2019.

———; Edward Stanley Roscoe; and Helenus Macaulay Robertson. *A Treatise on the Law of Collisions at Sea*, 6th ed. London: Stevens and Sons, Limited, 1910, https://ia600207.us.archive.org/26/items/cu31924022403921/cu31924022403921.pdf, accessed 3 June 2019.

Nordquist, Myron H. et al. (eds.). *UNCLOS 1982 Commentary. Supplementary Documents*. Leiden: Martinus Nijhoff Publishers, 2012.

———. *United Nations Convention on the Law of the Sea 1982 Commentary*. Vol. II. *Second Committee: Territorial Sea, Innocent Passage, Straits Used for International Navigation, Archipelagic States, the Exclusive Economic Zone, and the Continental Shelf*. Leiden: Martinus Nijhoff Publishers, 1993.

———. *United Nations Convention on the Law of the Sea 1982 Commentary*. Vol. V. *Settlement of Disputes, General and Final Provisions and related Annexes and resolutions*. Leiden: Martinus Nijhoff Publishers, 1989.

Oxman, Bernard. "The Duty to Respect Generally Accepted International Standards." *New York University Journal of International Law and Politics* 24 (1991): 109–59, https://repository.law.miami.edu/cgi/viewcontent.cgi?article=1403&context=fac_articles, accessed 5 June 2019.

———. "Le régime des navires de guerre dans le cadre de la Convention des Nations Unies sur le droit de la mer [The Regime of Warships Under the United Nations Convention on the Law of the Sea]." *Annuaire Français de Droit International* [French Yearbook of International Law] 28 (1982) : 811–50, https://www.persee.fr/docAsPDF/afdi_0066-3085_1982_num_28_1_2519.pdf,

———. "The Regime of Warships Under the United Nations Convention on the Law of the Sea." *Virginia Journal of International Law* 24 (1984): 809–63, https://repository.law.miami.edu/cgi/viewcontent.cgi?article=1401&context=fac_articles, accessed 5 June 2019.

Permanent Court of Arbitration. *The Arctic Sunrise Arbitration (Netherlands v. Russian Federation). Arbitral Tribunal Renders Award on the Merits*. Press Release of 24 August 2015, https://pcacases.com/web/sendAttach/1444, accessed 5 June 2019.

Philippines, Republic of the. Executive Order No. 459, providing for the Guidelines in the Negotiation of International Agreements and Its [sic] Ratification (25 November 1997), https://www.gppb.gov.ph/laws/laws/EO_459-1997.pdf, accessed 15 July 2021.

Request for Advisory Opinion submitted by the Sub-Regional Fisheries Commission. Advisory Opinion, 2 April 2015. ITLOS Reports 2015, 4–70, https://www.itlos.org/fileadmin/itlos/documents/cases/case_no.21/advisory_opinion_published/2015_21-advop-E.pdf, accessed 6 June 2019.

South China Sea Arbitration. Award of 12 July 2016, https://pcacases.com/web/sendAttach/2086, accessed 5 June 2019.

———. Award on Jurisdiction and Admissibility, 29 October 2015, https://pcacases.com/web/sendAttach/2579, accessed 5 June 2019.
———. Hearing on Jurisdiction and Admissibility. Final Transcript, Day 2 (8 July 2015), https://pcacases.com/web/sendAttach/1400, accessed 5 June 2019.
———. Hearing on the Merits and Remaining Issues of Jurisdiction and Admissibility. Final Transcript, Day 3 (26 November 2015), https://pcacases.com/web/sendAttach/1549, accessed 5 June 2019.
———. Independent Expert Report. Report of the International Navigational Safety Expert Appointed by the Permanent Court of Arbitration [sic], The Hague, The Netherlands, 15 April 2016, by Captain Gupreet S. Singhota, https://pcacases.com/web/sendAttach/1810, accessed 6 June 2019.
———. *Memorial of the Philippines* (30 March 2014). Vol. I, http://www.pcacases.com/pcadocs/Memorial%20of%20the%20Philippines%20Volume%20I.pdf, accessed 5 June 2019.
———. *Supplemental Written Submissions of the Philippines* (16 March 2015). Vol. I, https://files.pca-cpa.org/pcadocs/Supplemental%20Written%20Submission%20Volume%20I.pdf, accessed 5 June 2019.
———. Annex 467. People's Republic of China, Position Paper of the Government of the People's Republic of China on the Matter of Jurisdiction in the South China Sea Arbitration Initiated by the Republic of the Philippines (7 Dec. 2014). Vol. VIII, 19–34, https://files.pca-cpa.org/pcadocs/The%20Philippines%27%20Supplemental%20Written%20Submission%20-%20Volume%20VIII%20%28Annexes%20466-499%29.pdf, accessed 5 June 2019.
Treves, Tullio. "La navigation [Navigation]." *Traité du Nouveau droit de la mer* [Treatise on the New Law of the Sea], 687–808. Eds. René-Jean Dupuy and Daniel Vignes. Paris: Éditions Économica, 1985.
United Nations Codification Division. *United Nations Conference on the Law of the Sea (Geneva, 24 February–27 April 1958)*. New York: United Nations Codification Division, Office of Legal Affairs, 2019, http://legal.un.org/diplomaticconferences/1958_los/, accessed 5 June 2019.
United Nations Conference on the Law of the Sea. *Summary Record of the 19th Meeting* (28 March 1958). UN Doc. A/CONF.13/C.2/SR.19. *United Nations Conference on the Law of the Sea. Official records*. Vol. IV. *Second Committee (High Seas: General Regime). Summary records of meetings and Annexes, Geneva, 24 February–27 April 1958*. UN Doc. A/CONF.13/40. New York: United Nations, 1958, http://legal.un.org/docs/?path=../diplomaticconferences/1958_los/docs/english/vol_4.pdf&lang=Em, accessed 5 June 2019.
———. *Summary Record of the 22nd Meeting* (31 March 1958). UN Doc. A/CONF.13/C.2/SR.22. *United Nations Conference on the Law of the Sea. Official records*. Vol. IV. *Second Committee (High Seas: General*

Regime). Summary records of meetings and Annexes, Geneva, 24 February–27 April 1958. UN Doc. A/CONF.13/40. New York: United Nations, 1958, http://legal.un.org/docs/?path=../diplomaticconferences/1958_los/docs/english/vol_4.pdf&lang=Em, accessed 5 June 2019.

———. *Summary Record of the 23rd Meeting* (1 April 1958). UN Doc. A/CONF.13/C.2/SR.23. *United Nations Conference on the Law of the Sea. Official records*. Vol. IV. *Second Committee (High Seas: General Regime). Summary records of meetings and Annexes, Geneva, 24 February–27 April 1958*. UN Doc. A/CONF.13/40. New York: United Nations, 1958, http://legal.un.org/docs/?path=../diplomaticconferences/1958_los/docs/english/vol_4.pdf&lang=Em, accessed 5 June 2019.

———. *United Kingdom of Great Britain and Northern Ireland: Proposal*. UN Doc. A/CONF.13/C.2/L.49 (21 March 1958). *United Nations Conference on the Law of the Sea. Official records*. Vol. IV. *Second Committee (High Seas: General Regime). Summary records of meetings and Annexes, Geneva, 24 February–27 April 1958*. UN Doc. A/CONF.13/40. New York: United Nations, 1958, http://legal.un.org/docs/?path=../diplomaticconferences/1958_los/docs/english/vol_4.pdf&lang=Em, accessed 5 June 2019.

United Nations Convention on the Law of the Sea. Concluded at Montego Bay on 10 December 1982. Entered into force 16 November 1994. http://www.un.org/depts/los/convention_agreements/texts/unclos/unclos_e.pdf, accessed 6 June 2019.

United Nations. International Law Commission. *Mémorandum présenté par le Secrétariat* [Memorandum Submitted by the Secretariat]. UN Doc. A/CN.4/32 (14 juillet 1950). *Yearbook of the International Law Commission 1950*. Vol. II. *Documents of the second session including the report of the Commission to the General Assembly*, 67–113. UN Doc. A/CN. 4/SER.A/1950/Add. 1. New York: United Nations, 1957, http://legal.un.org/docs/?path=../ilc/publications/yearbooks/english/ilc_1950_v2.pdf&lang=E, accessed 5 June 2019.

———. *Régime of the High Seas. Rapport de J. P. A. François, rapporteur spécial* [Report of J. P. A. François, Special Rapporteur]. UN Doc. A/CN.4/17 (17 March 1950). *Yearbook of the International Law Commission 1950*. Vol. II. *Documents of the second session including the report of the Commission to the General Assembly*, 36–51. UN Doc. A/CN.4/SER.A/1950/Add. 1. New York: United Nations, 1957, http://legal.un.org/docs/?path=../ilc/publications/yearbooks/english/ilc_1950_v2.pdf&lang=E, accessed 5 June 2019.

———. *Régime of the High Seas. Deuxième rapport de M. J. P. A. François, rapporteur spécial* [Second Report of Mr. J. P. A. François, Special Rapporteur]. UN Doc. A/CN.4/42 (10 April 1951). *Yearbook of the International Law Commission 1951*. Vol. II. *Documents of the second session including the report of the Commission to the General Assembly*,

75–103. UN Doc. A/CN.4/SER.A/1951/Add. 1. New York: United Nations, 1957, http://legal.un.org/docs/?path=../ilc/publications/yearbooks/english/ilc_1951_v2.pdf&lang=E, accessed 5 June 2019.

———. *Régime of the High Seas. Troisième rapport par J. P. A. François, rapporteur spécial* [Third Report of J. P. A. François, Special Rapporteur]. UN Doc. A/CN.4/51 (28 February 1952). *Yearbook of the International Law Commission 1952.* Vol. II. *Documents of the second session including the report of the Commission to the General Assembly*, 44–50. UN Doc. A/CN.4/SER.A/1952/Add. 1. New York: United Nations, 1958, http://legal.un.org/docs/?path=../ilc/publications/yearbooks/english/ilc_1952_v2.pdf&lang=E, accessed 5 June 2019.

———. *Régime of the High Seas. Sixième rapport de J. P. A. François, rapporteur spécial* [Sixth Report of J. P. A. François, Special Rapporteur]. UN Doc. A/CN.4/79 (1 March 1954). *Yearbook of the International Law Commission 1954.* Vol. II. *Documents of the second session including the report of the Commission to the General Assembly*, 7–18. UN Doc. A/CN.4/SER.A/1954/Add. 1. New York: United Nations, 1960, http://legal.un.org/docs/?path=../ilc/publications/yearbooks/english/ilc_1954_v2.pdf&lang=E, accessed 5 June 2019.

———. *Summary Record of the 64*th *Meeting* (10 July 1950). UN Doc. A/CN.4/SR.64. *Yearbook of the International Law Commission* 1950. Vol. I, *Summary records of the second session*, 188–98. UN Doc. A/CN.4/SER.A/1950. New York: United Nations, 1958, http://legal.un.org/docs/?path=../ilc/publications/yearbooks/english/ilc_1950_v1.pdf&lang=E, accessed 5 June 2019.

———. *Summary Record of the 66th Meeting* (12 July 1950). UN Doc. A/CN.4/SR.66. *Yearbook of the International Law Commission 1950.* Vol. I. *Summary records of the second session*, 207–16. UN Doc. A/CN.4/SER.A/1950. New York: United Nations, 1958, http://legal.un.org/docs/?path=../ilc/publications/yearbooks/english/ilc_1950_v1.pdf&lang=E, accessed 5 June 2019.

———. *Summary Record of the 122nd Meeting* (11 July 1951). UN. Doc. A/CN.4/SR.122. *Yearbook of the International Law Commission 1951.* Vol. I. *Summary records of the third session, 16 May – 27 July 1951*, 336–46. UN Doc. A/CN.4/SER.A/1951. New York: United Nations, 1957, http://legal.un.org/docs/?path=../ilc/publications/yearbooks/english/ilc_1951_v1.pdf&lang=E, accessed 5 June 2019.

———. *Summary Record of the 123*rd *Meeting* (12 July 1951). UN Doc. A/CN.4/SR.123. *Yearbook of the International Law Commission 1951.* Vol. I. *Summary records of the third session, 16 May–27 July 1951*, 346–54. UN Doc. A/CN.4/SER.A/1951. New York: United

Nations, 1957, http://legal.un.org/docs/?path=../ilc/publications/yearbooks/english/ilc_1951_v1.pdf&lang=E, accessed 5 June 2019.

———. *Summary Record of the 285th Meeting* (5 May 1955). UN Doc. A/CN.4/SR.285. *Yearbook of the International Law Commission 1955.* Vol. I. *Summary records of the seventh session 2 May–8 July 1955*, 14–24. UN Doc. A/CN.4/SER.A/1955. New York: United Nations, 1960, http://legal.un.org/docs/?path=../ilc/publications/yearbooks/english/ilc_1955_v1.pdf&lang=E, accessed 5 June 2019.

———. *Summary Record of the 294th Meeting* (18 May 1955). UN Doc. A/CN.4/SR.294. *Yearbook of the International Law Commission 1955.* Vol. I. *Summary records of the seventh session 2 May-8 July 1955*, 61–68. UN Doc. A/CN.4/SER.A/1955. New York: United Nations, 1960, http://legal.un.org/docs/?path=../ilc/publications/yearbooks/english/ilc_1955_v1.pdf&lang=E, accessed 5 June 2019.

———. *Summary Record of the 321st Meeting* (28 June 1955). UN Doc. A/CN.4/SR.321. *Yearbook of the International Law Commission 1955.* Vol. I. *Summary records of the seventh session 2 May–8 July 1955*, 227–36. UN Doc. A/CN.4/SER.A/1955. New York: United Nations, 1960, http://legal.un.org/docs/?path=../ilc/publications/yearbooks/english/ilc_1955_v1.pdf&lang=E, accessed 5 June 2019.

———. *Summary Record of the 342nd Meeting* (8 May 1956). UN Doc. A/CN.4/SR.342. *Yearbook of the International Law Commission 1956.* Vol. I. *Summary records of the eighth session 23 April–4 July 1956*, 40–45. UN Doc. 1956.V.3, Vol. I. New York: United Nations, 1956, http://legal.un.org/docs/?path=../ilc/publications/yearbooks/english/ilc_1956_v1.pdf&lang=EFS, accessed 5 June 2019.

United Nations. Office of Legal Affairs. Treaty Section. *United Nations Treaty Collection, XXI6. Law of the Sea*, https://treaties.un.org/doc/Publication/MTDSG/Volume%20II/Chapter%20XXI/XXI-6.en.pdf, accessed 5 June 2019.

Vienna Convention on the Law of Treaties (with Annex). Concluded at Vienna on 23 May 1969. *United Nations Treaty Series.* Vol. 1155, 331–53. New York: United Nations, 1980, https://treaties.un.org/doc/publication/unts/volume%201155/volume-1155-i-18232-english.pdf, accessed 5 June 2019.

Vignes, Daniel. "La valeur juridique de certaines règles, normes ou pratiques, mentionnées au TNCO [Texte de négociation composite et officieux] comme 'généralement acceptées' [The Binding Force of Certain Rules, Norms or Practices Mentioned in the ICNT (Informal Composite Negotiating Text] as "Generally Accepted"]." *Annuaire Français de Droit International* [French Yearbook of International Law] 25 (1979): 712–18, https://www.persee.fr/doc/afdi_0066-3085_1979_num_25_1_2182, accessed 5 June 2019.

Zhao, Yuelin. "The Regulations for Preventing Collisions at Sea and Liability Apportionment in China." *The Asian Business Lawyer* 8 (Fall 2011): 100–15, https://asianbusinesslawyer.korea.ac.kr/xe/?module=file&act...file1_srl=436, accessed 24 September 2018.

CHAPTER 5

The Violations of the COLREGS as Violations of the United Nations Convention on the Law of the Sea

The starting point of the discussion is the Arbitral Tribunal's affirmation that since the Convention on the International Regulations for Preventing Collisions at Sea 1972 ("COLREGS 1972") are incorporated into the United Nations Convention on the Law of the Sea 1982 ("Convention") by Article 94 of the latter, the violation of the COLREGS as generally accepted international regulations constitutes a violation of the Convention itself.[1]

In applying the COLREGS, the Arbitral Tribunal, following well-established principles of the international law of State responsibility, considered that the conduct of each Chinese vessel—China Marine Surveillance ("CMS") 71, CMS 84, Fisheries Law Enforcement Command ("FLEC") 303, FLEC 306, and FLEC 310—was attributable to China. All these vessels belonged to CMS or FLEC. The actions having been undertaken by vessels directly under Chinese government command

[1] *South China Sea Arbitration*, Award of 12 July 2016, 429, para. 1083, https://pcacases.com/web/sendAttach/2086, accessed 5 June 2019. *Convention on the International Regulations for Preventing Collisions at Sea*, adopted 20 October 1972, entered into force 15 July 1977; consolidated text as amended in 1981, 1987, 1989, 1993, 2001 and 2007, http://www.ecolregs.com/index.php?option=com_k2&view=itemlist&layout=category&Itemid=505&lang=en, accessed 31 May 2019; *United Nations Convention on the Law of the Sea*, concluded at Montego Bay on 10 December 1982, entered into force 16 November 1994, http://www.un.org/depts/los/convention_agreements/texts/unclos/unclos_e.pdf, accessed 6 June 2019.

A. C. Robles Jr., *Vessel Collisions in the Law of the Sea*,
https://doi.org/10.1007/978-981-16-9793-7_5

and control, the vessel's behavior constituted official acts of China. Their conduct was automatically attributed to China.[2]

The Tribunal did not even consider the possibility, briefly raised and immediately rejected by the Philippines during the Hearing on the Merits, that the Chinese vessels' actions were not carried out under official orders—that their actions were unauthorized or *ultra vires* acts of State organs or entities. Under well-established principles of State responsibility, such acts are attributable to the State even if the State organ that committed them exceeded their authority or contravened instructions.[3] Consequently, even assuming that the officers of the FLEC and CMS vessels had exceeded their instructions—an argument that China had never put forward to excuse their actions—their acts would still have been attributed to China.

To evaluate China's conduct, the Tribunal took account of two expert reports. The first report was submitted by the Philippines together with

[2] Award of 12 July 2016, 431, para. 1090.

[3] *South China Sea Arbitration*, Hearing on the Merits and Remaining Issues of Jurisdiction and Admissibility, Final Transcript, Day 3 (26 November 2015), 72 ("Hearing on the Merits, Final Transcript, Day 3"), https://pcacases.com/web/sendAttach/1549, accessed 5 June 2019. The text of Article 7 (Excess of Authority or Contravention of Instructions) of the United Nations International Law Commission's Draft Articles on Responsibility of States for Internationally Wrongful Acts reads as follows:

> The conduct of an organ of a State or of a person or entity empowered to exercise elements of the governmental authority shall be considered an act of the State under international law if the organ, person or entity acts in that capacity, even if it exceeds its authority or contravenes instructions.

Draft Articles on Responsibility of States for Internationally Wrongful Acts, with Commentaries (2001). Report of the International Law Commission on the Work of its Fifty-third Session, 23 April–1 June and 2 July–10 August 2001, Official Records of the General Assembly, Fifty-sixth Session, Supplement No. 10, UN Doc. A/56/10, in *Yearbook of the International Law Commission 2001*, Vol. II, Part 2, *Report of the Commission to the General Assembly on the Work of its Fifty-third Session*. UN Doc. A/CN.4/SER.A/2001/Add.1 (Part 2) (New York: United Nations, 2007), 99, http://legal.un.org/docs/?path=../ilc/publications/yearbooks/english/ilc_2001_v2_p2.pdf&lang=EFSRAC, accessed 6 June 2019. On international State responsibility, see James Crawford, *The International Law Commission's Articles on State Responsibility* (Cambridge: Cambridge University Press, 2002); Eduardo Jiménez de Aréchaga, "International Responsibility," in Max Sørensen (ed.), *Manual of Public International Law* (London: Macmillan, 1968), 531–604; and Eduardo Jiménez de Aréchaga and Attila Tanzi, "International State Responsibility," in Mohammed Bedjaoui (ed.) *International Law: Achievements and Prospects* (Paris: UNESCO, 1991), 347–80.

its *Memorial*. Its author was Craig H. Allen, a lawyer and holder of a US merchant marine license as master of oceangoing vessels. During his 19-year service with the US Coast Guard (1975–1994), he performed, executed, and/or supervised more than 1000 collision avoidance maneuvers in various capacities, notably as operations officer, navigator, and commanding officer, on Coast Guard vessels. He also conducted over 100 investigations into vessel casualties and oil spills. He is the author of *Farwell's Rules of the Nautical Road* (Naval Institute Press, 8th ed., 2004), the leading book on the COLREGS in the US. He provided his expert opinion pro bono, as he has done as a member of several national and international litigation support projects.[4]

The second report was prepared by an expert who was appointed by the Tribunal in March 2016, several months after the closure of the oral phase on the merits.[5] Its author, Captain Gurpreet S. Singhota, had 14 years of seagoing experience, including six years– as commander on a supertanker, a bulk carrier, a chemical tanker, and other types of vessels. Among his important achievements in a 26-year career at the International Maritime Organization ("IMO") (1987–2013), he assisted in the preparation of amendments to the COLREGS 1972 and the revision of Chapter V (Safety of Navigation) of the International Convention for the Safety of Life at Sea 1974 ("SOLAS 1974").[6] His report, submitted in April 2016, was not annexed to the Award of 12 July 2016 but was made available online on the website of the Permanent Court of Arbitration after the Award of 12 July 2016 had been issued.

The two experts arrive at virtually identical conclusions regarding China's violations of the COLREGS. Any differences between the two are a matter of emphasis, as a result of which the two reports complement each other.

[4] *South China Sea Arbitration*, *Memorial of the Philippines* (30 March 2014), Annex 239, Opinion of Craig H. Allen, Judson Falknor Professor of Law, University of Washington (19 Mar. 2014) ("Allen Opinion"), vol. VII, 373, 380–87 ("*MP*"), https://files.pca-cpa.org/pcadocs/The%20Philippines%27%20Memorial%20-%20Volume%20VII%20%28Annexes%20222-255%29.pdf, accessed 6 June 2019.

[5] Award of 12 July 2016, 29–31, paras. 84–85, 91.

[6] *South China Sea Arbitration*, Independent Expert Report, Report of the International Navigational Safety Expert Appointed by the Permanent Court of Arbitration [sic], The Hague, The Netherlands, 15 April 2016, by Captain Gurpreet S. Singhota, 2, para. 1, Annex 2 ("Singhota Report"), https://pcacases.com/web/sendAttach/1810, accessed 6 June 2019.

The Tribunal did not categorize the Rules that the China's vessels had breached; rather, it analyzed them sequentially. A careful observer will realize that the conduct of China's official vessels on 28 April and 26 May 2012 implicated three sets of rules that are part of the COLREGS: the general rule on Responsibility (Part A of the COLREGS), steering and sailing rules concerning the conduct of vessels in any condition of visibility (Part B, Section 1 of the COLREGS, Rules 4–10), and steering and sailing rules concerning the conduct of vessels in sight of one another (Part B, Section 2, Rules 11–19) of the COLREGS. None of the Rules in Parts C (on Lights and Shapes, Rules 20–31), Part D (Sound and light signals, Rules 32–38), or in any of the four Annexes was implicated in the Chinese vessels' conduct.

Each of the following parts will first explore the scope of the rule(s) concerned before evaluating the conduct of China's official vessels in the light of the rule(s). As we shall see, the Chinese vessels' conduct violated Rule 2, concerning the general rule of responsibility, also known as the "good seamanship" rule. Among the rules applicable to vessels in any condition of visibility, the Chinese vessels' conduct breached Rules 6, 7, and 8. Among the rules applicable to vessels in sight of one another, the Chinese vessels' conduct violated Rules 15 and 16.

I. The General Rule of Responsibility

Rule 2(a) stresses the need for vessels, the owner, master, or crew to comply with the COLREGS, the precautions required by the ordinary practice of seamen, or the special circumstances.[7] The two experts and the Tribunal concluded that the conduct of the Chinese vessels breached the COLREGS and, consequently, the Convention, by neglecting the precautions required by good seamanship, without any special circumstances that could excuse their conduct.

A. Compliance with the COLREGS, Good Seamanship, and Special Circumstances

Rule 2 as a warning against failure to comply with the Rules might seem unnecessary, as mariners themselves recognize that the need to comply

[7] See Annex 5.1.

with them is self-evident. Rule 2 serves to guard against a tendency observed in the past to disregard the letter of the Regulations and to regard collision avoidance as a matter of individual common sense.[8]

Despite its importance—and perhaps because of its very nature—the second key concept listed in Rule 2, "the ordinary practice of seamen," is left undefined in the COLREGS. A British court ruled in 1939 that what constituted good seamanship, another term for "the ordinary practice of seamen," in a given instance was a question of fact to be decided upon consideration of all the relevant circumstances.[9] Fortunately, one of the commentaries on which the Philippines relied provided an easily comprehensible illustration of this key concept. Good seamanship requires that when a vessel anchors, it most do so without endangering other vessels that may be navigating close by; it must not anchor too close to other anchored vessels; sufficient cable must be put out according to the circumstances; and a second anchor should be used if necessary.[10]

There seems to be some divergence of views among commentators on the importance of good seamanship in preventing collisions. For some authors, the adoption of the COLREGS has reduced the role of this principle to a residual one. In the view of others, the principle underlies all the COLREGS, which form only a part of the concept of good seamanship.[11] Indeed, in his expert opinion, Allen, the expert appointed by the Philippines, described Rule 2 as the "good seamanship rule." As we shall see below, the concept of "good seamanship" was also crucial for the expert appointed by the Tribunal in assessing the conduct of the Chinese vessels.

The third concept, "special circumstances," which appears in paragraphs (a) and (b), might at first glance appear to offer an escape clause, a pretext not to comply with the COLREGS. Cockcroft and Lameijer

[8] Glen Plant, "The Collision Avoidance Regulations as a Regulator of International Navigation Rights: Underlying Principles and Their Adequacy for the Twenty-first Century," *Journal of Navigation* 88 (1996): 379 ("*JON*").

[9] Cited in *ibid.*, 387, note 2.

[10] Anthony Norman Cockcroft and J.N.F. Lameijer, *Guide to the Collision Avoidance Rules—International Regulations for Preventing Collisions at Sea Incorporating the 1981, 1987, 1989, 1993, 2001 and 2007 Amendments* (7th ed.; Amsterdam: Elsevier, 2012), 3. The Philippines relied on this commentary for its arguments relating to Rules 6, 8, and 15. See *South China Sea Arbitration, MP*, vol. I, 210, 211, http://www.pcacases.com/pcadocs/Memorial%20of%20the%20Philippines%20Volume%20I.pdf, accessed 7 June 2019.

[11] Plant, "The Collision Avoidance Regulations," 377.

warn that the Rule does not give any vessel the right to take any action contrary to the COLREGS whenever it is considered to be advantageous to do so. A departure from the Rules is only permitted when there are special circumstances and there is immediate danger of collision; both conditions must apply. Moreover, the departure must be of such a nature as to avoid the looming danger. But if the conditions were fulfilled, the vessel would not only be justified in departing from them; it may also be expected to do so.[12]

Only one type of special circumstance is specifically identified in Rule 2(b), the limitations of the vessels involved. One limitation may be physical, deriving from the ship's draft, defined as the depth in water at which a ship floats.[13] Draft limitations will prevent some vessels from turning in shallow water.[14] Other than this, the COLREGS do not provide a list of "special circumstances."

If we turn to State practice, the US case *Crowley Marine Services Inc. v. Maritrans Operating Company* illustrates the explanation provided by Cockcroft and Lameijer concerning the scope of the "special circumstances" exception.[15] The case arose over a collision between *Allegiance*, an oil tanker operated by Maritrans, and *Sea King*, one of two tugboats provided by Crowley to escort *Allegiance* as it transited a portion of Puget Sound in Washington State. The three vessels had agreed an escort maneuver under which *Allegiance* would gradually overtake the two tugboats and pass between them. The *Sea King* failed to make adjustments to its course required by the state of the wind and currents and came closer to *Allegiance*. The overtaking vessel, *Allegiance*, whose master confined himself to radioing the first vessel to inquire about its status, did not alter course or speed. As a result, the two vessels collided. Maritrans argued before the District Court that because the two vessels were operating according to agreed maneuvers, the COLREGS

[12] Cockcroft and Lameijer, *Guide*, 3.

[13] C. W. T. Layton et al., *Dictionary of Nautical Words and Terms* (2nd ed.; Glasgow: Brown, Son & Ferguson Ltd., Naval Publishers, 1982), 134.

[14] Christopher B. Llana and George P. Wisneskey, *Handbook of the Nautical Rules of the Road: A Convenient Take-Along Guide for Sail and Power Boaters* (3rd. [online] ed., 2009), 70, http://navruleshandbook.com/Rule1.html, accessed 7 June 2019.

[15] *Crowley Marine Services Inc. v. Maritrans Operating Company*, 530 F.3d 1167 (9th cir. 2006) [No. 04-35724. Decided: May 08, 2006], https://caselaw.findlaw.com/us-9th-circuit/1384355.html, accessed 7 June 2019.

rules on action to avoid collision (Rule 8) and on overtaking (Rule 13) did not apply.[16] The District Court accepted this argument but the Court of Appeals, noting "the dearth of available precedent," decided that the *Allegiance* had the responsibility of avoiding the *Sea King*, as required by Rule 13. The Court ruled that by its terms, Rule 2 limits "special circumstances" to those circumstances "which may make departure necessary to avoid immediate danger." Vessels may justify departure from COLREGS only in order to avoid immediate danger, not for more generic special circumstances, such as an agreed maneuver.[17] On this basis, Allen concluded that US courts strictly construe the "special circumstances" rule.[18]

The possibility that "special circumstances" existed that could justify the conduct of Chinese vessels was examined by the Tribunal, as we shall see in the next section.

B. Violations of Good Seamanship by the Chinese Vessels

The experts appointed by the Philippines and the Tribunal agreed that the conduct of Chinese vessels on 28 April and 26 May 2012 were in breach of Rule 2, an assessment that the Tribunal accepted.

During the Hearing on the Merits one can observe some uncertainty on the part of the Philippines concerning the importance of Rule 2. Its counsel first affirmed that Rule 2 plays a gap-filling role. This affirmation is consistent with the view that the value of "good seamanship" in the COLREGS framework is residual. But the Philippines immediately went on to say that Rule 2 could be an entirely separate ground for establishing a breach of the COLREGS.[19] As we shall see, it was this second conception that underlay the opinions of the two experts and the decision of the Tribunal itself.

We may recall that on 28 April 2012, FLEC 310 passed within 200 yards of *Barko ng Republika ng Pilipinas* (Ship of the Republic of the Philippines, "BRP") *Edsa II* and within 600 yards of BRP *Pampanga* at a speed of more than 20 knots. On 26 May 2012, CMS 71 and FLEC 303

[16] See Annex 5.1.

[17] *Crowley Marine Services Inc. v. Maritrans Operating Company.*

[18] Allen Opinion, 378.

[19] Hearing on the Merits, Final Transcript, Day 3, 69.

attempted to cut across the bow of Monitoring, Control and Surveillance ("MCS") 3008, on three occasions, once at a distance of less than 100 yards.[20]

Allen, the expert appointed by the Philippines, was of the view that the conduct of the vessels in the two incidents demonstrated serious and intentional breaches of the Rule 2 requirement for all vessels to take the precautions required by the ordinary practice of seamen. The Chinese vessels' high sped blocking or harassment maneuvers intentionally endangered other vessels, constituting flagrant disregard of the tenets of good seamanship.[21] Captain Singhota, the expert appointed by the Tribunal, analyzed each incident. In his view, the high-speed maneuvering by FLEC 310 and its veering away at an unsafe distance of just 0.32 nautical miles on 28 April 2012 was an example of unprofessional ship handling and was totally inconsistent with the practice of good seamanship.[22] He pointed out that a catastrophic collision would have inevitably resulted if the Chinese vessels' engine or steering gear had failed or if there had been a momentary lapse in decision-making on the part of the bridge team of the Chinese vessels.[23] Moreover, a head-on encounter, during which the bows of the two vessels would repel each other as they approach, could have increased a vessel's existing swing (the sideways movement at a constant distance from a point ahead). To prevent such risks, it would have been essential to maximize the distance between two vessels[24]—something that the Chinese vessels failed to do.

In Captain Singhota's view, all the Chinese vessels' maneuvers on 26 May 2012 demonstrated pre-determined attempts to intentionally "block" or hamper another vessel's passage by high-speed blocking or harassment through combined chasing as if in pursuit. Such conduct

[20] Award of 12 July 2016, 431, para. 1093.

[21] Allen Opinion, 376.

[22] Singhota Report, 4, para. 8; 9, para. 27.

[23] *Ibid.*, 4, para. 8. A bridge team, which supports the master in his decisions, consists at a minimum of the master, the officer on watch (OOW) and a sailor as helmsman and lookout. Captain Erik Blom, "Is the Pilot Part of the Bridge Team?" *Insight* 185 (2007), http://www.gard.no/web/updates/content/51708/is-the-pilot-part-of-the-bridge-team, accessed 7 June 2019.

[24] Singhota Report, 4, para. 9. See Annex 4 of the Report, UK Marine and Coastguard Agency, Marine Guidance Note, *Dangers of Interaction*, Doc. No. MGN 199(M)(April 2002), 2, para. 3 (ii).

demonstrated a total disregard of good seamanship and neglected any precaution that may be required by the ordinary practice of seamen.[25]

The Tribunal accepted Captain Singhota's characterization of the Chinese vessels' conduct as "in total disregard of good seamanship and the neglect of any precaution," describing their conduct in very strong language as "irreconcilable with the obligation of responsible navigation."[26] It concluded that Rule 2(a) had been breached by each incident. The Tribunal then sought to determine whether the exception posed by Rule 2(b) was applicable. This issue had not been addressed by Captain Singhota. Allen, on the other hand, acknowledged that US Coast Guard missions often required cutters to "approach" vessels to identify them, determine their flag, the nature of their activities and, if circumstances warranted, to intercept vessels in order to carry out law enforcement on board. Allen admitted that in such circumstances, there was an occasional tension between the COLREGS and the operational requirements of a public vessel engaged in constabulary operations. Nevertheless, the mission does not excuse the US Coast Guard from compliance with the COLREGS. Rule 2(b) permits departure from the rules only when necessary to "avoid immediate danger." He called the Tribunal's attention to the strict interpretation by US courts of the "special circumstances" rule. As seen above, under this interpretation, a departure from the COLREGS was limited to situations involving "an immediate danger, perfectly clear, and the departure from the rules must be more than necessary."[27] Following the opinion of Allen, the Philippines asserted at the Hearing on the Merits that there was no possible defense that China could make of its vessels' actions and that there were no special circumstances to make the exception in Rule 2(b) applicable. Indeed, far from avoiding immediate danger, the Chinese vessels' actions increased it.[28]

The Tribunal found that apart from the argument raised by Allen and presented by the Philippines, the high threshold established by the "special circumstances" exception could not be applied to the facts. The Tribunal was aware that for China its actions were justified as part of law enforcement activities in the vicinity of a maritime feature that

[25] Singhota Report, 6, para. 17; 9, para. 27.

[26] Award of 12 July 2016, 431, para. 1094.

[27] Allen Opinion, 376.

[28] Hearing on the Merits, Final Transcript, Day 3, 70.

China considered to be part of its sovereign territory. Despite this, the Tribunal recognized, in a far-reaching statement, that where the operational requirements of law enforcement ships stood in tension with the COLREGS, the latter must prevail. The Tribunal was unable to find any danger of collision justifying a departure from the COLREGS and did not hesitate to draw out the implications of the opinions of the two experts as well as that of the Philippines: "if anything, the record suggests that the Chinese manoeuvres themselves created immediate danger, rather than having been undertaken in response to a pre-existing threat."[29] To put it differently, Rule 2(b) would have justified a departure by the Chinese vessels from the COLREGS if a danger of collision had existed; but in reality it was the very departure by the Chinese vessels from the Rules that created the risk of collision.

By their conduct, the Chinese vessels also violated several Steering and Sailing Rules that govern the conduct of ships in any conditions of visibility.

II. The Conduct of Vessels in Any Condition of Visibility

The Steering and Sailing Rules applicable to vessels in any condition of visibility require that they proceed at safe speed; that they determine the risk of collision, and in case such a risk exists, that they take action to avoid collision. These rules were all infringed by the conduct of Chinese vessels on 28 April and 26 May 2012.

A. Safe Speed, Risk of Collision, and Action to Avoid a Collision

Three Rules in Part B, Section I of the COLREGS are relevant: Rule 6 on safe speed, Rule 7 on risk of collision, and Rule 8 on action to avoid collision.[30]

Rule 6 applies to all vessels, at all times, whether they are in view of one another or visibility is restricted. Prior to 1972, the COLREGS referred to speed only in restricted visibility, in which case "moderate speed" was required. The notion of "safe speed" in the COLREGS 1972 is broader

[29] Award of 12 July 2016, 431–32, para. 1095.

[30] See Annex 5.1.

than "moderate speed." It is based on the recognition that "moderate" speed might not necessarily be "safe," for example, if slow speed causes a loss of steerage.[31] Conversely, Rule 6 would not preclude the setting of high speed in appropriate circumstances.[32] The other paragraphs of Rule 6 identify some of the factors that have to be taken into account by all vessels. The state of visibility is perhaps appropriately mentioned first. In the experience of a mariner, the danger of collision is greatest in darkness and low visibility.[33] Next in the enumeration is the traffic density, including concentrations of fishing vessels or any other vessels. Traffic density has increased constantly since 1945, one reason why even the use of radar did not appreciably reduce the numbers of collisions in the early post-war period.[34] Attention to the presence of fishing vessels is essential, because small fishing vessels are not easily seen under the bow of large merchant vessels. They also stop or change course suddenly.[35] The other factors to be taken into account are the maneuverability of the vessel with special reference to stopping distance and turning ability in the prevailing conditions; at night, the presence of background light, such as from shore lights; the state of wind, sea and current, and the proximity of navigational hazards; and the draft in relation to the available depth of water (Rule 6(a)(i) to (vi)). Vessels with operational radar should take into account an additional number of factors (Rule 6(b)(i) to (vi)).[36]

Speed is an important factor in preventing collisions. The reason is that modern vessels are bigger and faster and may thus take longer to stop

[31] Nicholas J. Healy, "Collision Law During the Last Quarter-Century of the Millennium," *Tulane Law Review* 73 (1999): 1796. Steerage is defined as a ship's response to the helmsman's guidance. *Collins English Dictionary* (Glasgow: HarperCollins Publishers, 2019), https://www.collinsdictionary.com/dictionary/english/steerage, accessed 7 June 2019.

[32] Cockcroft and Lameijer, *Guide*, 22.

[33] Søren Thirslund, "Collision Avoidance at Sea in the Mid-20th Century. Thoughts from Denmark," *JON* 65 (2012): 201.

[34] Zdisław Kopacz et al., "An Attempt of [sic] the Specification of the Ship's Navigation Process," *Annals of Navigation* 3 (2001): 205.

[35] Anand Pillay and Jin Wang (eds.), *Technology and Safety of Marine Systems* (Killington, Oxford: Elsevier Science Ltd., 2003), 15.

[36] For a video explaining these factors, see The Casual Navigator, *COLREGS In Depth. Rule 6: Safe Speed*, published on 23 February 2018, at 0:56–4:54 ("*Rule 6*"), https://www.youtube.com/watch?v=f7654LIZ_GU&list=PL-bjik4MwIgI4gXgMTE1VJ6LGYQBhHkE&index=2, accessed 7 June 2019.

and maneuver. Even smaller vessels are much faster. Experience shows that vessels involved in collisions are likely to have been moving too fast. As Llana and Wisneskey put it facetiously, there are few collisions involving stopped vessels.[37] If a collision does occur, high speeds cause more damage than low speeds.[38]

The two objectives of maintaining safe speed are identified in Rule 6 itself. The first objective is to permit the vessel to take proper and effective action to avoid collision. To be able to maneuver as prescribed by the Rules, such as Rules 15 and 16, the vessel must be moving slowly enough to control its forward motion. In some cases, it must be moving fast enough for the rudder to effect a turn promptly.[39] The second objective is to enable the vessel to be stopped within a distance "appropriate to the prevailing circumstances and conditions." Crucial to understanding this objective is the notion of "stopping distance," which refers to the distance that a vessel will travel before stopping. Stopping distance will vary substantially, ranging from five to 15 ship lengths, depending on many factors, such as speed, displacement, type of machinery, and type of vessel.[40] Just to give an example of the importance of this last factor for setting safe speed: a supertanker will take three miles to stop, whereas a high-speed ferry can pull-up within its own length.[41]

Rule 7, according to Llana and Wisneskey, is an information collection and analysis rule. Determination of the risk of collision triggers the operation of other rules, such as Rules 15 and 16. Rule 7 does not define the key concept of "risk of collision."[42] In 1972, a definition was proposed at the London Conference that revised the COLREGS. According to this proposal, "risk of collision" exists between vessels when their projected courses and speeds place them at or near the same location simultaneously. This definition was rejected, on the grounds that it would have obliged a vessel detecting another at long range, slowly approaching from the port (left) side with little change of bearing, to keep its course and speed

[37] Llana and Wisneskey, *Handbook*, 37, 38.

[38] Mr. Justice Hewson, 1963, in *Niceto de Larrinaga–Sitala,* quoted in Cockcroft and Lameijer, *Guide*, 22.

[39] Llana and Wisneskey, *Handbook*, 87.

[40] Cockcroft and Lameijer, *Guide*, 21.

[41] The Casual Navigator, *Rule 6*, at 2:07–2:16.

[42] Llana and Wisneskey, *Handbook*, 92.

for a long period, possibly several hours.[43] Some professional mariners continue to believe that a risk exists for two vessels whose path would take them to the same spot in two minutes. A risk would not exist for two slow-moving vessels 20 miles apart heading for the same spot of water.[44]

Among the factors to be taken into account to determine whether risk of collision exists, Rule 7(d)(i) identifies the fact that the compass bearing of an approaching vessel does not appreciably change. However, a risk may still exist even when an appreciable bearing change is evident, particularly when approaching a very large vessel or a tow or when approaching a vessel at close range.[45] In all cases, the risk of collision must be discovered early enough, so that each vessel will be able to carry out its obligation under other Rules.[46]

Rule 7 warns that if there is any doubt whether a risk of collision exists, the risk should be deemed to exist.[47] Proper use should be made of radar equipment (Rule 7(b)) but assumptions should not be made on the basis of scanty information, especially scanty radar information (Rule 7(c)).

Once it has been determined that a risk of collision exists, succeeding Rules prescribe the action to be taken by vessels. The purpose of Rule 8 (Action to Avoid a Collision) was explained in 1993 by a British court:

> The structure of the Collision Regulations is designed to ensure that, whenever possible, ships will not reach a close-quarters situation in which there is risk of collision and in which decisions have to be taken without time for proper thought.[48]

[43] Cockcroft and Lameijer, *Guide*, 26.

[44] Llana and Wisneskey, *Handbook*, 93.

[45] For videos of the two situations, see The Casual Navigator, *COLREGS In Depth. Rule 7: Risk of Collision*, published on 9 March 2018, at 2:25–2:52, 3:10–4:25 ("*Rule 7*"), https://www.youtube.com/watch?v=pYWVp0Ujvw4&index=3&list=PL-Kbjik4MwIgI4gXgMTE1VJ6LGYQBhHkE, accessed 7 June 2019, and Maryland School of Sailing, *Collision Avoidance Nav Rules*, published on 11 April 2013, at 19:13–20:16, https://www.youtube.com/watch?v=19suVDp8GnMm, accessed 7 June 2019.

[46] Llana and Wisneskey, *Handbook*, 94.

[47] See Annex 5.1.

[48] Mr. Justice Sheen, in *Maloja II-John M* (1993), quoted in Cockcroft and Lameijer, *Guide*, 37. For the text of Rule 8, see Annex 5.1.

A nautical dictionary defines "close quarters" as "close proximity."[49] More informally, a close-quarters situation was defined by a professional mariner in the following terms: "if you could read the passing ship's name, then you were too close."[50] A close-quarters situation should be avoided wherever possible, although it must be recognized that in rivers, harbors, and other inland waterways close-quarters situations are unavoidable.[51] The distance at which a close-quarters situation first applies will depend on several factors, including visibility. In the open sea, in restricted visibility, distances of 2–3 nautical miles are the outer limits. When vessels are in sight of one another, smaller distances of around a mile would probably be accepted.[52]

To prevent a close-quarters situation from developing, Rule 8 provides instructions on the manner in which the collision avoidance maneuvers specified in other Rules are to be executed. It does not identify which vessels are required to take avoiding action; it is other Rules that do so. "Positive action" is identified by Rule 8(b) as "any alteration of course and/or speed." As will be seen below, in good visibility, one vessel will usually have the primary responsibility for taking avoiding action. "Ample time" "and "with due regard" are reminders to mariners to act early and to do more than is absolutely necessary to avoid the collision.[53]

Under Rule 8(b), if there is sufficient sea-room, a change in course alone may be and usually is the most effective action to avoid a close-quarters situation. Alterations of speed take longer to put into effect than alterations of course. A large vessel moving at high speed carries considerable momentum. Even if the engines are stopped on a tanker with 200,000-ton deadweight, it may take more than 20 minutes before its

[49] Layton et al., *Dictionary*, 95.

[50] Mike Bechley, "Collision Avoidance at Sea in the Mid-20th Century. Collision Avoidance in the 1960s," *JON* 65 (2012): 147.

[51] Llana and Wisneskey, *Handbook*, 99.

[52] Cockcroft and Lameijer, *Guide*, 38.

[53] Llana and Wisneskey, *Handbook*, 98.

speed is halved and over an hour before it can come to rest.[54] Furthermore, alterations of speed, even drastic ones, are less likely to be readily observed by the other vessel.[55]

But if a vessel is prevented from changing its course by a lack of sea-room or the presence of other vessels, the vessel required to take action will have to reduce its speed. Increases in speed are not prohibited as a means of avoiding collision but since many vessels already proceed at a speed that would not be considered safe, an increase in speed large enough to satisfy the requirements of Rule 8(a) would probably violate the Rule 6 requirement of proceeding at a safe speed.[56]

Rule 8(b) stresses that any change of course and/or speed should be large enough to be readily apparent. A school of sailing in the US suggests that a change in course of between 20° and 40° will meet this requirement.[57] Cockcroft and Lameijer believe that an alteration of course should be at least 30° and should preferably be between 60° and 90°.[58] In any event, a vessel that is required to take action under other Rules, such as Rule 15, should avoid making a series of small changes in course or speed, as they may not be perceived by the other vessel and may for this reason even increase the risk of collision.[59]

According to Rule 8(d), action taken to avoid a collision with another vessel should result in passing at a safe distance. The COLREGS do not define "safe distance." What is "safe" will depend on the circumstances, although Llana and Wisneskey observe that a "safe distance" represents a smaller distance than "close-quarters."[60] The Maryland School of Sailing appears to be more cautious, for it teaches that passing at a "safe distance" should not result in another "close-quarters" situation.[61] Rule

[54] Deadweight refers to the total weight in tons, of cargo, stores, and fuel carried by a vessel at her maximum permitted draft. Layton et al., *Dictionary*, 120.

[55] Cockcroft and Lameijer, *Guide*, 38, 41.

[56] *Ibid.*, 12.

[57] Maryland School of Sailing, *Collision Avoidance*, at 21:01.

[58] Cockcroft and Lameijer, *Guide*, 37.

[59] *Ibid.*, pp. 38, 40, 41. For a video of such a situation, see The Casual Navigator, *COLREGS In Depth. Rule 8: Action to Avoid Collision*, published on Mar 23, 2018, at 1:11–1:58, 2:14–2:51 ("*Rule 8*"), https://www.youtube.com/watch?v=uJShFEqKiIU&index=4&list=PL-Kbjik4MwIgI4gXgMTE1VJ6LGYQBhHkE, accessed 7 June 2019.

[60] Llana and Wisneskey, *Handbook*, 98–99.

[61] Maryland School of Sailing, *Collision Avoidance*, 20:35.

8(d) requires that the vessel should check the effectiveness of the action it has taken until the other vessel is finally past and clear. Only when the other vessel is finally past and clear can the vessel that has taken action alter back to its original heading.[62]

An American author argued that in 2009, the Chinese vessels involved in the *Impeccable* incident violated Rule 8 by taking action that could have easily led to a collision with the US vessel.[63] The Tribunal in the *South China Sea Arbitration* found that the conduct of Chinese vessels failed to comply with Rules 6, 7, and 8.

B. Violations of Rules 6, 7, and 8 by the Chinese Vessels

The Philippines acknowledged that the "safe speed" required by Rule 6 depends on the circumstances of the case, and that to determine "safe speed," one would have to examine factors such as traffic density, the maneuverability of the vessel, the state of the wind and current and other navigational hazards. That having been said, it argued, based on the Allen Opinion, that maneuvering in close proximity to the Philippine vessels by the Chinese vessels could not be considered safe. On 28 April, the Chinese vessel FLEC 310 approached the Philippine vessel BRP *Pampanga* (Search and Rescue Vessel 003 ["SARV-003"] in the Allen Opinion) at a speed of over 20 knots. Had FLEC 310 continued on its course, it would have collided with the BRP *Pampanga* in less than a minute.[64] The failure to proceed at a safe speed was aggravated by the size of the Chinese vessels compared with their smaller Philippine counterparts. The wake created by the Chinese ships' maneuver caused additional threat to the Philippine vessels.[65]

[62] The Casual Navigator, *Rule 8*, at 3:34.

[63] Jonathan G. Odom, "The True 'Lies' of the Impeccable Incident: What Really Happened, Who Disregarded International Law, and Why Every Nation (Outside of China) Should Be Concerned," *Michigan State University College of Law Journal of International Law* 18 (2010): 429, https://digitalcommons.law.msu.edu/cgi/viewcontent.cgi?article=1025&context=ilr, accessed 7 June 2019. This article was republished under the title "The Case of USNS Impeccable versus 5 Chinese Ships: A Close Examination of the Facts, the Evidence and the Law," in Jon M. Van Dyke et al. (eds.), *Governing Ocean Resources: New Challenges and Emerging Regimes. A Tribute to Judge Choon-Ho Park* (Leiden: Martinus Nijhoff Publishers, 2013), 307–43.

[64] *MP*, vol. I, p. 12, para. 6.141.

[65] Hearing on the Merits, Final Transcript, Day 3, 66–67.

Captain Singhota, clarifying that safe speed refers to speed through the water and not to engine speed, stressed that the requirement to observe safe speed is also a matter of good seamanship and not just of compliance with Rule 6. Excessive speed can reduce the time available in which clear-headed decisions leading to the avoidance of collisions can be made and increase the damage caused by any collision. He analyzed each incident. In a remarkable understatement, he described FLEC 310's high-speed passes on 28 April of 20.3 knots and 2.6 knots in extremely close proximity of 0.296 nautical miles from BRP *Pampanga* and 0.098 nautical miles from BRP *Edsa II* (SARV-002 in the Allen Opinion) "as certainly not good examples of observing safe speed."[66] He characterized the Chinese vessels' conduct on 26 May in stronger terms. Their attempts on 26 May to cut across the bow of Philippine vessel MCS 3008 at a distance of less than 0.049 nautical miles (100 yards) at speeds in excess of 20 knots were clear indications that they had no understanding of the concept of safe speed.[67] The Tribunal concurred with the two experts' view that the incidents occurred at unsafe speeds and therefore determined that the Chinese vessels' actions had breached Rule 6.[68]

Rule 7 was invoked by the Philippines in its *Memorial*, since the Rule set out the principles concerning the risk of collision. The Philippines recalled that in case of doubt, it must be presumed that a risk of collision exists. Therefore, the Chinese vessels were under an obligation to act as if the risk of collision—which their own maneuvers created—existed.[69] The two experts did not analyze the conduct of the Chinese vessels in terms of Rule 7, perhaps because what mattered was the actual conduct of the vessels. It could be plausibly argued that such conduct indirectly demonstrated that the Chinese vessels had not used all available means to determine if risk of collision existed, or that they had proceeded to act in such a way as to risk collision after having determined that risk of collision existed. Whatever may have been the reason for the two experts' silence on Rule 7, the Tribunal relied on Rule 7 as the basis of its finding that risk of collision existed on 28 April and 26 May 2012. The Tribunal went further than the two experts did and identified three instances in

66 Singhota Report, 5, para. 12.

67 *Ibid.*, 4, para. 11; 6, para. 20.

68 Award of 12 July 2016, 432, para. 1097.

69 *MP*, vol. I, 218, para. 6.137; 212, para. 6.143.

which Rule 7 was breached: (a) on 28 April, FLEC 303 closed at high speed within 600 yards of BRP *Pampanga* and passed BRP *Edsa II* within 200 yards; (b) on 26 May, CMS 71, FLEC 303, and CMS 84 passed Philippine vessels at distances of 100 yards or less; and (c) on 26 May, FLEC 306 nearly rammed MCS 3008. Consequently, the Tribunal considered the risk of collision identified under Rule 7 to have been clearly established.[70]

The nature of the Chinese vessels' violations of Rule 8 was the object of detailed attention on the part of the two experts and of the Philippines. For Allen, a "safe" passing distance should be large enough to leave a margin of error and allow for the unexpected, such as a mechanical malfunction on one of the vessels. Passing at a distance that does not provide such a margin violates Rule 8. The speed of a vessel is also a relevant consideration when determining a safe distance. Vessels traveling at high speeds, which Allen defined as any speed above 10–12 knots, require wider margins than vessels traveling at lower speeds. A further relevant consideration is the angle of approach. Passing astern of another vessel at a distance of 1000 yards might be deemed safe, but that same distance would almost certainly be deemed unsafe in an attempt to cross ahead of the vessel.[71] A temporary loss of steering or propulsion or a momentary distraction under these circumstances could quickly lead to collision. Allen was of the view that on 28 April, FLEC 310 failed to take positive action to avoid collision and to avoid a "close-quarters" situation. Instead, it intentionally passed at high speed to within 600 yards of BRP *Pampanga* at 0900H and 200 yards of BRP *Edsa II* at 0915H. On 26 May, CMS 71, FLEC 303, and FLEC 306 violated Rule 8 by failing to take timely and positive action to pass MCS 3008 at a safe distance.[72] As the Philippines put it in its *Memorial*, the Chinese vessels exacerbated, rather than mitigated, the risk of collision. They violated Rule 8, not only by failing to take actions to avoid collision but also by taking actions that made collision substantially more likely.[73]

[70] Hearing on the Merits, Final Transcript, Day 3, 65–66; Award of 12 July 2016, 432–433, para. 1098.

[71] "Astern" means outside a ship and directly behind her [sic]." Layton et al., *Dictionary*, 26.

[72] Allen Opinion, 377.

[73] *MP*, vol. I, 213, paras. 6.143–6.144.

Allen explained that the fact that collisions were avoided thanks to *in extremis* emergency maneuvers by the Philippine vessels in no way excused the violations of the rules. He stressed that it is the risk of collision that must be avoided, not just the collision itself.[74] The Philippines added at the Hearing on the Merits that Rule 8 is an obligation of conduct, rather than one of result. It is not concerned with attributing responsibility in cases of actual collision. Its aim is to ensure that steps are taken by vessels in order to avoid risk of collision.[75]

Captain Singhota emphasized the Chinese vessels' duty to take timely action to keep clear and to take action that was large enough as to leave the other vessel in no possible doubt as to what they were doing. For him, any action taken to avoid collision should be such as to result in passing at a safe distance. While the latter is not defined in the COLREGS, experienced mariners recognize that it will vary according to situation and the size of the vessels. A safe passing distance must also cater for human error on the bridge, engine, or steering gear failure at a critical phase of the maneuver and the interaction between passing vessels. FLEC 310's intentional closing in at high speed to within 600 yards (0.296 nautical miles) of BRP *Pampanga* (SARV-003 in the Singhota Report) at 0900H on 28 April and the subsequent pass of FLEC 310 from the starboard (right) quarter to the port (left) side of BRP *Edsa II* (SARV 002 in the Singhota Report) at a distance of barely 200 yards (0.098 nautical miles) were certainly not examples of safe distance.[76] On 26 May, CMS 71, FLEC 303, and FLEC 306 also violated Rule 8 by failing to take timely positive action with due regard to the observance of good seamanship to pass MCS 3008 at a safe distance.[77]

The Tribunal once more agreed with the opinions of the two experts and of the Philippines, declaring that the conduct of FLEC 303, FLEC 306, FLEC 310, and CMS 71 all fell short of any reasonable definition of safe distance. The Tribunal observed in damning terms that far from avoiding collision, the Chinese ships' actions made the possibility of collision substantially more likely. In its view, this fact alone—independent of the question as to whether collision, whether through the crew's effort

[74] *Ibid.*, 376.

[75] Hearing on the Merits, Final Transcript, Day 3, 5.

[76] Singhota Report, 5, paras. 13–14.

[77] *Ibid.*, 7.

or good fortune, was ultimately avoided—was sufficient to demonstrate the violation of COLREGS. For the same reasons as those underlying its conclusions regarding Rule 2(a), the Tribunal concluded that the other requirement imposed by Rule 8—due regard to the observance of good seamanship—had also been violated.[78]

Finally, the Chinese vessels' conduct during both incidents violated two Rules that are applicable to the conduct of vessels in sight of one another.

III. The Conduct of Vessels in Sight of One Another

On 28 April and 26 May 2012, Philippine and Chinese vessels nearly collided in a crossing situation. The conduct of Chinese vessels on both occasions violated Rules 15 and 16 of the COLREGS.

To understand the dangerous maneuvers undertaken by the Chinese vessels, one must first understand the nature of a crossing situation and the action required of the two vessels to avoid a collision in such a situation.

A. Crossing Situations and Actions by Give-Way and Stand-On Vessels

The two Rules in Part C of the COLREGS that were applicable to the two incidents, in the view of the two experts and of the Tribunal, were Rule15, which describes a crossing situation, and Rule 16 (Action by Give-way Vessel). Rule 15 does not define a crossing situation; for this reason, one must turn to Rules 13 and 14 to understand a crossing situation, by a process of elimination.[79]

Section II of the Steering and Sailing Rules distinguishes three types of encounters between vessels, or situations: overtaking, head-on, and crossing. According to Rule 13(b), a vessel is deemed to be overtaking

> when coming up with another vessel from a direction more than 22.5 degrees abaft her beam, that is, in such a position with reference to the

[78] Award of 12 July 2016, 433–34, paras. 1100–1101.

[79] See Annex 5.1 for the text of Rules 13 to 16.

> vessel she is overtaking, that at night she would be able to see only the sternlight of that vessel but neither of her sidelights.[80]

In a head-on situation, two power-driven vessels are meeting on reciprocal or nearly reciprocal courses (Rule 14(a)). "Reciprocal" simply means "180° degrees from the other." One vessel might be going north and the other is going south; alternatively, one vessel might be going east, while the other is going west.[81] According to Rule 14(b), a head-on situation is deemed to exist.

> when a vessel sees the other ahead or nearly ahead and by night she could see the masthead lights of the other in a line or nearly in a line and/or both sidelights and by day she observes the corresponding aspect of the other vessel.[82]

In the absence of a definition of a crossing situation in Rule 15, it may be assumed that a situation that does not correspond to the definition of overtaking or head-on must be a crossing situation.[83]

The distinctions matter because the conduct prescribed for the vessel(s) varies depending on the situation. In an overtaking situation, Rule 13(a) requires that a vessel overtaking another vessel must keep out of the way of the vessel being overtaken. Rule 13 was one of the COLREGS that the Chinese vessels violated during the *Impeccable* incident. They should have assumed that they were the vessels overtaking the *Impeccable* and should

[80] For videos of an overtaking situation, see The Casual Navigator, *COLREGS In Depth. Rule 13: Overtaking*, published on 15 December 2017, at 3:06–4:57, https://www.youtube.com/watch?v=zz8TZ7ataEo&index=8&list=PL-Kbjik4MwIgI4gXgMTE1VJ6LGYQBhHkE, accessed 7 June 2019, and Maryland School of Sailing, *Collision Avoidance*, at 35:08–36:30.

[81] The Casual Navigator, *COLREGS In Depth. Rule 14: Head-On Situation*, published on 22 December 2017, at 1:25 ("*Rule 14*"), https://www.youtube.com/watch?v=xGd_vJ9DMSE&list=PL-Kbjik4MwIgI4gXgMTE1VJ6LGYQBhHkE&index=9, accessed 7 June 2019.

[82] For videos of a head-on situation, see *ibid.* at 2:10–3:20 and 4:35–5:53, and Maryland School of Sailing, *Collision Avoidance*, at 38:12–38:44.

[83] The Casual Navigator, *COLREGS In Depth. Rule 15: Crossing Situation*, published on 29 December 2017, at 1:19–1:30 ("*Rule 15*"), https://www.youtube.com/watch?v=E11GonKFkUs&index=10&list=PL-Kbjik4MwIgI4gXgMTE1VJ6LGYQBhHkE, accessed 7 June 2019. For a diagram of a crossing situation, see *ibid.*, at 1:34–3:37, and Maryland School of Sailing, *Collision Avoidance*, at 39:03–40:12.

have remained clear and kept out of the way of the US vessel.[84] In a head-on situation, Rule 14(a) requires action on the part of both vessels. Each must alter its course to starboard (right), so that each shall pass on the port (left) side of the other. Rule 15 requires that in a crossing situation, the vessel that has the other on its starboard (right) side stay out of the way of the other. The vessel on the left is the give-way vessel and must follow Rule 16. The vessel on the right is the stand-on vessel and must follow Rule 17.[85]

The first part of Rule 15 does not indicate the action that the first vessel, the give-way vessel, must take. Thus, the first vessel is free to stop in the water and to let the other vessel pass ahead.[86] The second part does indicate that if circumstances permit, the give-way vessel must avoid crossing ahead of the other vessel. Experienced mariners believe that the most likely action to be taken by the give-way vessel would be a turn to starboard,[87] while commentators agree that alteration of course to starboard is usually the best method of keeping out of the way of a vessel that is on the starboard bow.[88] As we have seen, in the history of the COLREGS, the recommended maneuver for the give-way vessel is a turn to starboard, a maneuver first recommended by Lord Howe in 1776. Rule 15 was also violated by the Chinese vessels involved in the *Impeccable* incident, for they created a risk of collision by the failure to keep out of the way of the US vessel and by crossing the latter's bow.[89]

Whatever action the give-way vessel undertakes, Rule 16 directs it to take early and substantial action to keep well clear. As required by Rule 8(b), the action must be taken at an early stage and it must be large enough to be readily apparent to the other vessel. As explained in a British judgment, "the duty of the give-way vessel is to take timely action to keep clear… Moreover, it is her duty to act… handsomely, so as to leave the stand-on vessel in no possible doubt as to what the give-way vessel is

[84] Odom, "The True 'Lies'," 429.

[85] Llana and Wisneskey, *Handbook*, 122.

[86] The Casual Navigator, *Rule 15*, at 1:03.

[87] Norman Cockcroft, "Collision Avoidance at Sea in the Mid-20th Century. Two Incidents in the 1940s," *JON* 65 (2012): 203.

[88] Cockcroft and Lameijer, *Guide*, 77; Plant, "The Collision Avoidance Regulations," 383.

[89] Odom, "The True 'Lies'," 430.

doing."[90] If the method of giving way is to alter course to starboard, the give-way vessel must make a substantial alteration of course.[91] In a crossing situation, the obligation under Rule 8(d) to pass at a safe distance applies exclusively to the give-way vessel.[92] Rule 16 was also violated by the Chinese vessels that were involved in the *Impeccable* incident, because they failed to take early and substantial action to keep clear.[93]

As for the stand-on vessel, Rule 17(a)(i) requires it to stay its course and maintain its speed. However, under Rule 17(a)(ii), the stand-on vessel is permitted to take action to avoid collision as soon as it becomes apparent to it that the give-way vessel is not taking the appropriate action in compliance with the Rules. If the stand-on vessel finds itself so close that collision cannot be avoided by the action of the give-way vessel, the stand-on vessel will take action that can best avoid collision (Rule 17(b)). If the stand-on vessel does find itself in the latter situation, it is instructed not to alter course to port (Rule 17(c)). In this way, the area to the left of the stand-on vessel can be kept clear for the give-way vessel's maneuver to the right.[94] Otherwise the result would be a collision.

The commentator Cockcroft reported a personal experience of a near-collision in 1949, when he was an uncertified Third Mate on a tanker that was being approached by another vessel from 30° on the port bow. It was clearly the latter's duty to keep out of the way of the tanker, yet it failed to do so. The tanker's Master ordered a turn to port, a dangerous maneuver if the other ship turned to starboard at about the same time. No collision occurred because the give-way vessel did not take any action.[95]

Having in mind the nature of a crossing situation as well as of the duties of a give-way vessel and a stand-on vessel, we may now turn to the violations by the Chinese vessels of Rules 15 and 16.

[90] Mr. Justice Williams in the *Billings Victory-Warren Chase* case (1949), quoted in Cockcroft and Lameijer, *Guide*, 37.

[91] Cockcroft and Lameijer, *Guide*, 37.

[92] *Ibid.*, 39.

[93] Odom, "The True 'Lies'," 430.

[94] Llana and Wisneskey, *Handbook*, 123.

[95] Cockcroft, "Collision Avoidance," 203–4.

B. Violations of Rules 15 and 16 by the Chinese Vessels

The expert appointed by the Philippines and the expert appointed by the Tribunal were in agreement that the encounters on 28 April and 26 May occurred when the vessels were in sight of one another.[96] For this reason the applicable rules were those found in Part B, Section II of the COLREGS.[97] The two experts also agreed that the Chinese and Philippine vessels were in a crossing situation, and that in both incidents, it was the Chinese vessels that were the give-way vessels. In both incidents, they failed to take the action required by the COLREGS.

It may be recalled that on 28 April 2012, at 900H, FLEC 310 approached BRP *Pampanga* from port to dead ahead at a distance of about 600 yards, with a speed of 20.3 knots. In other words, FLEC 310 had BRP *Pampanga* on its starboard side. FLEC 310 thus created a dangerous situation that required it to assume the role of the give-way vessel in a crossing situation.[98] The duty of FLEC 310 was to keep out of the way of BRP *Pampanga*, under Rule 15, and to take early and substantial action to keep clear, according to Rule 16. Instead, FLEC 310 passed at 0915H from the starboard quarter of BRP *Pampanga* to the latter's port side at a distance of 200 yards with a speed of 20.6 knots. The Philippines argued that FLEC 310's approaches to the BRP *Pampanga* and the BRP *Edsa II* were the very opposite of keeping well clear and were therefore violations of Rule 16.[99]

In Captain Singhota's view, it was apparent that crossing a vessel at such a close distance did not amount to "keeping well clear," as required by Rule 16. It did not seem to him likely that FLEC 310's intent was to inspect BRP *Pampanga* at a close distance. It seemed more likely that it was an attempt to showcase the power of the larger Chinese vessel.[100] Based on the arguments of the Philippines and the conclusions of the Singhota report, the Tribunal concluded that FLEC 310, rather

[96] Allen Opinion, 376; Singhota Report, 2, para. 6.

[97] Allen Opinion, 376.

[98] *Ibid.*, 377.

[99] *MP*, vol. I, 213, para. 6.145.

[100] Singhota Report, 5, para. 15.

than complying with Rules 15 and 16 by "keeping out of the way" and avoiding BRP *Pampanga*, did exactly the opposite.[101]

On 26 May 2012, at around 1550H, CMS 71 was approaching MCS 3008 from the latter's port side. Hence CMS 71 was the "give-way vessel" in a crossing situation—it had MCS 3008 on its starboard side. Rule 15 required that CMS 71 keep out of the way of MCS 3008 and avoid, if the circumstances of the case admitted it, crossing ahead of MCS 3008.[102] What CMS 71 did was to cut across the bow of MCS 3008 at a distance of approximately 100 yards (0.049 nautical miles). The Philippines concluded that this action was a violation of Rule 16. Captain Singhota also judged CMS 71's attempt to cross MCS 3008's bow as a violation of Rule 15, adding that.

> [t]o cross another vessel's bow unnecessarily, where collision is probable, or even only possible, is an unseamanlike manoeuvre, and apart from the regulations would be held to be negligent in fact and in law.[103]

It may be recalled that subsequently, FLEC 310, together with FLEC 303, CMS 71, CMS 84, and FLEC 306, attempted to block and impede the passage of MCS 3008 to Scarborough Shoal. In Captain Singhota's opinion, the actions of the Chinese vessels created situations that required them to assume the role of the give-way vessels in a crossing situation. Under Rule 16, they should have taken early and substantial action to keep well clear.[104] On the basis of the reports of the two experts as well as of the arguments of the Philippines, the Tribunal concluded that the attempt of CMS 71 to cut across the bow of MCS 3008 from the port (left) side at a distance of merely 100 yards admitted of the same error as that committed by FLEC 310 on 28 April.[105]

The overall conclusions of the two experts were damning. Allen, who in the course of his career had been an investigator charged with the

[101] Award of 12 July 2016, 434, para. 1104.

[102] *MP*, vol. I, 213, para. 6.145; Allen Opinion, 377; Hearing on the Merits, Final Transcript, Day 3, 67.

[103] Singhota Report, 7, para. 22.

[104] *Ibid.*, 7, para. 23.

[105] Award of 12 July 2016, 434, para. 1104.

task of assessing whether vessel operators acted negligently by failing to adhere to the COLREGS, expressed the view that the incidents of April and May 2012 were fundamentally different, involving as they did "*intentional* violations of the most basic rules for preventing collisions at sea, such as proceeding at a safe speed and maneuvering to stay well clear of other vessels."[106] The Chinese vessels' acts endangered the lives of all the mariners involved, Chinese as well as Filipino, the vessels, and the marine environment, and would be condemned by all professional mariners.[107] The Tribunal-appointed expert, Captain Singhota, was no less forthright in his conclusions. It seemed to him fair to conclude that the Chinese vessels' ship handling maneuvers "demonstrated a complete disregard for the observance and practice of good seamanship including the ordinary practice of seamen but most importantly, a total disregard for the observance of the collision regulations."[108]

Once again, the Tribunal concurred with the two experts and with the Philippines. It considered that China repeatedly violated the COLREGS, as described by the crew of the Philippine vessels and as credibly assessed in the two expert reports. The Chinese vessels behaved in ways that were exactly the opposite of the conduct required by the Rules: "Where Chinese vessels were under an obligation to yield, they persisted; where the regulations called for a safe distance, they infringed it." Significantly, the Tribunal accepted Allen's view that the conduct of the Chinese vessels was not symptomatic of occasional negligence: [t]he actions are not suggestive of occasional negligence in failing to adhere to the COLREGS, but rather point to a conscious disregard of what the regulations require." The violations were aggravated by factors such as "the large disparity in size of the Chinese and Philippine vessels, the shallow waters in which the incidents took place, and the creation of a two metre-high wake causing additional risk to the Philippines' crews."[109]

The Tribunal, recalling Allen's statement that the occasional tension between the operational requirements of law enforcement and the obligations of the COLREGS did not diminish their binding force, found no

[106] Italics in the original.

[107] Allen Opinion, 378.

[108] Singhota Report, 10, para. 28.

[109] Award of 12 July 2016, 434, para. 1105.

convincing evidence that the violations by the Chinese vessels were excusable by any mitigating circumstances. For all these reasons, the Tribunal found that China had, "by virtue of the conduct of Chinese law enforcement vessels in the vicinity of Scarborough Shoal, created serious risk of collision and danger to Philippine vessels and personnel." The Tribunal found "China to have violated Rules 2, 6, 7, 8, 15, and 16 of the COLREGS and, as a consequence, to be in breach of Article 94 of the Convention."[110]

The Tribunal took great pains to emphasize that its decisions did not depend on and did not involve any finding of sovereignty over Scarborough Shoal and its waters; it would have reached the same conclusions concerning the violations of the navigational safety provisions of the Convention whichever State had sovereignty over Scarborough Shoal.[111] Alas! These reminders were futile. As we shall see in the next Chapter, the post-arbitration rationalizations by the Chinese Society of International Law ("CSIL") of the conduct of China's vessels centered on the right of China as the sovereign over Scarborough Shoal to resort to collisions as instruments of foreign policy.

Annex 5.1: International Regulations for Preventing Collisions at Sea, 1972 (Excerpts)

Part A: General

Rule 1. APPLICATION

(a) These Rules shall apply to all vessels upon the high seas and in all waters connected therewith navigable by seagoing vessels.
(b) Nothing in these Rules shall interfere with the operation of special rules made by an appropriate authority for roadsteads, harbours, rivers, lakes, or inland waterways connected with the high seas and navigable by seagoing vessels. Such special rules shall conform as closely as possible to these Rules.
(c) Nothing in these Rules shall interfere with the operation of any special rules made by the Government of any State with respect

[110] *Ibid.*, 435, para. 1109.

[111] *Ibid.*, para. 1108.

to additional station or signal lights or whistle signals for ships of war and vessels proceeding under convoy, or with respect to additional station or signal lights for fishing vessels engaged in fishing as a fleet. These additional station or signal lights or whistle signals shall, so far as possible, be such that they cannot be mistaken for any light or signal authorized elsewhere under these Rules.

Rule 2. RESPONSIBILITY

(a) Nothing in these Rules shall exonerate any vessel, or the owner, master, or crew thereof, from the consequences of any neglect to comply with these Rules or of the neglect of any precaution which may be required by the ordinary practice of seamen, or by the special circumstances of the case.
(b) In construing and complying with these Rules due regard shall be had to all dangers of navigation and collision and to any special circumstances, including the limitations of the vessels involved, which may make a departure from these Rules necessary to avoid immediate danger.

Part B: Steering and Sailing Rules

Section I: Conduct of Vessels in Any Condition of Visibility
Rule 4. APPLICATION
Rules in this Section apply in any condition of visibility.

Rule 5. LOOK-OUT
Every vessel shall at all times maintain a proper look-out by sight and hearing as well as by all available means appropriate in the prevailing circumstances and conditions so as to make a full appraisal of the situation and of the risk of collision.

Rule 6. SAFE SPEED
Every vessel shall at all times proceed at a safe speed so that she can take proper and effective action to avoid collision and be stopped within a distance appropriate to the prevailing circumstances and conditions.
In determining a safe speed the following factors shall be among those taken into account:

(a) by all vessels:

(i) the state of visibility;
(ii) the traffic density including concentrations of fishing vessels or any other vessels;
(iii) the manoeuvrability of the vessel with special reference to stopping distance and turning ability in the prevailing conditions;
(iv) at night the presence of background light such as from shore lights or from back scatter of her own lights;
(v) the state of wind, sea and current, and the proximity of navigational hazards;
(vi) the draught in relation to the available depth of water;

(b) additionally, by vessels with operational radar:

(i) the characteristics, efficiency and limitations of the radar equipment;
(ii) any constraints imposed by the radar range scale in use;
(iii) the effect on radar detection of the sea state, weather and other sources of interference;
(iv) the possibility that small vessels, ice and other floating objects may not be detected by radar at an adequate range;
(v) the number, location and movement of vessels detected by radar;
(vi) the more exact assessment of the visibility that may be possible when radar is used to determine the range of vessels or other objects in the vicinity.

Rule 7. RISK OF COLLISION

(a) Every vessel shall use all available means appropriate to the prevailing circumstances and conditions to determine if risk of collision exists. If there is any doubt such risk shall be deemed to exist.
(b) Proper use shall be made of radar equipment if fitted and operational, including long-range scanning to obtain early warning of risk of collision and radar plotting or equivalent systematic observation of detected objects.

(c) Assumptions shall not be made on the basis of scanty information, especially scanty radar information.
(d) In determining if risk of collision exists the following considerations shall be among those taken into account:

(i) such risk shall be deemed to exist if the compass bearing of an approaching vessel does not appreciably change;
(ii) such risk may sometimes exist even when an appreciable bearing change is evident, particularly when approaching a very large vessel or a tow or when approaching a vessel at close range.

Rule 8. ACTION TO AVOID COLLISION

(a) Any action taken to avoid collision shall, if the circumstances of the case admit, be positive, made in ample time and with due regard to the observance of good seamanship.
(b) Any alteration of course and/or speed to avoid collision shall, if the circumstances of the case admit, be large enough to be readily apparent to another vessel observing visually or by radar; a succession of small alterations of course and/or speed should be avoided.
(c) If there is sufficient sea room, alteration of course alone may be the most effective action to avoid a close-quarters situation provided that it is made in good time, is substantial and does not result in another close-quarters situation.
(d) Action taken to avoid collision with another vessel shall be such as to result in passing at a safe distance. The effectiveness of the action shall be carefully checked until the other vessel is finally past and clear.
(e) If necessary to avoid collision or allow more time to assess the situation, a vessel shall slacken her speed or take all way off by stopping or reversing her means of propulsion.

Section II. Conduct of Vessels in Sight of One Another
Rule 11. APPLICATION
Rules in this Section apply to vessels in sight of one another.

Rule 13. OVERTAKING

(a) Notwithstanding anything contained in the Rules of this Section, any vessel overtaking any other shall keep out of the way of the vessel being overtaken.
(b) A vessel shall be deemed to be overtaking when coming up with another vessel from a direction more than 22.5 degrees abaft her beam, that is, in such a position with reference to the vessel she is overtaking, that at night she would be able to see only the sternlight of that vessel but neither of her sidelights.
(c) When a vessel is in any doubt as to whether she is overtaking another, she shall assume that this is the case and act accordingly.
(d) Any subsequent alteration of the bearing between the two vessels shall not make the overtaking vessel a crossing vessel within a meaning of these Rules or relieve her of the duty of keeping clear of the overtaken vessel until she is finally past and clear.

Rule 14. HEAD-ON SITUATION

(a) When two power-driven vessels are meeting on reciprocal or nearly reciprocal courses so as to involve risk of collision, each shall alter her course to starboard so that each shall pass on the port side of the other.
(b) Such a situation shall be deemed to exist when a vessel sees the other ahead or nearly ahead and by night she could see the masthead lights of the other in a line or nearly in a line and/or both sidelights and by day she observes the corresponding aspect of the other vessel.
(c) When a vessel is in any doubt as to whether such a situation exists, she shall assume that it does exist and act accordingly.

Rule 15. CROSSING SITUATION
When two power-driven vessels are crossing so as to involve risk of collision, the vessel which has the other on her own starboard side shall keep

out of the way and shall, if the circumstances of the case admit, avoid crossing ahead of the other vessel.

Rule 16. ACTION BY GIVE-WAY VESSEL
Every vessel which is directed to keep out of the way of another vessel shall, so far as possible, take early and substantial action to keep well clear.

Source: *United Nations Treaty Series*, Vol. 1050, 1-15824 (New York: United Nations, 1993), 19–43, https://treaties.un.org/doc/Publication/UNTS/Volume%201050/volume-1050-I-15824-English.pdf, accessed 21 October 2018.

References

Blom, Captain Erik. "Is the Pilot Part of the Bridge Team?" *Insight* 185 (2007), http://www.gard.no/web/updates/content/51708/is-the-pilot-part-of-the-bridge-team, accessed 7 June 2019.

The Casual Navigator. *COLREGS In Depth. Rule 6: Safe Speed*. 6:35. Published on 23 February 2018, https://www.youtube.com/watch?v=f7654LIZ_GU&list=PL-Kbjik4MwIgI4gXgMTE1VJ6LGYQBhHkE&index=2, accessed 7 June 2019.

———. *COLREGS In Depth. Rule 7: Risk of Collision*. 5:05. Published on 9 March 2018, https://www.youtube.com/watch?v=pYWVp0Ujvw4&index=3&list=PL-Kbjik4MwIgI4gXgMTE1VJ6LGYQBhHkE, accessed 7 June 2019.

———. *COLREGS In Depth. Rule 8: Action to Avoid Collision*. 8:00. Published on 23 March 23, 2018, https://www.youtube.com/watch?v=uJShFEqKiIU&index=4&list=PL-Kbjik4MwIgI4gXgMTE1VJ6LGYQBhHkE, accessed 7 June 2019.

———. *COLREGS In Depth. Rule 13: Overtaking*. 9:22. Published on 15 December 2017, https://www.youtube.com/watch?v=zz8TZ7ataEo&index=8&list=PL-Kbjik4MwIgI4gXgMTE1VJ6LGYQBhHkE, accessed 7 June 2019.

———. *COLREGS In Depth. Rule 14: Head-On Situation*. 6:50. Published on 22 December 2017, https://www.youtube.com/watch?v=xGd_vJ9DMSE&list=PL-Kbjik4MwIgI4gXgMTE1VJ6LGYQBhHkE&index=9, accessed 7 June 2019.

———. *COLREGS In Depth. Rule 15: Crossing Situation*. 4:26. Published on 29 December 2017, https://www.youtube.com/watch?v=E11GonKFkUs&index=10&list=PL-Kbjik4MwIgI4gXgMTE1VJ6LGYQBhHkE, accessed 7 June 2019.

Cockcroft, Anthony Norman, and J.N.F. Lameijer. *Guide to the Collision Avoidance Rules—International Regulations for Preventing Collisions at Sea Incorporating the 1981, 1987, 1989, 1993, 2001 and 2007 Amendments*, 7th ed. Amsterdam: Elsevier, 2012.

Cockcroft, Norman. "Collision Avoidance at Sea in the Mid-20th Century. Two Incidents in the 1940s." *Journal of Navigation* 65 (2012): 203–4.

Collins English Dictionary. Glasgow: HarperCollins Publishers, 2019, https://www.collinsdictionary.com/dictionary/english, accessed 7 June 2019.

Convention on the International Regulations for Preventing Collisions at Sea. Adopted 20 October 1972. Entered into force 15 July 1977. Consolidated text as amended in 1981,1987, 1989, 1993, 2001 and 2007, http://www.ecolregs.com/index.php?option=com_k2&view=itemlist&layout=category&Itemid=505&lang=en, accessed 31 May 2019.

Crawford, James. *The International Law Commission's Articles on State Responsibility*. Cambridge: Cambridge University Press, 2002.

Healy, Nicholas J. "Collision Law During the Last Quarter-Century of the Millennium." *Tulane Law Review* 73 (1999): 1789–1802.

Jiménez de Aréchaga, Eduardo. "International Responsibility." *Manual of Public International Law*, 531–604. Ed. Max Sørensen. London: Macmillan, 1968.

——— and Attila Tanzi. "International State Responsibility." *International Law: Achievements and Prospects*, 347–80. Ed. Mohammed Bedjaoui. Paris: UNESCO, 1991.

Kopacz, Zdisław *et al.* "An Attempt of [sic] the Specification of the Ship's Navigation Process." *Annals of Navigation* 3 (2001): 99–109.

Layton, C. W. T. *et al. Dictionary of Nautical Words and Terms*, 2nd ed. Glasgow: Brown, Son & Ferguson Ltd., Naval Publishers, 1982.

Llana, Christopher B., and George P. Wisneskey. *Handbook of the Nautical Rules of the Road: A Convenient Take-Along Guide for Sail and Power Boaters*, 3rd. [online] ed., 2009, http://navruleshandbook.com/, accessed 7 June 2019.

Maryland School of Sailing. *Collision Avoidance Nav Rules*. 1:42:04. Published on 11 April 2013, https://www.youtube.com/watch?v=19suVDp8GnMm, accessed 7 June 2019.

Pillay, Anand, and Jin Wang (eds.). *Technology and Safety of Marine Systems*. Killington, Oxford: Elsevier Science Ltd., 2003.

Plant, Glen. "The Collision Avoidance Regulations as a Regulator of International Navigation Rights: Underlying Principles and Their Adequacy for the Twenty-first Century." *Journal of Navigation* 88 (1996): 377–93.

South China Sea Arbitration. Award of 12 July 2016, https://pcacases.com/web/sendAttach/2086, accessed 5 June 2019.

———. Hearing on the Merits and Remaining Issues of Jurisdiction and Admissibility. Final Transcript, Day 3 (26 November 2015), https://pcacases.com/web/sendAttach/1549, accessed 5 June 2019.

———. Independent Expert Report. Report of the International Navigational Safety Expert Appointed by the Permanent Court of Arbitration [sic], The Hague, The Netherlands, by Captain Gurpreet S. Singhota, 15 April 2016, https://pcacases.com/web/sendAttach/1810, accessed 6 June 2019.

———. *Memorial of the Philippines* (30 March 2014). Vol. I, http://www.pcacases.com/pcadocs/Memorial%20of%20the%20Philippines%20Volume%20I.pdf, accessed 7 June 2019.

———. Annex 239. Opinion of Craig H. Allen, Judson Falknor Professor of Law, University of Washington (19 Mar. 2014). Vol. VII, 371–88, https://files.pca-cpa.org/pcadocs/The%20Philippines%27%20Memorial%20-%20Volume%20VII%20%28Annexes%20222-255%29.pdf, accessed 6 June 2019.

Thirslund, Søren. "Collision Avoidance at Sea in the Mid-20th Century. Thoughts from Denmark." *Journal of Navigation* 65 (2012): 201–3.

United Nations Convention on the Law of the Sea. Concluded at Montego Bay on 10 December 1982. Entered into force 16 November 1994, http://www.un.org/depts/los/convention_agreements/texts/unclos/unclos_e.pdf, accessed 6 June 2019.

United Nations. International Law Commission. *Draft Articles on Responsibility of States for Internationally Wrongful Acts, with Commentaries (2001). Report of the International Law Commission on the work of its fifty-third session, 23 April–1 June and 2 July–10 August 2001. Official Records of the General Assembly, Fifty-sixth session. Supplement No. 10*. UN Doc. A/56/10. *Yearbook of the International Law Commission 2001*. Vol. II, Part 2. *Report of the Commission to the General Assembly on the work of its fifty-third session*. UN Doc. A/CN.4/SER.A/2001/Add.1 (Part 2). New York: United Nations, 2007, http://legal.un.org/docs/?path=../ilc/publications/yearbooks/english/ilc_2001_v2_p2.pdf&lang=EFSRAC, accessed 6 June 2019.

United States. Court of Appeals for the Ninth Circuit. *Crowley Marine Services Inc. v. Maritrans Operating Company*, 530 F.3d 1167 (9th cir. 2006) [No. 04-35724. Decided: May 08, 2006], https://caselaw.findlaw.com/us-9th-circuit/1384355.html, accessed 7 June 2019.

CHAPTER 6

Toward a Critique of the Rationalizations of Collisions as Instruments of Chinese Foreign Policy

China's rationalizations of collisions as instruments of its foreign policy were laid out in a Note Verbale to the Philippines following the latter's protest over the incident of 28 April 2012. First, China asserted that

> The various jurisdiction measures adopted by the ·Chinese government over Huangyan Island [Scarborough Shoal] and its waters, and activities by Chinese ships, including government public service ships and fishing boats, in Huangyan Island and its waters are completely within China's sovereignty.[1]

Second, China claimed that during an incident that occurred on 10 April 2012, a Philippine warship not only "violated severely" China's territorial sovereignty but also allegedly harassed "with force" and severely infringed the human rights of Chinese fishermen working in the waters of Scarborough Shoal.[2]

[1] *South China Sea Arbitration, Memorial of the Philippines* (30 March 2014), Annex 211, Note Verbale from the Embassy of the People's Republic of China in Manila to the Department of Foreign Affairs of the Republic of the Philippines, No. (12) PG-239 (25 May 2012), vol. VI, 403 ("*MP*"), http://www.pcacases.com/pcadocs/The%20Philippines%27%20Memorial%20-%20Volume%20VI%20%28Annexes%20158-221%29.pdf, accessed 9 June 2019.

[2] *Ibid.*

A. C. Robles Jr., *Vessel Collisions in the Law of the Sea*,
https://doi.org/10.1007/978-981-16-9793-7_6

China's response, together with its failure to deny the facts, leads the reader to understand that in China's view the actions of the Chinese vessels that nearly provoked collisions with Philippine vessels, being "completely within China's sovereignty," were legal. Several incidents that occurred in the following years cannot but prompt the observer to hypothesize that for China, collisions are instruments of foreign policy.[3] In these incidents, Chinese vessels rammed—deliberately collided with—vessels from other littoral States of the South China Sea. These occurred as the arbitral proceedings were ongoing and after the Tribunal had rendered its decision that China had breached the COLREGS.

On 29 January 2015, Chinese Coast Guard vessel Haijing 3412 rammed one Philippine fishing vessel that it encountered near Scarborough Shoal. China tacitly admitted the fact, alleging that the fishing vessel ignored Coast Guard warnings and that the vessels sustained only slight scratches during the confrontation.[4] On 5 March 2016, a Chinese Coast Guard vessel rammed a Philippine fishing vessel near Scarborough Shoal.[5] On 22 March 2016, a Chinese Coast Guard vessel rammed a Philippine fishing vessel approaching Scarborough Shoal.[6] On 9 July 2016 two Chinese Coast Guard vessels, Haijing 46,101 and Haijing 34,103, rammed one of two Vietnamese fishing vessels operating in waters near Discovery Reef in the Paracel Islands.[7] On 13 October 2016, Chinese Coast Guard vessel Haijing 45,103 rammed a Vietnamese fishing vessel KH 97,850 TS that was fishing near the Paracel Islands, chased it from the area, and trailed it for several hours. That evening, the Chinese vessel encountered the same Vietnamese vessel between Woody Island and Lincoln Island and repeatedly rammed it.[8] This account excludes two incidents in which the responsibility of Chinese vessels is disputed. On 1 May 2014, following China's deployment of an oil rig in the waters off

[3] As we are not in a position to determine whether China's official vessels ram other vessels as part of law enforcement operations in China's internal waters, we simply refer to collisions as instruments of China's foreign policy.

[4] Center for Strategic and International Studies (CSIS), "Are Maritime Law Enforcement Forces Destabilizing Asia?" *China Power Project* (2021), https://chinapower.csis.org/maritime-forces-destabilizing-asia/, accessed 13 October 2021.

[5] *Ibid.*

[6] *Ibid.*

[7] *Ibid.*

[8] *Ibid.*

the Paracel Islands, collisions occurred between Vietnamese Coast Guard and Chinese official vessels for which each side blamed the other.[9] On the night of 29 September 2015, a Vietnamese fishing vessel was rammed by a Chinese vessel and sunk 12 hours after the ramming. Although Vietnam admitted that there was no indication that the Chinese ship was owned by the Chinese government, China asserted that Chinese authorities had the right to take law enforcement measures in accordance with the law on boats that have illegally entered waters that China claimed as its territory.[10]

The doctrinal rationalizations of the resort to collisions as instruments of China's foreign policy were elaborated in the CSIL's critique, carried out under the leadership and supervision of China's Ministry of Foreign Affairs, of the Tribunal's decision on the merits of Philippine Submission No. 13.[11] The critique followed two tracks that elaborated on ideas already laid out in China's response to the Philippine protest. The first is the idea that the activities of China's official vessels were "completely within China's sovereignty." The second alleges that the Tribunal engaged in "cherry picking" by isolating the incidents of 26 April and 28 May 2012, ignoring the incident of 10 April 2012.

In this chapter, the critique of the rationalizations of collisions as instruments of foreign policy will be carried out in three stages. It will be demonstrated that at each stage, the rationalizations lack legal foundations.

First, we examine the CSIL's allegation that the Arbitral Tribunal engaged in "cherry-picking" the incidents on 28 April and 25 May, which it described as part of a "Scarborough Shoal incident" that included the incident of 10 April.[12] At this stage one might already ask whether in the CSIL's view, the alleged fact that the two incidents were part of a larger incident constituted "special circumstances" within the incident and justifying departure by the Chinese vessels from the Convention on the

[9] *Ibid.*

[10] *Ibid.*

[11] Chinese Society of International Law ("CSIL"), "The South China Sea Arbitration Awards: A Critical Study," *Chinese Journal of International Law* 17 (2018): 594–607, paras. 827–57.

[12] *Ibid.*, 595, para. 830; 596, para. 832.

International Regulations for Preventing Collisions at Sea 1972 ("COL-REGS 1972") on the same day (10 April), 18 days later (on 28 April), and/or 46 days later (on 26 May).[13]

In the second and third parts of the chapter, we examine the CSIL argument that the Philippine vessels were not engaged in innocent passage in the territorial sea of Scarborough Shoal, forcing China to conduct law enforcement activities that entailed the use of force and a departure by the Chinese vessels from the COLREGS. The CSIL's assumption that its vessels can conduct law enforcement activities with respect to foreign warships—vessels that enjoy sovereign immunity—can be approached in two ways. The first emphasizes the status of the Philippine vessels as official vessels—as warships—and examines State practice on the use of force against foreign warships. That practice demonstrates that while there may be a debate on the permissibility of the use of force by a coastal State against foreign warships, States refrain from using force against foreign warships and clearly draw the line at deliberate attempts to provoke collisions between vessels. The second approach downplays the status of the vessels as official vessels enjoying sovereign immunity, as China and the CSIL seem to have done, and asks the question whether the use of force, including collision and ramming, in law enforcement operations at sea is justified under international law. An examination of State practice on the use of force in law enforcement shows that States, while allowing the use of force as a last resort in law enforcement against ordinary vessels, draw the line at collisions, which they consider unacceptable. Italy went to the extent of prosecuting the commander of an Italian warship that had failed to comply with the COLREGS and caused a collision in the course of a law enforcement operation against illegal migration.

[13] *Convention on the International Regulations for Preventing Collisions at Sea*, adopted at London on 20 October 1972, entered into force 15 July 1977, consolidated text as amended in 1981, 1987, 1989, 1993, 2001 and 2007, http://www.ecolregs.com/index.php?option=com_k2&view=itemlist&layout=category&Itemid=505&lang=en, accessed 31 May 2019.

I. The Incident of 10 April 2012: Absence of Special Circumstances Creating Immediate Danger and Justifying Departure from the Colregs

On 10 April 2012, a Philippine vessel was dispatched to conduct maritime patrol in the waters of Scarborough Shoal. Philippine and Chinese accounts of the conduct of the Philippine vessel differ dramatically. Even assuming that the Chinese account is accurate, the conduct of the boarding procedure that allegedly violated Chinese sovereignty and the human rights of Chinese fishermen can in no way be considered "special circumstances" creating "immediate danger," as required by Rule 2 of the COLREGS, and justifying departure from the COLREGS by Chinese vessels, whether on the same day or weeks and months after the incident.

A. The Conduct of Maritime Patrol and the Absence of Immediate Danger

On 8 April 2012, a Philippine Navy vessel observed six Chinese fishing vessels anchored inside Scarborough Shoal. BRP *Gregorio del Pilar* was then redeployed from Palawan to the waters of Northern Luzon, the main island of the Philippines, and arrived at Scarborough Shoal at 0326H on 10 April. At 0720H, a team of five persons was launched aboard two rubber boats to collect images of the Chinese fishing vessels, but since the deck of the fishing vessels was covered by a high free board, the vessel requested clearance to conduct a boarding procedure, with the aim of determining whether corals or sea turtles were on board the Chinese fishing vessels.[14]

At 0910H, the Philippine vessel BRP *Gregorio del Pilar* started to conduct Visit, Board, Search, and Seizure ("VBSS") on the eight Chinese vessels. The Philippine team documented the presence of assorted corals and giant clams on board two Chinese fishing vessels and assorted endangered species and corals on board the other six. By 1420H, the boarding procedure was terminated. At 1610H, the Philippine vessel observed two Chinese survey ships, Zhongguo Haijian 75 and Zhongguo Haijan 64,

[14] *MP*, Annex 77, Memorandum from Col. Nathaniel Y. Casem, Philippine Navy, to Chief of Staff, Armed Forces of the Philippines, No. N2E-0412-008 (11 April 2012), vol. IV, 133–34, https://files.pca-cpa.org/pcadocs/The%20Philippines%27%20Memorial%20-%20Volume%20IV%20%28Annexes%2061-102%29.pdf, accessed 9 June 2019.

moving toward Scarborough Shoal. The two Chinese vessels, through a series of maneuvers, managed to position themselves at the mouth of the entrance of Scarborough Shoal and place themselves between the BRP *Gregorio del Pilar* and the eight Chinese fishing vessels. The Philippine vessel then departed the scene.[15]

From the perspective of China, which claims sovereignty over Scarborough Shoal, the Philippine vessel's conduct of boarding procedure "severely" violated its sovereignty.[16] The question that must be raised, though, is whether the Philippine vessel's conduct of the boarding procedure in any way created special circumstances that would have created immediate danger and justified departure from the COLREGS on the same day, 18 days later, and/or 46 days later.

As we have seen above, the COLREGS do not provide a comprehensive definition, much less a complete list, of special circumstances. Chris Llana, a former US Coast Guard Officer, and George Wisnesky, former head of the US Coast Guard's Rules of the Road Branch, acknowledge that during routine operations, virtually all vessels engage in maneuvers that are not covered by the COLREGS. These routine operations, which normally take a very short time, may occur near other vessels.[17] For example, vessels entering or leaving a slip do not follow the steady course needed for the application of the Rules.[18] Vessels proceeding stern-first are also considered to be in special circumstances. Vessels not making way may be in special circumstances.[19] A vessel stopping in a high-traffic area may create special circumstances. Normally, a vessel should avoid stopping in such an area, and when it decides to stop, it should make its intentions clear to other vessels in the area. If the stopped vessel is large, it may not be able to move out of the way of a fast-oncoming vessel. The presence of

[15] *Ibid.*, 135.

[16] *MP*, Annex 211, 403.

[17] Christopher B. Llana and George P. Wisneskey, *Handbook of the Nautical Rules of the Road: A Convenient Take-Along Guide for Sail and Power Boaters* (3rd. [online] ed., 2009), 70, http://navruleshandbook.com/Rule1.html, accessed 9 June 2019.

[18] A slip is an inclined bed of masonry, sloping toward water, on which ships are built; it is also an inclined bed, often fitted with rollers, on to which vessels can be hauled for examination of underwater body, for painting and for repairing. C. W. T. Layton et al., *Dictionary of Nautical Words and Terms* (2nd ed.; Glasgow: Brown, Son & Ferguson Ltd., Naval Publishers, 1982), 357.

[19] A vessel making way is moving ahead or astern through the water. *Ibid.*, 241.

more than two vessels may preclude full compliance with the COLREGS, as the action required with respect to one vessel may conflict with the action required with respect to one or more of the other vessels.[20]

The Chinese vessels apparently did not report, and China certainly did not communicate to the Philippines, any maneuvers by the Philippine vessels that corresponded to the "special circumstances" described above, or indeed any maneuvers that created immediate danger. Certainly, the reactions of the Chinese official vessels did not seem to signal that they considered any immediate danger to exist, nor did they violate the COLREGS on the very day. Had there been any immediate danger and had the CSIL wished to excuse the conduct of the Chinese vessels on 28 April and 26 May on that basis, it should still have explained how immediate danger on 10 April could be grounds for departure by Chinese vessels from the COLREGS on 28 April and, even more improbably, on 26 May.

Equally puzzling is the importance attributed by the Chinese government and the CSIL, in their attempts to find grounds for the violations by the Chinese vessels of the COLREGS on 28 April and 26 May, to the alleged violation of the human rights of the Chinese fishermen on 10 April.

B. The Alleged Violation of Human Rights as a Pretext for the Violations of the COLREGS

The Philippine Navy reported to the Chief of Staff of the Armed Forces of the Philippines that during the conduct of the boarding procedure on 10 April incident, "strict adherence to human rights in the treatment of the crew was observed."[21] As this was a confidential report that was not intended for production as evidence in any international judicial proceedings, the mere possibility of which could not have been anticipated by the personnel concerned at the time, there is no reason to doubt its veracity. The Report added that as a result of the language barrier, communication between the Philippine boarding team and the Chinese fishermen was

[20] Llana and Wisnesky, *Handbook*, 70–71.

[21] *MP*, Annex 77, 133.

through sign language, and some boarding documents were not properly accomplished.[22]

Rejecting the Philippine protest over the incident, China characterized the maritime patrol as "harassment with force" of the Chinese fishermen. It claimed that the attempt to arrest and prosecute Chinese fishermen "infringed the human rights" of the fishermen.[23] One should of course rejoice that China is concerned about the human rights of its citizens. Unfortunately, China's claim is undermined by its failure to identify the human rights of the Chinese fishermen that had been violated and the ways in which they had been violated.[24] The CSIL adds that the personnel of BRP *Gregorio del* Pilar questioned and "toughened up [sic]" the Chinese fishermen and searched their boats. Their behavior was said to have been "rude and rough."[25] These statements still do not identify the human rights of the Chinese fishermen that were violated. If anything, they muddy the waters further, through the use of the expression "toughen up." The latter means "to make someone stronger,"[26] a meaning that could not possibly have been intended by the CSIL.

One might ask whether China's silence may be attributed to the Chinese fishermen's failure to give details of the alleged human rights violations that they suffered. Otherwise, the silence of China and of the CSIL on the matter would be inexplicable. The lack of detail concerning the alleged human rights violations that the Chinese fishermen suffered is curious, to say the least, and is in sharp contrast to the precise and vivid details that Filipino fishermen recalled, weeks or months after the events, regarding the actions of Chinese authorities who sought to prevent them from fishing at Scarborough Shoal. One Filipino fisherman reported that he and other fishermen who attempted to evade Chinese authorities by waiting for nighttime before starting to fish found that the Chinese lay

[22] *Ibid.*, 136.

[23] *Ibid.*, Annex 211, 404.

[24] Unless China was referring to the "right" to fish endangered species, like corals and sea turtles.

[25] CSIL, "The South China Sea Arbitration Awards," 596, para. 831.

[26] *Cambridge English Dictionary* (Cambridge: Cambridge University Press, 2019), https://dictionary.cambridge.org/dictionary/english/toughen-someone-up, accessed 9 June 2019.

in wait for them.[27] According to another fishermen, while they were still far from reaching Scarborough Shoal, the Chinese already gave them the signal not to proceed further and used water cannons against them.[28] A third fishermen testified that the Filipinos were harassed through water cannon and sound blares, and were threatened with guns.[29]

Whatever might be the reason for the failure of China and the CSIL to identify and describe the human rights of Chinese fishermen that were allegedly violated, neither China nor the CSIL spelled out the implications of these violations for their defense of the conduct of the Chinese vessels on 28 April and 26 May. The reasons for this restraint are readily understandable. Had the alleged violations indeed occurred, they would in all likelihood still not have been considered "special circumstances" creating immediate danger and providing a pretext to the Chinese vessels for departing from the COLREGS on any day—on the same day, 18 days later, or 46 days later.

Any attempt to rationalize violations of the COLREGS endangering the lives of Filipino mariners as a response to alleged human rights violations committed by Philippine vessels against Chinese fishermen would immediately bring to mind the judgment of the International Court of Justice ("ICJ") in the *Nicaragua* case. One of the reasons that the US had adduced to excuse the placing of mines in Nicaraguan ports, the destruction of Nicaraguan oil installations, and the training, arming, and equipping of Nicaraguan rebels was that the Nicaraguan government had allegedly violated human rights. The ICJ made short shrift of this pathetic argument:

[27] *South China Sea Arbitration, Supplemental Documents of the Philippines* (19 November 2015), Annex 697, Affidavit of Mr. Crispen Talatagod (12 November 2015), vol. II, 210, para. A24 ("*SDP*"), https://files.pca-cpa.org/pcadocs/The%20Philippines%27%20Supplemental%20Documents%20-%20Volume%20II%20%28Annexes%20608-709%29.pdf, accessed 9 June 2019.

[28] *Ibid.*, Annex 698, Affidavit of Mr. Cecilio Taneo (12 November 2015), vol. II, 227, para. A30, https://files.pca-cpa.org/pcadocs/The%20Philippines%27%20Supplemental%20Documents%20-%20Volume%20II%20%28Annexes%20608-709%29.pdf, accessed 9 June 2019.

[29] *Ibid.*, Annex 696, Affidavit of Mr. Jowe Legaspi (12 November 2015), vol. II, 193, para. A27, https://files.pca-cpa.org/pcadocs/The%20Philippines%27%20Supplemental%20Documents%20-%20Volume%20II%20%28Annexes%20608-709%29.pdf, accessed 9 June 2019.

> the use of force could not be the appropriate method to monitor or ensure such respect [i.e., for human rights]. …[T]he protection of human rights, a strictly humanitarian objective, cannot be compatible with the mining of ports, the destruction of oil installations, or again with the training, arming and equipping of the contras….[T]he argument derived from the preservation of human rights in Nicaragua cannot afford a legal justification for the conduct of the United States….[30]

The same reasoning could be applied to any Chinese rationalization of the violations of the COLREGS on the basis of alleged human rights violations by Philippine vessels. It would be paradoxical, to say the least, if a humanitarian objective—enforcing the human rights of Chinese fishermen—were to be achieved through a non-humanitarian action—endangering the lives of Filipino mariners. It is probably for this reason that all references to the human rights of Chinese fishermen, after making a brief appearance, disappeared without a trace in the CSIL's elaborate rationalization of the conduct of Chinese vessels on 28 April and 26 May.

The CSIL concentrated on the alleged violations by Philippine vessels on 28 April and 26 May of China's laws and regulations on innocent passage in the territorial sea. This rationalization neglected the fact that the Philippine vessels concerned, as warships, enjoyed sovereign immunity.

II. The Incidents of 28 April and 26 May 2012: The Use of Force Against Warships

The CSIL asserts that the actions of the Chinese vessels were law enforcement actions in response to the activities of the Philippine vessels in violation of Chinese laws and regulations governing innocent passage through the territorial sea. It argues that since the Philippine vessels' activities in China's territorial sea did not constitute innocent passage, China was entitled, under the terms of Article 25 of the United Nations Convention on the Law of the Sea ("Convention"), "to take the necessary

[30] *Military and Paramilitary Activities in and against Nicaragua (Nicaragua v. United States of America), Merits, Judgment, I.C.J. Reports 1986*, 134–35, para. 268, https://www.icj-cij.org/files/case-related/70/070-19860627-JUD-01-00-BI.pdf, accessed 9 June 2019.

steps in its territorial sea to prevent passage which is not innocent."[31] It claims that on 26 May Philippine vessels entered into Scarborough Shoal's waters, bypassed a blockage [sic] formed by Chinese law enforcement vessels in a dangerous manner, through a sharp turn and stop, eventually intruded into the lagoon, and anchored there. These actions allegedly forced Chinese vessels to take the necessary response measures.[32]

Two observations are in order concerning the account of the 26 May incident. First, we should note that the CSIL still refrained from claiming that the allegedly dangerous maneuvers undertaken by the Philippine vessels created immediate danger justifying a departure from the COLREGS. Second, the CSIL fails to mention that the vessels entered the lagoon after the Chinese vessels had already violated the COLREGS by provoking near-collisions with them.

Beyond the observations on details of this incident, it is remarkable that nowhere is there any recognition that the Philippine vessels involved were warships and as such, enjoyed sovereign immunity. The omission of this fact is a fatal flaw in the CSIL's rationalization of the violations of the COLREGS by Chinese vessels. As Bernard Oxman put it in a comprehensive treatment of the regime of warships under the Convention, the concept of "law enforcement" properly applies only to the relationship between a State and persons or ships subject to the State's enforcement jurisdiction (the State's power to enforce its laws). Any attempt to exercise law enforcement jurisdiction against a foreign warship is in reality an attempt to threaten or use force against the sovereign instrumentality of a foreign State. Thus it is a subject matter that falls within the scope of the international law on the use of force.[33] The question, therefore, is not

[31] CSIL, "The South China Sea Arbitration Awards," 594–95, para. 829. *United Nations Convention on the Law of the Sea*, concluded at Montego Bay on 10 December 1982, entered into force 16 November 1994, http://www.un.org/depts/los/convention_agreements/texts/unclos/unclos_e.pdf, accessed 9 June 2019.

[32] CSIL, "The South China Sea Arbitration Awards," 596, para. 822.

[33] Bernard Oxman, "The Regime of Warships Under the United Nations Convention on the Law of the Sea," *Virginia Journal of International Law* 24 (1984): 815, https://repository.law.miami.edu/cgi/viewcontent.cgi?article=1401&context=fac_articles, accessed 9 June 2019. This article is an English adaptation of an article in French by the same author, "Le régime des navires de guerre dans le cadre de la Convention des Nations Unies sur le droit de la mer [The Regime of Warships Under the United Nations Convention on the Law of the Sea]," *Annuaire Français de Droit International* [French Yearbook

whether the Chinese vessels were justified in carrying out law enforcement measures directed against the Philippine vessels, but whether the Chinese vessels were justified in using force against sovereign immune Philippine vessels.

The warship's sovereign immunity does not exempt the warship from the duty to comply with the Convention's provisions on the regulation of innocent passage in the territorial sea. Whether the permissible response of the coastal State in the event that a foreign warship fails to do so includes the use of force is the object of scholarly debate. The concept of use of force includes the threat or attempt by a State's public vessels to intentionally collide with a foreign vessel.[34] State practice demonstrates that States refrain from using force against a foreign warship, such as a submarine, that has infringed the coastal State's territorial sovereignty. State practice also demonstrates that when a coastal State warship deliberately provokes a collision in order to compel a foreign warship to comply with its laws, such attempts are considered to be in contravention of international law.

A. The Scope of Sovereign Immunity

Article 29 of the Convention defines a "warship" as

> a ship belonging to the armed forces of a State bearing the external marks distinguishing such ships of its nationality, under the command of an officer duly commissioned by the government of the State and whose name

of International Law] 28 (1982): 811–50 ("*AFDI*"), https://www.persee.fr/docAsPDF/afdi_0066-3085_1982_num_28_1_2519.pdf, accessed 9 June 2019. See also Francesco Francioni, "Peacetime Use of Force, Military Activities, and the New Law of the Sea," *Cornell International Law Journal* 18 (1985): 215, https://scholarship.law.cornell.edu/cgi/viewcontent.cgi?article=1152&context=cilj, accessed 9 June 2019; Patricia Jimenez Kwast, "Maritime Law Enforcement and the Use of Force: Reflections on the Categorisation of Forcible Action at Sea in the Light of the *Guyana/Suriname* Award," *Journal of Conflict and Security Law* 13 (2008): 84, 85; Yoshifumi Tanaka, "Navigational Rights and Freedoms," in Donald Rothwell et al. (eds.), *The Oxford Handbook of the Law of the Sea* (Oxford: Oxford University Press, 2015), 547.

34 *MP*, Annex 239, Opinion of Craig H. Allen, Judson Falknor Professor of Law, University of Washington (19 March 2014), vol. VII, 376, https://files.pca-cpa.org/pcadocs/The%20Philippines%27%20Memorial%20-%20Volume%20VII%20%28Annexes%20222-255%29.pdf, accessed 9 June 2019.

appears in the appropriate service list or its equivalent, and manned by a crew which is under regular armed forces discipline.

Although this definition is to be found in Part II of the Convention on the territorial sea, the definition is "for the purposes of the Convention," rather than for this "part" or "section," which implies that the definition refers to the entire Convention.[35] The International Tribunal for the Law of the Sea ("ITLOS") has confirmed that the definition of warships provided for in Article 29 of the Convention is "applicable to all maritime areas," including internal waters.[36]

The sovereign immunity of warships is recognized by customary international law and is taken for granted by the Convention.[37] Article 32 of the Convention, on "Immunities of warships and other government ships operated for non-commercial purposes," stipulates that "[w]ith such exceptions as are contained in subsection A and in articles 30 and 31, nothing in this Convention affects the immunities of warships and other government ships operated for non-commercial purposes."[38] The justification for sovereign immunity lies in the fact that the warship is "an expression of the sovereignty of the State whose flag it flies."[39]

[35] Oxman, "The Regime of Warships," 812.

[36] *"ARA Libertad" (Argentina v. Ghana), Provisional Measures, Order of 15 December 2012, ITLOS Reports 2012*, 344, para. 64; 348, para. 95, https://www.itlos.org/fileadmin/itlos/documents/cases/case_no.20/published/C20_Order_151212.pdf, accessed 9 June 2019.

[37] *Ibid.*, Joint Separate Opinion of Judge Wolfrum and Judge Cot, 373, para. 41, https://www.itlos.org/fileadmin/itlos/documents/cases/case_no.20/published/C20_Wolfrum_Cot_151212.pdf, accessed 9 June 2019.

[38] Article 30, on "Non-compliance by Warships with the Laws and Regulations of the Coastal State," reads as follows: "If any warship does not comply with the laws and regulations of the coastal State concerning passage through the territorial sea and disregards any request for compliance therewith which is made to it, the coastal State may require it to leave the territorial sea immediately." Article 31, on the "Responsibility of the Flag State for Damage Caused by a Warship or Other Government Ship Operated for Non-commercial Purposes," states: The flag State shall bear international responsibility for any loss or damage to the coastal State resulting from the non-compliance by a warship or other government ship operated for non-commercial purposes with the laws and regulations of the coastal State concerning passage through the territorial sea or with the provisions of this Convention or other rules of international law.

[39] *"ARA Libertad," Provisional Measures Order*, 348, para. 94. One can already find a clear explanation of the rationale for sovereign immunity in the nineteenth century. Théodore Ortolan, *Règles internationales et diplomatie de la mer* [International Rules and

The immunity of warships covers attempts to arrest, detain, or impose coercive measures against it.[40] The warship navigating in the territorial sea of another State in the regime of innocent passage enjoys sovereign immunity, but its passage must comply with the requirements of innocent passage, laid down by Articles 18, 19, and 20 of the Convention, on the one hand, and with the laws and regulations relating to innocent passage that Article 21 authorizes the coastal State to adopt in a specified number of fields, on the other. According to Article 18, innocent passage must be "continuous and expeditious." Article 19 defines passage as innocent "so long as it is not prejudicial to the peace, good order and security of the coastal State." It provides a list of activities that are considered to be prejudicial to the "peace, good order or security of the coastal State." Some of these activities are clearly military in nature and could be carried out only by warships.[41] Article 20 stipulates that submarines and other underwater vehicles must navigate on the surface and show their flag. Article 21 permits the coastal State to adopt laws and regulations relating to innocent passage in a specified number of fields: safety of navigation and regulation of maritime traffic; the protection of navigational aids and facilities and other facilities or installations; the protection of cables and pipelines; the prevention of infringement of its fisheries laws and regulations; the preservation of its marine environment and the prevention,

the Diplomacy of the Sea], vol. I (Paris: H. Plon, 1864), 188–89, https://ia800308.us.archive.org/23/items/rglesinternatio03ortogoog/rglesinternatio03ortogoog.pdf, accessed 9 June 2019.

[40] James Kraska, "Putting Your Head in the Tiger's Mouth: Submarine Espionage in Territorial Waters," *Columbia Journal of Transnational Law* 54 (2015): 229, 236–37, http://jtl.columbia.edu/wp-content/uploads/sites/4/2015/12/Kraska_54-CJTL-164.pdf, accessed 9 June 2019. See also *"ARA Libertad"*, *Provisional Measures Order*, 349, para. 99.

[41] Francioni, "Peaceful Use of Force," 205. These military activities are "any threat or use of force against the sovereignty, territorial integrity or political independence of the coastal State, or in any other manner in violation of the principles of international law embodied in the Charter of the United Nations" (Article 19(2)(a)); "any exercise or practice with weapons of any kind" (Article 19(2)(b)); "any act aimed at collecting information to the prejudice of the defence or security of the coastal State" (Article 19(2)(c)); "any act of propaganda aimed at affecting the defence or security of the coastal State" (Article 19(2)(d)); "the launching, landing or taking on board of any aircraft" (Article 19(2)(e)); "the launching, landing or taking on board of any military device" (Article 19(2)(f)).

reduction and control of pollution; marine scientific research and hydrographic surveys; and the prevention of the infringement of its customs, fiscal, immigration, or sanitary laws and regulations.

In the event of non-innocent passage by any type of ships, the coastal State is authorized by Article 25 of the Convention "to take the necessary steps in its territorial sea to prevent passage which is not innocent." Article 30 envisages a scenario in which a foreign warship does not comply with the coastal State's laws and regulations relating to innocent passage. In such a scenario, the coastal State has the right to request compliance by the warship with the said laws and regulations. If the warship disregards the request for compliance, the coastal State may require it to leave the territorial sea immediately. The coastal State's right to order a warship to leave the territorial sea is analogous to the territorial State's right to expel a foreign diplomat who carries out activities incompatible with his/her diplomatic function. In both cases, the territorial State has a duty to refrain from exercising coercion against the foreign entity; in both cases, the territorial State's recourse is to "expel" the foreign entity.[42]

From the point of view of China, which claims sovereignty over Scarborough Shoal, the Philippine warships were not engaged in innocent passage, for two reasons. First, the purpose of their activities, law enforcement, was not consistent with the purposes and manner of innocent passage. Under Article 18(1) of the Convention, foreign vessels conducting innocent passage in the territorial sea will pass for the purposes of navigation. On the contrary, the purpose of the warships was to conduct maritime patrol and law enforcement activities in the area of Scarborough Shoal.[43] Second, the manner of passage of the Philippine warships was not consistent with the requirement of Article 18(2) of the Convention that the passage should be "continuous and expeditious." The CSIL points out that after entering Scarborough Shoal's

[42] Claudio Baldoni, "Les navires de guerre dans les eaux territoriales étrangères [Warships in Foreign Territorial Waters]," *Recueil des Cours de l'Académie de Droit International de La Haye* [Collected Courses of the Hague Academy of International Law], t. 65 (1938-III), 283; see also Oxman, "The Regime of Warships," 817. On Articles 25 and 30 of the Convention, see Richard A. Barnes, "Article 25. Right of Protection of the Coastal State," and "Article 30. Non-compliance by Warships with the Laws and Regulations of the Coastal State," in Alexander Proelss et al. (eds.), *United Nations Convention on the Law of the Sea: A Commentary* (München: Verlag C.H. Beck, oHG, 2017), 222–26, 244–47.

[43] CSIL, "The South China Sea Arbitration Awards," 603, para. 851.

territorial Sea, military personnel was transferred between two Philippine Coast Guard vessels,[44] while the BFAR vessel approached and resupplied the Coast Guard vessel anchored there earlier.[45] The CSIL argues that these activities could not be characterized as "continuous and expeditious passage."[46]

To justify the dangerous maneuvers of the Chinese vessels that could have resulted in collisions, the CSIL quotes Article 25 of the Convention, while conveniently forgetting Article 30. Taking into consideration Article 30 obliges us to examine two issues. The first is whether ordering the foreign warship to leave the territorial sea is also the only recourse of the coastal State in the event that the warship violates the coastal State's laws and regulations relating to innocent passage. The second is whether the coastal State is authorized to use force against the foreign warship under either or both articles. The answers to both questions are interrelated. At one end of the continuum is the view that the foreign warship enjoys complete immunity; hence, the use of force by the coastal State is admissible only in self-defense.[47] Presumably, this applies both to cases of non-innocent passage (Article 25) and violation of a coastal State's

[44] BRP *EDSA II* and BRP *Pampanga*. We should note that the CSIL was aware that the Philippine vessels involved belonged to the Philippine Coast Guard. As Moore observes, law enforcement is an act of sovereignty. Cameron Moore, "The Arbitral Award in the Matter of the South China Sea Between the Philippines and China: What Are the Implications for Freedom of Navigation and the Use of Force?" *Asia–Pacific Journal of Ocean Law and Policy* 2 (2017): 124; *Freedom of Navigation and the Law of the Sea Warships, States and the Use of Force* (Kindle edition; London: Routledge, 2021), Ch. 4, 111.

[45] MCS 3008 and BRP *Corregidor*, respectively.

[46] CSIL, "The South China Sea Arbitration Awards," 604, para. 851.

[47] Francioni, "Peacetime Use of Force," 208; Baldoni, "Les navires de guerre," 32. Francioni does not identify any authors who hold this view, but there is no doubt that the idea that a coastal State may use force in self-defense against a warship that commits forcible acts or acts of violence in the coastal State's territorial sea has a very long pedigree. See, for example, Ortolan, *Règles internationales*, vol. I, 190–91; Ferdinand Perels, *Das internationale öffentliche Seerecht der Gegenwart* [Contemporary Public International Law of the Sea] (Berlin: Ernst Siegfried Mittler und Sohn, 1882), 102, https://ia902701.us.archive.org/5/items/dasinternationa01peregoog/dasinternationa01peregoog.pdf, accessed 9 June 2019; Ferdinand Perels, *Manuel de droit maritime international* [Manual of International Maritime Law], transl. L. Arendt (Paris: Librairie Guillaumin & Cie, 1884), 111, https://ia802606.us.archive.org/33/items/manueldedroitma00arengoog/manueldedroitma00arengoog.pdf, accessed 9 June 2019; Baldoni, "Les navires de guerre," 191.

laws and regulations (Article 31). In this view, the only measures that the coastal State may take to protect itself against non-innocent passage and to respond to violations of its laws and regulations relating to innocent passage are to request compliance and failing compliance, to ask the foreign warship to leave the territorial sea immediately.

At the other end of the continuum, Froman argues that one must separate the issue of non-innocent passage from that of non-compliance with the coastal State's laws and regulations. The reason for this would be that the actions that render a warship's passage non-innocent do not overlap any of the areas in which the coastal State is allowed to adopt laws and regulations. The first type of actions is said to refer to coastal State security; the second type, to safety. Consequently, violation of a coastal State's laws and regulations would not necessarily render passage non-innocent. The distinction between non-innocent passage and violation of a coastal State's laws and regulations would supposedly entail a difference in sanctions. In the event of non-innocent passage, ships—presumably, including warships—are treated legally as though they were passing through the coastal State's internal waters. Against this type of passage, the coastal State has the right of protection, embodied in Article 25. The warship would theoretically fall under the complete jurisdiction of the coastal State, including enforcement jurisdiction. In contrast, the breach of coastal State laws and regulations alone would not warrant a forceful response.[48] These considerations lead one to infer that Froman's answer to the second question is affirmative, that in the event of non-innocent passage, the foreign warship cannot expect to be spared the use of force and be asked simply to comply with the conditions for innocent passage or leave the territorial sea immediately. Somewhat perversely, Froman admits that the foreign warship's immunity would compel the

[48] F. David Froman, "Uncharted Waters: Non-innocent Passage of Warships in the Territorial Sea," *San Diego Law Review* 21 (1984): 659, 661, 664. An earlier version of this article is available as "Uncharted Waters: Non-innocent Passage of Warships in the Territorial Sea," M.A. Thesis, Naval Postgraduate School, 1983, https://calhoun.nps.edu/bitstream/handle/10945/20015/unchartedwatersn00from.pdf, accessed 9 June 2019. Moore also argues that a warship engaged in non-innocent passage, for example, by fishing, may still not pose a threat to a coastal State. In that case, the use of force in self-defense by the coastal State would not be justifiable. Moore, *Freedom of Navigation*, Ch. 4, 104.

coastal State to take less intrusive measures than those taken against non-innocent passage of merchant vessels.[49] He also believes that prudence dictates that a coastal State should follow the special procedures applicable to warships in breach of a coastal State's laws and regulations.[50] These qualifications blur the distinctions that Froman attempts to make.

Unlike Froman, Francioni believes that conceptually and practically, one cannot separate violations of a coastal State's regulations from violations of the "peace, good order and security" of the coastal State. The list of activities that render passage non-innocent includes "any other activity not having a direct bearing on passage (Article 19(2)(l))," thus leaving little margin for the possibility that a foreign warship's operation may constitute a violation of a coastal State's laws and regulations without at the same time violating the requirements of innocent passage.[51] This approach seems to be appropriate for assessing the legality of the Chinese vessels' actions, for China alleged that the Philippine vessels violated its laws and regulations concerning innocent passage, rendering their passage non-innocent.

Francioni's approach still does not provide an answer to the question of the way in which a coastal State may put into effect its request that a foreign warship leaves its territorial sea, and more specifically, the question of the way in which the coastal State may respond if the foreign warship disregards the request. Froman seems to think it unlikely that the foreign warship will refuse to heed such a request. He explains that a warship in innocent passage, unless it is proceeding to internal waters, is by definition only passing through the territorial sea. Since it is in the process of leaving it, he thinks it unlikely that the vessel will disregard a request to leave the territorial sea.[52] But as the "bumping incident" discussed below shows, it is possible that the request is made when the foreign warship has just entered the territorial sea and that it may take some time for it to exit the territorial sea. In such a situation, one still cannot avoid the question whether the use of force by the coastal State is justified. In the view of some authoritative commentators, the sole recourse of the coastal State in case of non-compliance by a foreign warship with its laws and regulations

[49] Froman, "Uncharted Waters," 664.

[50] *Ibid.*, 674.

[51] Francioni, "Peacetime Use of Force," 209.

[52] Froman, "Uncharted Waters," 665.

regarding innocent passage is to request the warship to leave the territorial sea immediately.[53]

Most authors accept that the use of force is permitted, but that such use must be in conformity with international law and the UN Charter.[54] The principles governing the use of force in maritime law enforcement were restated by the ITLOS in its judgment in the *M/V "Saiga" (No. 2)* case:

> Although the Convention does not contain express provisions on the use of force in the arrest of ships, international law, which is applicable by virtue of article 293 of the Convention, requires that the use of force must be avoided as far as possible and, where force is unavoidable, it must not go

[53] Béla Vitányi, "L'immunité des navires d'État – I [The Immunity of Government Vessels—I]," *Netherlands International Law Review* 10 (1963): 44; Myron H. Nordquist et al. (eds.), United Nations Convention on the Law of the Sea 1982: A *Commentary*, vol. II, *Second Committee: Territorial Sea, Innocent Passage, Straits Used for International Navigation, Archipelagic States, the Exclusive Economic Zone, and the Continental Shelf* (Leiden: Martinus Nijhoff Publishers, 1993), 255.

[54] On the use of force with respect to foreign warships, see Axel Berg, "Das sowjetische U-Boot 137 in schwedischen Hoheitsgewässern. Fragen der Immunität fremder Kriegsschiffe [Soviet Submarine 137 in Swedish Territorial Waters. Questions on the Immunity of Foreign Warships]," *Zeitschrift für ausländisches öffentliches Recht und Völkerrecht* [Journal for Foreign Public Law and International Law] 42 (1982): 315, http://www.zaoerv.de/42_1982/42_1982_2_a_295_326.pdf, accessed 9 June 2019; Valentín Bou Franch, "El derecho de paso inocente de los buques de guerra en tiempos de paz [The Innocent Passage of Warships in Peacetime]," *Anuario de Derecho Marítimo* [Yearbook of Maritime Law] 11 (1994): 93–135, https://core.ac.uk/download/pdf/80525575.pdf, accessed 9 June 2019; Carlos Espaliú Berdud, *Le passage inoffensif des navires de guerre étrangers dans la mer territoriale. Portée du régime contenu dans la Convention des Nations Unies sur le droit de la mer* [Innocent Passage of Foreign Warships in the Territorial Sea. The Scope of the Regime Contained in the United Nations Convention on the Law of the Sea] (Bruxelles: Établissements Bruylant, 2007), 62–66; Carlos Espaliú Berdud and Rafael Casado Raigón, "El paso inocente de buques de guerra extranjeros por mar territorial: alcance del régimen de la CNUDM [The Innocent Passage of Foreign Warships in the Territorial Sea: The Scope of the UNCLOS Regime]," *Revista Española de Derecho Internacional* [Spanish Journal of International Law] 57 (2005): 790 ("*REDI*"); Francioni, "Peacetime Use of Force," 209–10; Jimenez Kwast, "Maritime Law Enforcement," 61; Tullio Treves, "La navigation [Navigation]," in René-Jean Dupuy and Daniel Vignes (eds.), *Traité du Nouveau droit de la mer* [Treatise on the New Law of the Sea] (Paris: Éditions Économica, 1985), 758.

> beyond what is reasonable and necessary in the circumstances. Considerations of humanity must apply in the law of the sea, as they do in other areas of international law.[55]

The application of these principles in maritime law enforcement will be discussed in the third part of this chapter. Suffice it to say at this point that the violations of these principles could not be excused by the pretext that the purpose of the use of force is to respond to alleged violations of the Convention, including non-innocent passage.[56] If the warship has not used deadly force, these requirements would exclude the use of deadly force with the intent of sinking a vessel or of causing serious physical injury.[57] What forceful measures aimed at compelling a foreign warship to leave the territorial sea would meet the *Saiga* principles? Moore cites as examples the placing of obstructions in the water to impede or direct

[55] *M/V "SAIGA" (No. 2) (Saint Vincent and the Grenadines v. Guinea), Judgment, ITLOS Reports 1999*, 61, para. 155, https://www.itlos.org/fileadmin/itlos/documents/cases/case_no_2/published/C2-J-1_Jul_99.pdf, accessed 9 June 2019. This formulation had been anticipated by Ivan Shearer, "The Development of International Law with respect to the Law Enforcement Roles of Navies and Coast Guards in Peacetime," in Michael N. Schmitt and Leslie C. Green (eds.), *The Law of Armed Conflict: Into the Next Millennium* (Newport, RI: Naval War College, 1998), 440–41, https://ia801601.us.archive.org/1/items/lawofarmedconfli71schm/lawofarmedconfli71schm.pdf, accessed 9 June 2019. For commentaries on the "saga of the Saiga," see Louise de la Fayette, "International Tribunal for the Law of the Sea: *The M/V "Saiga" (No. 2) Case (St. Vincent and the Grenadines v. Guinea), Judgment*," *International and Comparative Law Quarterly* 49 (2000): 467–76; Louise de La Fayette, "ITLOS and the Saga of the Saiga: Peaceful Settlement of a Law of the Sea Dispute," *International Journal of Marine and Coastal Law* 15 (2000): 355–92; Malcolm D. Evans and Vaughan Lowe, "The M/V Saiga: the First Case in the International Tribunal for the Law of the Sea," *International and Comparative Law Quarterly* 48 (1999): 187–99; Bernard H. Oxman, "The M/V 'Saiga' (Saint Vincent and the Grenadines v. Guinea). ITLOS Case No. 1," *American Journal of International Law* 92 (1998): 278–82 ("*AJIL*").

[56] Oxman, "The Regime of Warships," 815.

[57] Francioni, "Peacetime Use of Force," 220.

passage, shouldering of the foreign warship,[58] and the firing of warning shots.[59]

There have been few instances of disputes involving violations by sovereign immune vessels of the requirements of innocent passage and of the laws and regulations of the coastal State relating to innocent passage that have been brought before international tribunals—all the more reason why particular attention should be paid to State practice, which reveals that States avoid the use of force as far as possible and condemn the use of force through collisions in response to such violations.

B. State Practice: The Avoidance of the Use of Force and the Condemnation of Collisions

When a Soviet submarine ran aground in 1981 in its security zone, Sweden refrained from using force against the submarine. Sweden's restraint did not leave it without protection, for it negotiated with the USSR a more flexible interpretation of the sovereign immunity of the submarine as a condition of its investigation into the incident. In 1988, the USSR resorted to force by "bumping" US warships that the USSR accused of violating its laws and regulations relating to innocent passage, prompting protests from the US. The incident led to negotiation of an agreement between the two States that reaffirmed the customary rule embodied in Article 30 of the Convention.

Submarines are the warships that are most likely to violate the requirements of innocent passage, due to their capability of carrying out covert operations. During the Cold War, submarine intrusions into Swedish and Norwegian territorial waters were the most serious type of non-innocent

[58] The US Department of Defense defines shouldering as "maneuvering a vessel in contact with the opposing vessel to cause the opposing vessel to turn away." It is undertaken with the intent of minimizing damage to the opposing vessel. "Shouldering (US DoD Definition)," *Military Factory* (2021), https://www.militaryfactory.com/dictionary/military-terms-defined.php?term_id=4876, accessed 19 October 2021.

[59] Moore, *Freedom of Navigation*, Chapter 4, p. 115. As we shall see bellow, the *Commander's Handbook on the Law of Naval Operations*, published by the US Navy, the US Marine Corps, and the US Coast Guard, clarifies that under international law, warning shots do not constitute a use of force.

passage; the submarines often penetrated completely through the territorial sea and deep into internal waters.[60] When they were detected, it was often not possible to identify their nationality, but one such vessel, Soviet W-137 submarine, belonging to the "Whiskey" class, became famous when it ran aground in a Swedish fjord at 2157H on 27 October 1981, 15 km from the most important naval base in the south of the country and located in a military security zone.[61] Sweden protested that the submarine had intentionally violated Swedish territory in order to undertake illegal activities and suspected that the submarine was carrying nuclear weapons. Sweden rejected Soviet explanations implying distress that forced the submarine to enter the area as well as the Soviet request to allow Soviet vessels to refloat the submarine. Sweden did not release W-137 until the USSR had apologized, agreed to pay for the cost of the refloating operation, and agreed to an investigation.

The Swedish reaction should serve as a model for States, like China, that seek to justify a resort to force on the basis of violations of laws and regulations relating to innocent passage. Froman and Berg believe that Sweden would have been justified in using force to protect itself against the W-137, either for engaging in non-innocent passage or for violation of its borders and unauthorized stay in its territory.[62] Even so, any use of force on Sweden's part would have been constrained by the sovereign immunity of warships under customary international law as well as the international law governing the use of force. Kraska reminds us that the mere presence of a submarine, even combined with the suspicion of spying, would have been insufficient grounds to destroy the submarine. The unauthorized entry of the submarine could be considered analogous

[60] Froman, "Uncharted Waters," 679 and note 247.

[61] Unless otherwise indicated, this account is summarized from Aleth Manin, "L'échouement du Whiskey 137 dans les eaux suédoises [The Stranding of Whisky 137 in Swedish Waters]," *AFDI* 27 (1981): 689–710, https://www.persee.fr/docAsPDF/afdi_0066-3085_1981_num_27_1_2468.pdf, accessed 9 June 2019. For information on the Whiskey class of submarines, see "The Whiskey Class," *Weapons and Warfare: History and Hardware of Warfare* (10 June 2017), https://weaponsandwarfare.com/2017/06/10/the-whiskey-class/, accessed 9 June 2019. For foreign submarine incursions in the post-Cold War period, see Nils-Ove Jansson, "Submarine Intrusions in Swedish Waters," *Handlingar och Tidskrift. Kungl Krigsvetenskapsakademien. Proceedings and Journal. Royal Swedish Academy of War Sciences* 1 (2016): 52–59, http://kkrva.se/hot/2016:1/jansson_subm_instrusions.pdf, accessed 9 June 2019.

[62] Manin, "L'échouement," 691–92; Berg, "Das sowjetische U-Boot 137," 302.

to illegal overflight, which is not considered an armed attack or an act of aggression, following the 1960 precedent of the US U-2 flying over Soviet territory.[63]

The fact remains that Sweden did not resort to the use of force. It did not seize the W-137. Furthermore, in order to avoid creating the impression that it was forcibly boarding the vessel, the Swedish authorities left the submarine where it had run aground, refraining from refloating it or from towing it to a dock. Sweden even went to the extent of not intervening to help the W-137 when very strong winds caused it to list, until it received distress calls from the submarine.[64] Nor were any coercive measures directed against the crew.[65]

But Sweden was not left without any measures of protection against the violation of its laws and regulations relating to innocent passage by W-137. The USSR had insisted that a warship enjoyed total immunity from the jurisdiction of any other State except the flag State, wherever the warship might be found and whatever the breaches of which it was accused.[66] From the Soviet perspective, the proper and only course of action would have been to require the submarine to leave Swedish territorial waters immediately. This interpretation of the principle of sovereign immunity was unacceptable to Sweden, first because it could not be applied in the case of a vessel that had run aground and could not set out to sea using its own means, and second, because the breaches imputable to the W-137 were extremely grave. Sweden insisted on negotiating derogations from the principle of sovereign immunity to enable it to carry out its investigation into the incident, derogations that the USSR was finally compelled to accept.

An exclusively Swedish Commission of Inquiry was established to investigate the incident "among mariners," the report of which was submitted only to the Swedish government. The commander of the W-137 was forced to give testimony on the incident, although the place where the testimony was heard was the result of a compromise. For the USSR, he should have been heard on board the W-137. For its part,

[63] Kraska, "Putting Your Head," 229, 236–37; Berg, "Das sowjetische U-Boot 137," 300.

[64] Manin, "L'échouement," 703, note 66.

[65] *Ibid.*, 708.

[66] *Ibid.*, 702.

Sweden insisted that the hearing should take place anywhere but on the W-137. As a compromise, he gave his testimony on board a Swedish vessel in Swedish internal waters but outside the military security zone. Sweden was able to inspect the technical facilities and the navigational documents of the W-137, but when the Soviet commander refused a request that the Swedish team be allowed to enter the torpedo chamber, the team did not insist. Sweden rejected USSR requests to allow Soviet vessels to refloat the W-137. In the end it was Swedish vessels that refloated the W-137, the cost of the operation being borne by the USSR.[67]

The W-137 incident shows that it is possible for a coastal State to respond to violations by foreign warships of the requirements of innocent passage and of its laws and regulations relating to innocent passage without resorting to the use of force, while at the same time negotiating with the flag State derogations from the principle of the sovereign immunity of warships.

That the prohibition of the use of force extends to the prohibition of deliberate collisions is confirmed by the "bumping" incident of 12 February 1988, in the course of which two Soviet warships intentionally "bumped" (defined as "physically nudging away from shore" or "coming more less violently in contact with") the USS *Caron*, a heavily armed destroyer configured for intelligence gathering, and the USS *Yorktown*, a heavily-armed guided missile cruiser.[68] The two US warships had entered the Soviet territorial sea off the southwest tip of the Crimean peninsula in the Black Sea, following a route that was not included among the "routes ordinarily used for international navigation" that the Soviet Law on the State Boundary 1982 had predesignated as routes for the innocent passage of warships. Within 15 minutes of the two US warships' entry into the Black Sea, they were shadowed by two Soviet naval vessels, the *Bezzavetny* and the *SKR-6*. About eight miles off the southern tip of Crimea, between Sevastopol and Yalta, the Soviet vessels assumed positions between the US warships and the Crimean coastline and began

[67] *Ibid.*, 704–8.

[68] The first definition of "bumping" is provided by John C. Hitt, Jr., "Oceans Law and Superpower Relations: The Bumping of the *Yorktown* and the *Caron* in the Black Sea," *Virginia Journal of International Law* 29 (1989): 713, note 1. The second definition is given by John W. Rolph, "Freedom of Navigation and the Black Sea Bumping Incident: How 'Innocent' Must Innocent Passage Be?" *Military Law Review* 135 (1992): 144, note 28. The following account is summarized from the article by Rolph. See also Bou Franch, "El derecho de paso inocente," 126.

to "parallel" the movements of the latter. Each Soviet warship maneuvered to within 50 meters of the US warship that it was shadowing. The commander of the *Bezzavetny* radioed the *Yorktown* that it had entered the Soviet territorial sea and that his vessel was authorized to strike the US warship. The *Yorktown* commander acknowledged the communication but maintained its course and speed, as did the *Caron*. The Soviets issued another radio warning, which was unacknowledged by the two US warships. Each US warship was then bumped on the port side by the Soviet vessel shadowing it. Overall damage to the US warships was negligible, since the Soviet vessels were significantly smaller. There was even speculation at the time that the USSR had intentionally dispatched warships one-seventh the size of the US warships to minimize the potential for actual hostilities.[69] The US warships remained under escort until they reentered the high seas.

The US protested that the Soviets had deliberately rammed US vessels that were engaged in innocent passage. The USSR claimed that the US warships violated its border, did not react to warning signals, did not make suggested changes in their course, went a considerable distance into Soviet territorial waters, and undertook dangerous maneuvering that led to the collision. When the US Navy produced videotapes that had recorded both bumping episodes and demonstrated that neither US warship had been "maneuvering dangerously," the USSR shifted tack and contended that the passage of the two warships was illegal because they did not observe the coastal State's laws and regulations relating to safety and good order and they were not innocent because they were navigationally unnecessary.[70]

The incident prompted negotiations between the two States that concluded with the adoption of a "Joint Statement With Attached Uniform Interpretation of Rules of International Law Governing Innocent Passage."[71] Paragraph 4 of the "Joint Statement" provided that if a

[69] Rolph, "Freedom of Navigation," 144, note 30.

[70] *Ibid.*, 144–45.

[71] Union of Soviet Socialist Republics-United States: Joint Statement With Attached Uniform Interpretation of Rules of International Law Governing Innocent Passage, entered into at Jackson Hole, Wyoming, 23 September 1989, https://cil.nus.edu.sg/wp-content/uploads/formidable/18/1989-USA-USSR-Joint-Statement-with-Attached-Uniform-Interpretation-of-Rues-of-International-Law-Governing-Innocent-Passage.pdf, accessed 9 June 2019.

coastal State questioned whether the particular passage of a ship through its territorial sea is innocent, it should inform the ship of the reasons why it questions the innocence of the passage and provide the ship an opportunity to clarify its intentions or correct its conduct in a reasonably short period of time. Paragraph 5 stipulated that a warship exercising the right of innocent passage should comply with all the laws and regulations of the coastal State relating to innocent passage in conformity with international law as reflected in Articles 21, 22, 23, and 25 of the Convention. If the warship violates such laws or regulations or renders its passage not innocent and does not take corrective action upon request, the coastal State may request it to leave the territorial sea, as set forth in Article 30 of the Convention, in which case the warship should do so immediately, according to paragraph 7. All disputes regarding innocent passage through the territorial sea should be settled through diplomatic channels or other agreed means, according to paragraph 8.

The US-USSR Uniform Statement is noteworthy in that it prescribes the same course of action for the coastal State in two situations: one in which the foreign warship violates its rules and regulations, corresponding to Article 25 of the Convention, and the other in which the foreign warship undertakes non-innocent passage, under the terms of Article 19 of the Convention. That course of action is to require that the foreign warship leaves the territorial sea, a request that the foreign warship must comply with immediately. The distinction between the two situations proposed by Froman and implying that the coastal State had the right to take different courses of action depending on the situation is not accepted by the two States. Furthermore, the US-USSR Uniform Statement stipulates that any disputes regarding innocent passage through the territorial sea, which might arise if the foreign warship refuses to leave the territorial sea when requested to do so, should be settled exclusively through peaceful means. In this manner, "bumping" or any other use of force is clearly excluded. Finally, the US-USSR Uniform Interpretation is remarkable in that it invoked several articles of the Convention at a time when neither of the two States was a party to the Convention. It was only on 12 March 1997 that Russia, the successor State of the USSR, ratified the Convention; the US, to this date, still has not ratified the Convention. That they were guided by the provisions of the Convention, as indicated in the Joint Statement accompanying the Uniform Interpretation, reflects the belief, at least on the US side, that the provisions of the Convention that they invoked were reflective of the customary law of innocent passage and for this reason are binding even on States that were not parties to the Convention.[72] As for Russia, there is no doubt that as a party to the Convention, it has been bound by all its provisions (and not just the provisions on innocent passage) since 1997.

This brief survey of State practice should suffice to demonstrate that the use of force against a foreign warship that is accused by a coastal State of engaging in non-innocent passage or violating its laws and regulations relating to innocent passage is prohibited, unless it complies with the provisions governing the use of force under general international law and as embodied in the UN Charter.

So far, our attention has focused on the question of whether the use of force against warships—even those that are allegedly in breach of the requirements of innocent passage or the laws and regulations of the coastal State relating to innocent passage—is permissible. If, against all logic, no account is taken of the immunity of warships, one must still confront the question of whether the Chinese vessels were justified in using force in the course of ordinary law enforcement.

III. The Incidents of 28 April and 26 May 2012: The Use of Force in Maritime Law Enforcement

The CSIL argues that the COLREGS apply only to normal navigation and to questions of collision arising in normal circumstances. In this view, the COLREGS do not apply when law enforcement vessels or warships take necessary measures to approach, intercept, or board another vessel for law enforcement purposes.[73] It pointed out that a law enforcement vessel pursuing a foreign vessel might be forced to cross ahead of the vessel, a maneuver that is clearly in conflict with COLREGS rules, such as maintaining "safe speed" and keeping a "safe distance."[74]

In support of its view, the CSIL cites State practice and international case law. The CSIL finds it significant that in the US, Coast Guard vessels are entitled to take all necessary measures, including approaching and intercepting vessels, for law enforcement purposes.[75] The CSIL invokes

[72] Hitt, "Oceans Law," 715.

[73] CSIL, "The South China Sea Arbitration Awards," 599–600, paras. 840, 841, 843.

[74] *Ibid.*, 601, para. 843.

[75] *Ibid.*, 602, para. 845.

for the international level the judgment of the ITLOS in *Saiga (No. 2)* and quoted the relevant (but not the entire) passage:

> Although the Convention does not contain express provisions on the use of force in the arrest of ships, international law, which is applicable by virtue of article 293 of the Convention, requires that the use of force must be avoided as far as possible and, where force is unavoidable, it must not go beyond what is is reasonable and necessary in the circumstances.[76]

The CSIL then quoted some (not all) guidelines to maritime law enforcement activities laid down by the ITLOS:

> These principles have been followed over the years in law enforcement operations at sea. The normal practice used to stop a ship at sea is first to give an auditory or visual signal to stop, using internationally recognized signals. Where this does not succeed, a variety of actions may be taken, including the firing of shots across the bows of the ship. It is only after the appropriate actions fail that the pursuing vessel may, as a last resort, use force.[77]

It is understandable that the CSIL cited the *Saiga* case. As the ITLOS itself noted, the Convention does not contain express provisions on the use of force in the arrest of ships.[78] The principles it laid down in the *Saiga* case governing the use of force in maritime law enforcement, principles have been variously described as "authoritative articulation" and customary international law.[79] Unfortunately, when quoting from the

[76] *M/V "SAIGA" (No. 2) (Saint Vincent and the Grenadines v. Guinea), Judgment*, 61, para. 155, quoted in CSIL, 606, para. 855.

[77] *M/V "SAIGA" (No. 2)*, 61, para. 156, quoted in CSIL, 606, para. 855.

[78] *Ibid.*, para. 155. On this point, see Shearer, "The Development," 441; Matteo Tondini, "The Use of Force in the Course of Maritime Law Enforcement Operations," *Journal on the Use of Force and International Law* 4 (2017): 254.

[79] The first view is held by Jimenez Kwast, "Maritime Law Enforcement," 56, and the second, by Cameron Moore, "The Use of Force," in Robin Warner and Stuart Kaye (eds.), *Routledge Handbook of Maritime Regulation and Enforcement* (Milton Park, Abingdon, Oxon: Routledge, 2016), 38. For the debate on the use of force in maritime law enforcement, see also David H. Anderson, "Some Aspects on the Use of Force in Maritime Law Enforcement Operations," in Bernard H. Oxman et al. (eds.), *International Courts and the Development of International Law: Essays in Honour of Tullio Treves* (The Hague: T.M.C. Asser Press, 2013), 233–43; M. Paz Andrés Saenz de Santa María, "Incidentes

ITLOS *Saiga* Judgment, the CSIL omitted two important sentences. From the first passage, it dropped the following sentence: "Considerations of humanity must apply in the law of the sea, as they do in other areas of international law." From the second passage, it deleted the following sentence: "Even then, appropriate warning must be issued to the ship and all efforts should be made to ensure that life is not endangered."[80]

It is also understandable that the CSIL omitted these sentences, for the Chinese official vessels violated both requirements: they failed to give warning of their action to the Philippine vessels and their conduct showed disregard for the safety of human life. In so doing, they seem to have neglected "considerations of humanity." The Chinese vessels' conduct in contravention of the *Saiga* principles and of the COLREGS cannot be excused by invoking State practice, which shows that States seek to avoid collisions even when resorting to force in the course of maritime law enforcement operations. This is the conclusion that may be derived from the Canadian response to a European complaint that its law enforcement vessels brushed against a Spanish fishing vessel that they were pursuing in 1996, and the prosecution and sentencing by the Italian authorities of the commander of an Italian naval vessel that collided with a vessel transporting illegal migrants from Albania in 1997.

A. Warning Shots and Considerations of Humanity in Maritime Law Enforcement

It is not even necessary to enter into the debate whether the Chinese vessels, on 28 April and 26 May 2012, employed force as a last resort. In the scenario most favorable to them, which assumes that force was indeed a last resort, they were still not relieved of the duty to warn the Philippine vessels of their resort to force and of the duty to have regard for the safety of human life.

pesqueros y recurso a la fuerza. Estudio del apresamiento de buques pesqueros como medida de ejecución en el régimen internacional de pesquerías [Fishing Incidents and the Resort to Force. A Study of the Arrest of Fishing Vessels as a Measure of Execution in the International Regime of Fisheries]," *REDI* 41 (1989): 7–41; Francioni, "Peacetime Use of Force," 218–20; Donald R. Rothwell and Tim Stephens, *The International Law of the Sea* (2nd ed.; Oxford: Hart Publishing, 2016), 232–33; Shearer, "The Development," 440–41.

80 *M/V "SAIGA" (No. 2)*, 61, para. 156.

US practice, by which the CSIL seems to set great store, is explicit on the need to fire warning shots before using force. The *Commander's Handbook on the Law of Naval Operations*, published by the US Navy, the US Marine Corps, and the US Coast Guard, under the heading of Use of Force in Maritime Law Enforcement, defines a warning shot as "a signal - usually to warn an offending vessel to stop or maneuver in a particular manner or risk the employment of disabling fire or more severe measures." The *Commander's Handbook* clarifies that under international law, warning shots do not constitute a use of force. It is only if firing shots are not heeded that they may be followed by disabling fire—"firing under controlled conditions into a noncompliant vessel's rudder, propeller area/outboard engine, or engine room for the sole purpose of stopping it…."[81]

The firing of warning shots is also required before resort to the use of force under Canada's Coastal Fisheries Protection Regulations Amendment of 25 May 1994, which implements the Act to Amend the Coastal Fisheries Protection Act of 12 May 1994. The purpose of the latter Act is to enable Canada "to take urgent action necessary to prevent further destruction" of the straddling fish stocks on the Grand Banks of Newfoundland and "to permit their rebuilding."[82] As conservation and management measures may be undermined by the activities of foreign fishing vessels in the area, the Regulations authorize a protection officer to use force in order to arrest the master of a foreign fishing vessel committing an offense under the Act, after he/she has considered all less violent means reasonable in the circumstances to stop the foreign fishing vessel and decided that those means would not suffice to stop the vessel. Before using force, the protection officer must

[81] US Navy, US Marine Corps, and US Coast Guard, *Commander's Handbook on the Law of Naval Operations Edition July 2007*, Doc. NWP1-14 M/MCWP 5-12.1/COMDTPUB P5800.7A ([Washington, DC:] Department of the Navy, Office of the Chief of Naval Operations and Headquarters, US Marine Corps, Department of Homeland Security, and US Coast Guard, 2007), 3–16, http://www.jag.navy.mil/documents/NWP_1-14M_Commanders_Handbook.pdf, accessed 9 June 2019.

[82] "An Act to Amend the Coastal Fisheries Protection Act [Assented to 12 May 1994]," Section 5.1, Annexe 14 in *Fisheries Jurisdiction (Spain v. Canada), Mémoire du Royaume d'Espagne (Compétence) (Septembre 1995)* [Memorial of the Kingdom of Spain (Jurisdiction) (September 1995)], International Court of Justice, 147–48, https://www.icj-cij.org/files/case-related/96/096-19950928-WRI-01-01-BI.pdf, accessed 9 June 2019. The *Memorial* is available only in French.

(a) fire a warning shot or. if the protection officer considers it advisable, a series of warning shots in the vicinity of the foreign fishing vessel but at a safe distance and give the master or other person on board a reasonable opportunity to bring to; and
(b) signal the foreign fishing vessel by Signal SQ 1 and give the master or other person on board a reasonable opportunity to bring to.[83]

The Signal SQ 1 is taken from the International Code of Signals, approved by the International Maritime Organization ("IMO"), and means "You should stop, or otherwise I shall open fire on you."[84] The use of warning shots at a safe distance is a well-known international practice, designed to minimize risks to the safety of life at sea.[85] It should be noted here that the Canadian regulations also provide for the use of Signals taken from the International Code to signal the vessel to stop (Signal L, "you should stop your vessel instantly") and to signal to the vessel that the protection officer will board it (Signal SQ 3, "You should stop, or heave to. I am going to board you").[86]

The Soviet vessels that were shadowing US naval vessels in Soviet territorial waters in the Black Sea in 1988 did not fire warning shots to signal their intentions, perhaps because the US vessels involved were warships, but they communicated twice with the US naval vessels, to inform them that they had entered Soviet territorial waters and that the Soviet vessels

[83] "Coastal Fisheries Protection Regulations, Amendment," 25 May 1994, Annexe 17 in *Fisheries Jurisdiction (Spain v. Canada), Mémoire du Royaume d'Espagne*, 155–56.

[84] *International Code of Signals As adopted by the Fourth Assembly of the Inter-Governmental Maritime Consultative Organization in 1965 For Visual, Sound, and Radio Communications United States Edition, 1969 (Revised 2003)*, Publ. 102 (Washington, DC: Government Printing Office, 2003), 83, http://www.seasources.net/PDF/PUB102.pdf, accessed 9 June 2019.

[85] *Fisheries Jurisdiction (Spain v. Canada)*, Verbatim record 1998/11 (11 June 1998), International Court of Justice, 59, para. 35, https://www.icj-cij.org/files/case-related/96/096-19980611-ORA-01-00-BI.pdf, accessed 9 June 2019.

[86] Coastal Fisheries Protection Regulations, Amendment, 156. The Canadian Law and Regulations were severely criticized by at least one foreign observer for authorizing the use of force by Canadian authorities against foreign fishing vessels on the high seas. See Laurent Lucchini, "La loi canadienne du 12 mai 1994: la logique extrême de la théorie du droit préférentiel de l'Etat côtier en haute mer au titre des stocks chevauchants [The Canadian Law of 12 May 1994: The Extreme Logic of the Theory of the Preferential Right of the Coastal State on the High Seas with Respect to Straddling Stocks]," *AFDI* 40 (1994): 864–75, https://www.persee.fr/doc/afdi_0066-3085_1994_num_40_1_3226, accessed 9 June 2019.

had orders to strike the US naval vessels if the latter did not leave the Soviet territorial sea. In April and May 2012, the Chinese vessels made no effort to warn the Philippine vessels of their action through warning shots or in any other way. Technical reasons could not have possibly explained the absence of communication. As the International Code of Signals indicates, there are many methods of signaling: through flags, flashing lights, using Morse signals, sound signaling, using Morse signals; voice over loud hailer,[87] radiotelegraphy,[88] or radiotelephony.[89] Nor did the Chinese authorities communicate with the Philippine authorities in Manila or even the Philippine representatives in Beijing, to signal that the Chinese vessels would employ force on 28 April or 26 May if the Philippine vessels did not leave on those days.[90]

At the international level, the failure to issue a warning signal is one reason that may be considered in judging that the use of force by a law enforcement authority against a foreign commercial vessel is excessive. The *"M/V Saiga"* case concerned an oil tanker, which was registered in

[87] A "loud-hailer" in British English is a portable loudspeaker having a built-in amplifier and microphone. In the US and Canada, it is called a "bullhorn." *Collins English Dictionary* (Glasgow: HarperCollins Publishers, 2019). https://www.collinsdictionary.com/dictionary/english/loud-hailer, accessed 9 June 2019.

[88] "Radiotelegraphy" in British English refers to a type of telegraphy in which messages (usually in Morse code) are transmitted by radio waves; its use is no longer widespread as it has been superseded by satellite technology. It is also called "wireless telegraphy." *Collins English Dictionary*, https://www.collinsdictionary.com/dictionary/english/radiotelegraphy, accessed 9 June 2019.

[89] A "radiotelephone" in British English, also called "radiophone" or "wireless telephone," is a device for communication by means of radio waves rather than by transmitting along wires or cables, *Collins English Dictionary*, https://www.collinsdictionary.com/dictionary/english/radiotelephone, accessed 9 June 2019.

[90] One cannot help but recall the complaint of counsel for Spain during hearings at the ICJ concerning Canada's use of force against Spanish fishing vessels in March 1995:

> Canada has not put in one shred of evidence that warnings were given to the *Estai* [the Spanish fishing vessel]; or to Spain; or to Spain and the *Estai*; or to [the European Commission in] Brussels and Spain; or to the owners of the *Estai*; or to the *Estai*, to Brussels, and Spain. Not a shred. Not a single radio transmission. Not a single fax. Not a single telex. Nothing.

Fisheries Jurisdiction (Spain v. Canada), Verbatim record 1998/10 (10 June 1998), 18, https://www.icj-cij.org/files/case-related/96/096-19980610-ORA-01-00-BI.pdf, accessed 9 June 2019.

Saint Vincent and the Grenadines and was engaged in selling gas oil as bunker and occasionally water to fishing and other vessels off the coast of West Africa. On 28 October 1997, when it was at a point south of the southern limit of the Exclusive Economic Zone of Guinea, awaiting the arrival of fishing vessels to which it was to supply gas oil, a Guinean patrol boat fired shots at it, injuring four members of the crew, before taking control of the vessel.[91] Guinea claimed that the patrol boat had sent out radio messages to *Saiga* ordering it to stop and that these were ignored. Guinea also claimed that another patrol boat gave auditory and visual signals to *Saiga* when it came within sight and hearing of the latter. Guinean officers who arrested the ship testified that the patrol boat sounded its siren and switched on its blue revolving signals.[92] On the other hand, the master of *Saiga* who was on the bridge at the time and another crew member who was on deck both categorically denied that such signals had been given. The ITLOS found that the Guinean evidence did not support the Guinean claims.[93] The ITLOS concluded that there was no excuse for the firing by the Guinean officers at the ship with live ammunition "without issuing any of the signals and warnings required by international law and practice."[94]

It goes without saying that it is not sufficient to issue signals and warnings for the use of force to be legitimate. As the ITLOS put it, when force is finally employed, all efforts should be made to ensure that life is not endangered.[95] Once again, it is appropriate to refer to US practice. According to US Navy Regulations, when domestic and international rules and regulations for regulating traffic and preventing collisions on the high seas, in inland waters, or in the air are not applicable to naval vessels

[91] *M/V "SAIGA" (No. 2)*, 28, paras. 31–33; *The M/V "SAIGA" Case (Saint Vincent and the Grenadines v. Guinea), Prompt Release*, ITLOS, *Application submitted by Saint Vincent and the Grenadines* (11 November 1997), 6, para. 1, https://www.itlos.org/fileadmin/itlos/documents/cases/case_no_1/application_without_annexes__svg_131197_eng.pdf, accessed 9 June 2019.

[92] *M/V "SAIGA" (No. 2)*, 58, para. 143.

[93] *Ibid.*, 60, para. 148.

[94] *Ibid.*, 63, para. 157.

[95] *Ibid.*, 62, para. 156.

and to aircraft, these should be operated "with due regard for the safety of others."[96]

Sweden's response to the spotting of foreign submarines in Harsfjarden, near the top-secret naval base of Musko, on 1 October 1982, nearly a year after W-137 had run aground in its internal waters, demonstrates regard for the safety of life. Initially, a depth charge was dropped from a helicopter, to signal to the submarine that it had been discovered and that it should surface; the area was searched by boats and helicopters. On the following day, four more depth charges were dropped and metal barriers were placed across the two main entrances to Harsfjarden to prevent conventional submarines from leaving. On the following days, after further indications of submarine presence were recorded, 14 more depth charges were dropped. On the sixth day, minesweepers, submarine rescue vessels, anticraft units, and military police were brought into action to prepare for mine detonation. On the seventh day, the Navy dropped six depth charges. Only then were three mines detonated in the vicinity of Malsten, for the purpose of forcing the submarine to surface, not to destroy it. The personnel in charge of the detonation deliberately refrained from automatically detonating the mines and attempted instead a more flexible, more sophisticated technique of delayed detonation after indication. Recognizing the risks to human life posed by the detonation, the Swedish authorities prepared an internment center for any rescued crew and alerted hospitals to prepare to receive possible injured seamen who would be suffering from detonation shock. The search for submarines continued until 1 November in the area as well as in other areas to the north and to the south, in the course of which more controlled mines were laid and depth charges dropped, but the search proved fruitless.[97]

It was the failure to ensure the safety of life that motivated the two earlier decisions cited in the *Saiga* Judgment that the use of force in law enforcement was excessive. The first case arose from the sinking on 22

[96] US Department of the Navy, *United States Navy Regulations 1990*, Doc. PCN 50100370000 (Washington, DC: Department of the Navy, 1990), p. 108, Article 1139, para. 2, https://www.marines.mil/Portals/59/Publications/United%20States%20Navy%20Regulations.pdf?ver=2012-10-11-164138-043, accessed 9 June 2019.

[97] Roma Sadurska, "Foreign Submarines in Swedish Waters: The Erosion of an International Norm," *Yale Journal of International Law* 10 (1984): 37–38, 43, http://digitalcommons.law.yale.edu/cgi/viewcontent.cgi?article=1314&context=yjil, accessed 9 June 2019.

March 1929 of the vessel *I'm Alone*, a British ship of Canadian registry, on the high seas in the Gulf of Mexico, by a US revenue cutter.[98] The *I'm Alone* was engaged in rum running during the Prohibition period in the US.[99] At the time of its sinking, it was carrying liquor from Belize (British Honduras) to locations in the Gulf of Mexico, near Louisiana. Under the terms of a 1924 treaty between the UK and the US, the former had agreed not to object to the latter's boarding, searching, seizing, and bringing into port of suspected vessels flying the British flag within certain limits and under certain conditions. The two-man Commission to which the dispute was submitted decided that the US was authorized to use necessary and reasonable force to board, search, seize, and bring the ship into port. If the sinking occurred accidentally as a result, then the US would not be held responsible. However, the intentional sinking of the ship was unlawful.[100] In Shearer's view, the Commission's conclusions meant that the State undertaking law enforcement must weigh the gravity of the offense (in this case, smuggling of liquor) against the value of human life.[101]

The second case involved the British-flagged trawler, the *Red Crusader*, which was suspected of illegally fishing in May 1961 in the Faroe Islands, "a self-governing nation with extensive autonomous powers and responsibilities within the Kingdom of Denmark."[102] The

[98] A revenue cutter was a small sailing vessel, cutter rigged and armed, manned by the Royal Navy and used for prevention of smuggling and for maintaining order on the fishing grounds; it has been superseded by mechanically propelled fishery protection vessels. Layton et al., *Dictionary*, 316.

[99] "Prohibition" refers to the legal prevention of the manufacture, sale, and transportation of alcoholic beverages in the US from 1920 to 1933 under the terms of the Eighteenth Amendment. Editors of Encyclopaedia Britannica, "Prohibition United States History [1920–1933]," *Encyclopaedia Britannica* (2019), https://www.britannica.com/event/Prohibition-United-States-history-1920-1933, accessed 9 June 2019.

[100] *S.S. "I'm Alone" Case (Canada/United States, 30 June 1933 and 5 January 1935), Reports of International Arbitral Awards*, vol. III (New York: United Nations, 2006), 1609–18, http://legal.un.org/riaa/cases/vol_III/1609-1618.pdf, accessed 9 June 2019. For commentaries, see William C. Dennis, "The Sinking of the *I'm Alone*," *AJIL* 23 (1929): 351–62; G. G. Fitzmaurice, "The Case of the *I'm Alone*," *British Yearbook of International Law* 17 (1936): 82–111; Charles Cheney Hyde, "The Adjustment of the *I'm Alone* Case," *AJIL* 29 (1935): 296–301.

[101] Shearer, "The Development," 441.

[102] Føroya landsstýri, *Faroe Islands: Government* (2019), https://www.faroeislands.fo/government-politics/, accessed 9 June 2019.

Danish vessel *Niels Ebbesen* arrested it and ordered it to follow the Danish vessel to the nearest port. After initially following the *Niels Ebbesen*, the *Red Crusader* decided to flee to Aberdeen, taking with them two Danish officers who had boarded the vessel. After firing warning shots over four minutes, to no avail, the *Niels Ebbesen* fired at the *Red Crusader*, within a space of 13 minutes, 8 machine-gun shots at the ship's scanner, 21 machine-gun shots at the ship's mast, a round of 40 mm gun shots at the masthead light, a round of 40 mm gun shots at the mast, two rounds of 40 mm gun at the stern (resulting in some damage), and a round of 10 mm gun at the stern. The three-man Commission of Inquiry to which the dispute was submitted decided that the Danish vessel had exceeded the legitimate use of armed force, for firing without warning of solid gun shot and creating danger to human life on board the *Red Crusader*, without proved necessity, by firing at the vessel. The Commission of Inquiry acknowledged that the *Red Crusader*'s escape, the seclusion on board of two Danish officers and the ship's refusal to stop could explain the resentment felt by the pursuing vessel's commander, but it believed that the circumstances did not justify such violent action. In the Commission's view, other means should have been attempted that, "if duly persisted in," might have persuaded the *Red Crusader* to stop.[103] Francioni concludes from this that international law prohibits the use of force in the pursuit of an offending fishing vessel unless required by self-defense.[104]

In the *Saiga* case, the ITLOS found that Guinean officers who boarded the ship appeared to have attached little or no importance not only to the safety of the ship but also to the safety of the persons on board. They fired indiscriminately on deck, despite the fact that there had been no resistance to boarding and there was no evidence of the use or threat of force from the crew.[105]

[103] *The Red Crusader Case (Commission of Enquiry, Denmark—United Kingdom, 1962)*, *Reports of International Arbitral Awards*, vol. 29 (New York: United Nations, 2012), 521–39, http://legal.un.org/riaa/cases/vol_XXIX/521-539.pdf, accessed 9 June 2019. For a commentary, see Gérard Timsit, "Le fonctionnement de la procédure d'enquête dans l'affaire du Red Crusader [The Functioning of the Procedure of Inquiry in the Red Crusader Case]," *AFDI* 9 (1963): 460–72, https://www.persee.fr/doc/afdi_0066-3085_1963_num_9_1_1040, accessed 9 June 2019.

[104] Francioni, "Peacetime Use of Force," 205.

[105] *M/V "SAIGA" (No. 2)*, 63, para. 158.

Less well-known than these instances of State practice and international caselaw is the practice of States when their vessels fail to comply with the COLREGS in maritime law enforcement.

B. Compliance of States with the COLREGS in Maritime Law Enforcement

As seen above, Canada's Coastal Fisheries Protection Regulations Amendment of 12 May 1994 authorized the use of force as a last resort. Yet Canada denied that one of its vessels intentionally brushed against a Spanish ship that was allegedly violating the Coastal Fisheries Protection Act in April 1995. The Italian authorities went further and prosecuted the commander of an Italian ship that had failed to comply with the COLREGS and collided with a vessel transporting illegal Albanian migrants in March 1997.

On the morning of 5 April 1995, the Spanish-flagged vessel *Ana María Gandán*, which was at a point 230 nautical miles from the coast of Canada, was surrounded by two Canadian patrol vessels, which attempted to cut its nets. The Spanish vessel called for help from other fishing vessels. One of the vessels that responded to its call, a Spanish-flagged refrigerator vessel, the *José María Nores*, was surrounded by another Canadian patrol boat. The weather was stormy and visibility was close to zero. The master of the *José María Nores* reported that the Canadian patrol boat came upon his vessel "like a pirate ship," until it was astern. At that point it brushed against the Spanish vessel. The dangerous maneuvering continued for an hour and a half. The incident prompted a complaint from the President of the European Commission to Canada and a call from the Vice-President of the Commission, who was concurrently Trade and External Relations Commissioner, to the Canadian ambassador to the EU. The latter responded that the incident was "unintended."[106]

Canada's denial that its official vessel deliberately intended to brush the Spanish vessel, which sounded very much like an apology, should be contrasted with its lack of reaction to Spanish complaints of two incidents that had occurred in the previous month. Early in the morning of 9 March 1995, three Canadian patrol boats had thrown ropes with hooks

[106] Xosé Hermida and Xavier Vidal-Folch, "Conflicto pesquero [Fisheries Conflict]," *El País* [The Country], 5 April 1995, https://elpais.com/diario/1995/04/07/economia/797205622_850215.html, accessed 9 June 2019.

and claws on the deck of the Spanish-flagged vessel *Estai*, in preparation for boarding. As the Canadian vessels approached the *Estai*, the vessel's captain ordered his crew to cut the ropes thrown by the Canadians and their own nets, so that they could flee to Spain. Five Spanish fishing vessels responded to the *Estai*'s call for help and through their maneuvers were able to prevent the boarding of the *Estai* for five hours. When the latter was finally surrounded, the Canadian patrol boats fired water cannon against it. When the water cannon seemed to produce no effect, the commander of the Canadian flotilla gave the order to fire cannon with live rounds. It was only then that the *Estai* surrendered. The officers of the Spanish vessel were handcuffed and the Canadians took control of the *Estai*, taking it to the nearest Canadian port, St. John's in Newfoundland.[107] Spain later declared that the safety and integrity of the vessel and of its crew had been endangered by the coercive action of Canadian vessels.[108] On 26 March 1995, a Canadian patrol vessel attempted to board the Spanish-flagged fishing vessel *Pescamoro I*, ordering it to stop its engines and using water cannons. The Canadian patrol vessel cut a large part of the fishing nets of the Spanish vessel, thus endangering the lives of the crew.[109] There is no public record of Canada presenting excuses or explanations of any kind for the conduct of its vessels on these two other occasions. The marked contrast implies that Canada, while affirming the legitimacy of the use of force in maritime law enforcement, attached great importance to avoiding collisions, even in the course of maritime law enforcement. Nor does one get the impression that Canadian vessels deliberately sought to provoke collisions with the Spanish fishing vessels.

The conduct of Italian authorities in seeking to prevent illegal migration from Albania in 1997 provides further confirmation that States are conscious of the need to comply with the COLREGS, even in the course of maritime law enforcement operations. As we shall see, the Italian

[107] Primitivo Carbajo, "Canadá apresa al pesquero español 'Estai' tras cinco horas de persecución en aguas internacionales [Canada Arrests the Spanish Fishing Vessel 'Estai' After a Five-Hour Chase in International Waters]," *El País* [The Country], 10 March 1995, https://elpais.com/diario/1995/03/10/economia/794790035_850215.html, accessed 9 June 2019.

[108] *Fisheries Jurisdiction (Spain v. Canada), Mémoire du Royaume d'Espagne*, 12, para. 13.

[109] *Ibid.*, 12–13, para. 13.

authorities instructed Italian warships to comply with the COLREGS in efforts to board and search Albanian vessels. The commander of an Italian warship, who was charged in court for the collision with and the sinking of an Albanian vessel, argued, in his defense, that the COLREGS were not applicable in law enforcement operations. This defense was rejected on the basis of the COLREGS by the Italian courts at all levels, from the court of first instance to the Supreme Court.

Italy and Albania had concluded an agreement on 23 March 1997 providing for a "naval blockade" in Albanian territorial waters and on the high seas. The following day all Italian authorities in charge of public safety were instructed to prevent the illegal entry of Albanians into Italy. A second Italo-Albanian agreement, signed on 25 March 1997, authorized Italian authorities to board and search, in international waters or in Albanian territorial waters, any vessel transporting Albanian citizens who had managed to avoid checks carried out by Albanian authorities on Albanian territory.[110]

On 28 March 1997, the Albanian-flagged vessel *Kater I Rades A-451*, carrying illegal Albanian migrants, sank in the Strait of Otranto, in the Adriatic sea, approximately 35 nautical miles from the Italian coast, as a result of a collision with the Italian warship *Sibilla*, which had attempted to stop and board it.[111] The number of people who perished was variously reported to be 58, 84, and 108.[112] The reaction of the Italian authorities

[110] The facts are summarized from a judgment of the European Court of Human Rights. See *Viron Xhavara et quinze autres contre l'Italie et l'Albanie* [Viron Xhavara and Fifteen Others v. Italy and Albania] Requête [Application] n° 39473/98 (jugement) [Judgment] [2001] Cour européenne des droits de l'homme [European Court of Human Rights], 3–4, http://hudoc.echr.coe.int/eng?i=001-31884, accessed 9 June 2019. The Judgment is available in French only. For a summary, see European Court of Human Rights, *Information Note No. 26 on the case-law of the Court January 2001*, 4, https://www.echr.coe.int/Documents/CLIN_2001_01_26_ENG_815318.pdf, accessed 9 June 2019.

[111] *Viron Xhavara et quinze autres*, 2.

[112] The first estimate is that of the European Court of Human Rights, *Viron Xhavara et quinze autres*, 2. The second is provided in "Strage del Venerdì Santo, i due comandanti condannati anche in Cassazione [The Good Friday Carnage: The Two Commanders Also Convicted on Appeal before the Supreme Court]," *Brindisi Report*, 12 May 2014, http://www.brindisireport.it/cronaca/strage-del-venerdi-santo-i-due-comandanti-condannati-anche-in-cassazione.html, accessed 7 June 2019. The third is found in "Naufragio del venerdì santo, la Cassazione conferma le condanne [The Good Friday Shipwreck, The Supreme Court Affirms Convictions]," *La Repubblica* [The Republic],

to this tragedy should be exemplary for China. They prosecuted not only the master of the Albanian vessel, but also the commander of the Italian warship. The latter, who was convicted for culpable sinking, multiple manslaughter, and culpable injury by the Court of First Instance in Brindisi, saw his appeal rejected in 2011 by the Court of Appeals in Lecce and finally in 2014 by the Italian Supreme Court (*Corte di Cassazione*).[113]

It is instructive to examine the details of the case.[114] On 24 March, the *Sibilla*'s commander had been ordered by the chief commander of the naval team to operate safely. Further instructions on 27 March specified that kinematic maneuvers should be undertaken in formal compliance with rules for preventing collisions at sea.[115] The investigation found that after a series of maneuvers intended to compel the *Kater I Rades* to reverse course, the *Sibilla* found itself at the derisory[116] lateral distance smaller than the safe distance, estimated at 10 meters or less, from the Albanian vessel. Indeed, it almost brushed against the stern and the side of the *Kater I Rades*. Despite the fact that the commander of *Sibilla* gave the order of "full speed astern," a collision was inevitable.[117]

The Italian courts found that the *Sibilla*'s commander had violated his instructions, which included compliance with the COLREGS. According to the courts, he had undertaken the irresponsible and imprudent pursuit of the *Kater I Rades*, when he could not have been unaware, in view of his competency as a mariner, of the sea conditions, the almost zero

12 May 2014, https://bari.repubblica.it/cronaca/2014/05/12/news/naufragio_del_venerd_santo_la_cassazione_conferma_le_condanne-85930009/, accessed 9 June 2019.

113 "Strage del Venerdì Santo"; "Naufragio del venerdì santo."

114 The following is summarized from the Judgment of the Court. Repubblica Italiana, Corte Suprema di Cassazione. Sez. Quarta Penale [Italian Republic, Supreme Court of Cassation, Fourth Criminal Section], Sentenza Num. 24527 del 10/06/2014 [Judgment No. 24527 of 10/06/2014] (ECLI:IT:CASS:2014:24527PEN), http://www.italgiure.giustizia.it/xway/application/nif/clean/hc.dll?verbo=attach&db=snpen&id=./20140611/snpen@s40@a2014@n24527@tS.clean.pdf, accessed 9 June 2019. The Judgment is cited in Tondini, 258, note 22, although there is no indication that the Judgment was delivered by the Fourth Criminal Section of the Italian Supreme Court.

115 Sentenza Num. 24527 del 10/06/2014, 5. Kinematics refers to the study of the motion of bodies without reference to mass or force. *Collins English Dictionary*, https://www.collinsdictionary.com/dictionary/english/kinematics, accessed 9 June 2019.

116 The adjective used by the Italian courts could also be translated as "ridiculous."

117 Sentenza Num. 24527 del 10/06/2014, 4–5.

visibility, and the difficulty that the *Kater I Rades* would have experienced in maneuvering, as a result of the ship's poor condition and the large number of people on board. The *Sibilla*'s commander had failed to calculate the roll of the *Kater I Rades* that would have been caused by the movement of the waves; the repellent and then attracting effect of the whirlpools formed by the movement of the vessels in the water; and the possibility of a mistaken maneuver on the part of the commanders of the two vessels, keeping in mind the route taken, the distance between the two vessels, the speed and the headway following a stoppage in the direction of travel, or a reversal of the direction that would have been rendered indispensable in case of emergency and that became indeed necessary.[118] In effect, the courts charged the commander with poor seamanship, a crucial element of Rule 2 of the COLREGS.

In their judgments, the lower and appeals courts invoked two rules of the COLREGS. Rule 6 provided that vessels should always proceed at a safe speed, in such a way that they can act in an appropriate and efficient manner to avoid collisions and can be stopped within a distance appropriate to the circumstances and to the conditions of the moment. Rule 13 provides that a vessel that overtakes another vessel should keep out of the way of the vessel being overtaken. The lower and appeals courts concluded that the *Sibilla*'s commander had violated his instructions to operate safely and to comply with the COLREGS.[119]

Among the arguments on which the *Sibilla*'s commander based his appeal to the Supreme Court was the inapplicability of the COLREGS to vessels undertaking police operations in compliance with a legitimate order issued by the military and governmental authority.[120] The Italian Supreme Court ruled that the argument was manifestly devoid of any legal basis. In its view, the commander's conduct could not plausibly fall within the scope of any legal framework of any kind or source, whether domestic or "supranational [sic]." The implementing regulations of the Italo-Albanian Agreement aimed to recommend, ensure, and impose in every case strict respect for the safety of Albanian vessels and of the refugees. The rules of engagement of the *Sibilla* stipulated among others that interdiction maneuvers should be carried out in formal compliance

[118] *Ibid.*, 5.

[119] *Ibid.*

[120] *Ibid.*, 10.

with the rules concerning collisions at sea. The appropriate legal conduct on the part of the *Sibilla*'s commander would have consisted, among others, in maintaining distance from the *Kater I Rades* that would have been suitable for preventing any possible form of collision between the two vessels.[121] The Italian commander did not find himself in a situation of risk for the safety of the two vessels and even less in a situation of "agreed risk" on the basis of any domestic or international rule. According to the Italian Supreme Court, no rule of domestic or international law, whether customary law or treaty law, would ever have authorized the commander—since a rule to cause the sinking of the *Kater I Rades* and the death of its passengers was inconceivable—to endanger the integrity and safety of the *Kater I Rades*, which were already precarious as a result of the condition of the vessel, the high number of passengers, and the conduct of its helmsman. The risky conduct of the commander, who approached the Albanian vessel at a distance that was not appropriate for taking precautions against the possibility of a foreseeable collision, was the expression of an imprudent choice on the part of the commander.[122] The Italian commander had illegally assumed the risk of collision, caused by approaching the *Kater I Rades* beyond the limits of safety required in the circumstances of the case. The risk was foreseeable given the reckless conduct of the helmsman of the latter vessel, and the risk was easily avoidable.[123] Even if the commander had alleged that he was complying with superior orders, his conduct could not be justified, as the content of any such order would be criminal in character.The Supreme Court rejected the commander's appeal; it was only the prescription of the crime of manslaughter that caused the Supreme Court to reduce slightly his sentence from two years and four months to two years. The commander and the Italian Ministry of Defense were also ordered to pay damages to the relatives of the victims.[124]

The judgment of the Italian Supreme Court should be the final nail in the coffin containing the CSIL's post-arbitration rationalization of the conduct of Chinese vessels on 28 April and 26 May 2012. It is now appropriate to formulate our conclusions.

121 *Ibid.*, 21.

122 *Ibid.*, 23.

123 *Ibid.*, 24.

124 "Strage del Venerdì Santo."

References

Anderson, David H. "Some Aspects on the Use of Force in Maritime Law Enforcement Operations." *International Courts and the Development of International Law: Essays in Honour of Tullio Treves*, 233–43. Eds. Bernard H. Oxman et al. The Hague: T.M.C. Asser Press, 2013.

Andrés Saenz de Santa María, M. Paz. "Incidentes pesqueros y recurso a la fuerza. Estudio del apresamiento de buques pesqueros como medida de ejecución en el régimen internacional de pesquerías [Fishing Incidents and the Resort to Force. A Study of the Arrest of Fishing Vessels as a Measure of Execution in the International Regime of Fisheries]." *Revista Española de Derecho Internacional* [Spanish Journal of International Law] 41 (1989): 7–41.

"*ARA Libertad*" *(Argentina v. Ghana). Provisional Measures. Order of 15 December 2012. ITLOS Reports 2012*, 332–51, https://www.itlos.org/fileadmin/itlos/documents/cases/case_no.20/published/C20_Order_151212.pdf, accessed 9 June 2019.

———. Joint Separate Opinion of Judge Wolfrum and Judge Cot. *ITLOS Reports 2013*, 363–81, https://www.itlos.org/fileadmin/itlos/documents/cases/case_no.20/published/C20_Wolfrum_Cot_151212.pdf, accessed 9 June 2019.

Baldoni, Claudio. "Les navires de guerre dans les eaux territoriales étrangères [Warships in Foreign Territorial Waters]." *Recueil des Cours de l'Académie de Droit International de La Haye* [Collected Courses of the Hague Academy of International Law], t. 65 (1938-III): 185–304.

Barnes, Richard A. "Article 25. Right of Protection of the Coastal State." *United Nations Convention on the Law of the Sea: A Commentary*, 222–26. Eds. Alexander Proelss et al. München: Verlag C.H. Beck, oHG, 2017.

———. "Article 30. Non-compliance by Warships with the Laws and Regulations of the Coastal State." *United Nations Convention on the Law of the Sea: A Commentary*, 244–47. Eds. Alexander Proelss et al. München: Verlag C.H. Beck, oHG, 2017.

Berg, Axel. "Das sowjetische U-Boot 137 in schwedischen Hoheitsgewässern. Fragen der Immunität fremder Kriegsschiffe [Soviet Submarine 137 in Swedish Territorial Waters. Questions on the Immunity of Foreign Warships]." *Zeitschrift für ausländisches öffentliches Recht und Völkerrecht* [Journal for Foreign Public Law and International Law] 42 (1982): 295–326, http://www.zaoerv.de/42_1982/42_1982_2_a_295_326.pdf, accessed 9 June 2019.

Bou Franch, Valentín. "El derecho de paso inocente de los buques de guerra en tiempos de paz [The Innocent Passage of Warships in Peacetime]." *Anuario de Derecho Marítimo* [Yearbook of Maritime Law] 11 (1994): 93–135, https://core.ac.uk/download/pdf/80525575.pdf, accessed 9 June 2019.

Cambridge English Dictionary. Cambridge: Cambridge University Press, 2019, https://dictionary.cambridge.org/dictionary/english/, accessed 9 June 2019.

Canada. "An Act to Amend the Coastal Fisheries Protection Act [Assented to 12 May 1994]." Annexe 14. *Fisheries Jurisdiction (Spain v. Canada). Mémoire du Royaume d'Espagne* (28 Septembre 1995) [Memorial of the Kingdom of Spain (Jurisdiction) (September 1995)], 147–54. International Court of Justice, https://www.icj-cij.org/files/case-related/96/096-19950928-WRI-01-01-BI.pdf, accessed 9 June 2019.

Carbajo, Primitivo. "Canadá apresa al pesquero español 'Estai' tras cinco horas de persecución en aguas internacionales [Canada Arrests the Spanish Fishing Vessel 'Estai' After a Five-Hour Chase in International Waters]." *El País* [The Country], 10 March 1995, https://elpais.com/diario/1995/03/10/economia/794790035_850215.html, accessed 9 June 2019.

Center for Strategic and International Studies. "Are Maritime Law Enforcement Forces Destabilizing Asia?" *China Power Project* (2018), https://chinapower.csis.org/maritime-forces-destabilizing-asia/, accessed 9 June 2019.

Chinese Society of International Law. "The South China Sea Arbitration Awards: A Critical Study." *Chinese Journal of International Law* 17 (2018): 207–748.

Collins English Dictionary. Glasgow: HarperCollins Publishers, 2019, https://www.collinsdictionary.com/dictionary/english/, accessed 9 June 2019.

de la Fayette, Louise. "International Tribunal for the Law of the Sea: *The M/V 'Saiga' (No. 2) Case (St. Vincent and the Grenadines v. Guinea), Judgment*." *International and Comparative Law Quarterly* 49 (2000): 467–76.

———. "ITLOS and the Saga of the Saiga: Peaceful Settlement of a Law of the Sea Dispute." *International Journal of Marine and Coastal Law* 15 (2000): 355–92.

Dennis, William C. "The Sinking of the *I'm Alone*." *American Journal of International Law* 23 (1929): 351–62.

Editors of Encyclopaedia Britannica. "Prohibition United States History [1920–1933]." *Encyclopaedia Britannica* (2019), https://www.britannica.com/event/Prohibition-United-States-history-1920-1933, accessed 9 June 2019.

Espaliú Berdud, Carlos. *Le passage inoffensif des navires de guerre étrangers dans la mer territoriale. Portée du régime contenu dans la Convention des Nations Unies sur le droit de la mer* [Innocent Passage of Foreign Warships in the Territorial Sea. The Scope of the Regime Contained in the United Nations Convention on the Law of the Sea]. Bruxelles: Établissements Bruylant, 2007.

Espaliú Berdud, Carlos, and Rafael Casado Raigón. "El paso inocente de buques de guerra extranjeros por mar territorial: alcance del régimen de la CNUDM [Innocent Passage of Foreign Warships in the Territorial Sea: The Scope of the UNCLOS Regime]." *Revista Española de Derecho Internacional* [Spanish Journal of International Law] 57 (2005): 777–98.

European Court of Human Rights. *Information Note No. 26 on the Case-Law of the Court January 2001*, https://www.echr.coe.int/Documents/CLIN_2001_01_26_ENG_815318.pdf, accessed 9 June 2019.

Evans, Malcolm D., and Vaughan Lowe. "The M/V Saiga: The First Case in the International Tribunal for the Law of the Sea." *International and Comparative Law Quarterly* 48 (1999): 187–99.

Fisheries Jurisdiction (Spain v. Canada). Verbatim Record 1998/10 (10 June 1998). International Court of Justice, https://www.icj-cij.org/files/case-related/96/096-19980610-ORA-01-00-BI.pdf, accessed 9 June 2019.

———. Verbatim Record 1998/11 (11 June 1998). International Court of Justice, https://www.icj-cij.org/files/case-related/96/096-19980611-ORA-01-00-BI.pdf, accessed 9 June 2019.

Fitzmaurice, G. G. "The Case of the *I'm Alone*." *British Yearbook of International Law* 17 (1936): 82–111.

Føroya landsstýri. *Faroe Islands: Government* (2019), https://www.faroeislands.fo/government-politics/, accessed 9 June 2019.

Francioni, Francesco. "Peacetime Use of Force, Military Activities, and the New Law of the Sea." *Cornell International Law Journal* 18 (1985): 203–26, https://scholarship.law.cornell.edu/cgi/viewcontent.cgi?article=1152&context=cilj, accessed 9 June 2019.

Froman, F. David. "Uncharted Waters: Non-innocent Passage of Warships in the Territorial Sea." M.A. Thesis, Naval Postgraduate School, 1983, https://calhoun.nps.edu/bitstream/handle/10945/20015/unchartedwatersn00from.pdf, accessed 9 June 2019.

———. "Uncharted Waters: Non-innocent Passage of Warships in the Territorial Sea." *San Diego Law Review* 21 (1984): 626–89.

Hermida, Xosé, and Xavier Vidal-Folch. "Conflicto pesquero [Fisheries Conflict]." *El País* [The Country], 5 April 1995, https://elpais.com/diario/1995/04/07/economia/797205622_850215.html, accessed 9 June 2019.

Hitt, John C. Jr. "Oceans Law and Superpower Relations: The Bumping of the *Yorktown* and the *Caron* in the Black Sea." *Virginia Journal of International Law* 29 (1989): 713–43.

Hyde, Charles Cheney. "The Adjustment of the *I'm Alone* Case." *American Journal of International Law* 29 (1935): 296–301.

International Code of Signals as adopted by the Fourth Assembly of the Inter-Governmental Maritime Consultative Organization in 1965 for Visual, Sound, and Radio Communications United States Edition, 1969 (Revised 2003). Publ. 102. Washington, DC: Government Printing Office, 2003, http://www.seasources.net/PDF/PUB102.pdf, accessed 9 June 2019.

International Convention on the International Regulations for Preventing Collisions at Sea. Adopted at London on 20 October 1972. Entered into force 15 July 1977. Consolidated text as amended in 1981, 1987, 1989,

1993, 2001 and 2007, http://www.ecolregs.com/index.php?option=com_k2&view=itemlist&layout=category&Itemid=505&lang=en, accessed 31 May 2019.

Italy. Repubblica Italiana. Corte Suprema di Cassazione. Sez. Quarta Penale [Italian Republic. Supreme Court of Cassation. Fourth Criminal Section]. Sentenza Num. 24527 del 10/06/2014 [Judgment No. 24527 of 10/06/2014] (ECLI:IT:CASS:2014:24527PEN), http://www.italgiure.giustizia.it/xway/application/nif/clean/hc.dll?verbo=attach&db=snpen&id=./20140611/snpen@s40@a2014@n24527@tS.clean.pdf, accessed 9 June 2019.

Jansson, Nils-Ove. "Submarine Intrusions in Swedish Waters." *Handlingar och Tidskrift. Kungl Krigsvetenskapsakademien. Proceedings and Journal. Royal Swedish Academy of War Sciences* 1 (2016): 52–59, http://kkrva.se/hot/2016:1/jansson_subm_instrusions.pdf, accessed 9 June 2019.

Jimenez Kwast, Patricia. "Maritime Law Enforcement and the Use of Force: Reflections on the Categorisation of Forcible Action at Sea in the Light of the *Guyana/Suriname* Award." *Journal of Conflict and Security Law* 13 (2008): 49–91.

Kraska, James. "Putting Your Head in the Tiger's Mouth: Submarine Espionage in Territorial Waters." *Columbia Journal of Transnational Law* 54 (2015): 164–247, http://jtl.columbia.edu/wp-content/uploads/sites/4/2015/12/Kraska_54-CJTL-164.pdf, accessed 9 June 2019.

Layton, C. W. T. et al. *Dictionary of Nautical Words and Terms*, 2nd ed. Glasgow: Brown, Son & Ferguson Ltd., Naval Publishers, 1982.

Llana, Christopher B., and George P. Wisneskey. *Handbook of the Nautical Rules of the Road: A Convenient Take-Along Guide for Sail and Power Boaters*, 3rd. [online] ed., 2009, http://navruleshandbook.com/, accessed 9 June 2019.

Lucchini, Laurent. "La loi canadienne du 12 mai 1994 : la logique extrême de la théorie du droit préférentiel de l'Etat côtier en haute mer au titre des stocks chevauchants [The Canadian Law of 12 May 1994: The Extreme Logic of the Theory of the Preferential Right of the Coastal State on the High Seas with respect to Straddling Stocks]." *Annuaire Français de Droit International* [French Yearbook of International Law] 40 (1994): 864–75, https://www.persee.fr/doc/afdi_0066-3085_1994_num_40_1_3226, accessed 9 June 2019.

Manin, Aleth. "L'échouement du Whiskey 137 dans les eaux suédoises [The Stranding of Whisky 137 in Swedish Waters]." *Annuaire Français de Droit International* [French Yearbook of International Law] 27 (1981): 689–710, https://www.persee.fr/docAsPDF/afdi_0066-3085_1981_num_27_1_2468.pdf, accessed 9 June 2019.

Military and Paramilitary Activities in and against Nicaragua (Nicaragua v. United States of America). Merits. Judgment. I.C.J. Reports 1986, 14–150, https://www.icj-cij.org/files/case-related/70/070-19860627-JUD-01-00-BI.pdf, accessed 9 June 2019.

Moore, Cameron. "The Arbitral Award in the Matter of the South China Sea Between the Philippines and China: What Are the Implications for Freedom of Navigation and the Use of Force?" *Asia-Pacific Journal of Ocean Law and Policy* 2 (2017): 117–39.

———. *Freedom of Navigation and the Law of the Sea: Warships, States and the Use of Force*, Kindle edition. London: Routledge, 2021.

———. "The Use of Force." *Routledge Handbook of Maritime Regulation and Enforcement*, 27–40. Eds. Robin Warner and Stuart Kaye. Milton Park, Abingdon, Oxon: Routledge, 2015.

The M/V "SAIGA" Case (Saint Vincent and the Grenadines v. Guinea). Prompt Release. ITLOS. *Application submitted by Saint Vincent and the Grenadines* (11 November 1997), https://www.itlos.org/fileadmin/itlos/documents/cases/case_no_1/application_without_annexes__svg_131197_eng.pdf, accessed 9 June 2019.

M/V "SAIGA" (No. 2) (Saint Vincent and the Grenadines v. Guinea). Judgment. ITLOS Reports 1999, 10–70, https://www.itlos.org/fileadmin/itlos/documents/cases/case_no_2/published/C2-J-1_Jul_99.pdf, accessed 9 June 2019.

"Naufragio del venerdì santo, la Cassazione conferma le condanne [The Good Friday Shipwreck, The Supreme Court Affirms Convictions]." *La Repubblica* [The Republic], 12 May 2014. https://bari.repubblica.it/cronaca/2014/05/12/news/naufragio_del_venerd_santo_la_cassazione_conferma_le_condanne-85930009/, accessed 9 June 2019.

Nordquist, Myron H. et al. (eds.). *United Nations Convention on the Law of the Sea 1982: A Commentary*. Vol. II. *Second Committee: Territorial Sea, Innocent Passage, Straits Used for International Navigation, Archipelagic States, the Exclusive Economic Zone, and the Continental Shelf*. Leiden: Martinus Nijhoff Publishers, 1993.

Ortolan, Théodore. *Règles internationales et diplomatie de la mer* [International Rules and the Diplomacy of the Sea]. Vol. I. Paris: H. Plon, 1864, https://ia800308.us.archive.org/23/items/rglesinternatio03ortogoog/rglesinternatio03ortogoog.pdf, accessed 9 June 2019.

Oxman, Bernard. "Le régime des navires de guerre dans le cadre de la Convention des Nations Unies sur le droit de la mer [The Regime of Warships Under the United Nations Convention on the Law of the Sea]." *Annuaire Français de Droit International* [French Yearbook of International Law] 28 (1982): 811–50, https://www.persee.fr/docAsPDF/afdi_0066-3085_1982_num_28_1_2519.pdf, accessed 9 June 2019.

———. "*The M/V "Saiga" (Saint Vincent and the Grenadines v. Guinea)*. ITLOS Case No. 1." *American Journal of International Law* 92 (1998): 278–82.

———. "The Regime of Warships Under the United Nations Convention on the Law of the Sea." *Virginia Journal of International Law* 24 (1984): 809–63, https://repository.law.miami.edu/cgi/viewcontent.cgi?article=1401&context=fac_articles, accessed 9 June 2019.

Perels, Ferdinand. *Das internationale öffentliche Seerecht der Gegenwart* [Contemporary Public International Law of the Sea]. Berlin: Ernst Siegfried Mittler und Sohn, 1882, https://ia902701.us.archive.org/5/items/dasinternationa01peregoog/dasinternationa01peregoog.pdf, accessed 9 June 2019.

———. *Manuel de droit maritime international* [Manual of International Maritime Law]. Transl. L. Arendt. Paris: Librairie Guillaumin & Cie, 1884, https://ia802606.us.archive.org/33/items/manueldedroitma00arengoog/manueldedroitma00arengoog.pdf, accessed 9 June 2019.

The Red Crusader Case (Commission of Enquiry, Denmark—United Kingdom, 1962). Reports of International Arbitral Awards. Vol. 29, 521–39. New York: United Nations, 2012, http://legal.un.org/riaa/cases/vol_XXIX/521-539.pdf, accessed 9 June 2019.

Rolph, John W. "Freedom of Navigation and the Black Sea Bumping Incident: How 'Innocent' Must Innocent Passage Be?" *Military Law Review* 135 (1992): 137–65.

Rothwell, Donald R., and Tim Stephens. *The International Law of the Sea*, 2nd ed. Oxford: Hart Publishing, 2016.

Sadurska, Roma. "Foreign Submarines in Swedish Waters: The Erosion of an International Norm." *Yale Journal of International Law* 10 (1984): 34–58, http://digitalcommons.law.yale.edu/cgi/viewcontent.cgi?article=1314&context=yjil, accessed 9 June 2019.

Shearer, Ivan. "The Development of International Law with Respect to the Law Enforcement Roles of Navies and Coast Guards in Peacetime." *The Law of Armed Conflict: Into the Next Millennium*, 429–53. Eds. Michael N. Schmitt and Leslie C. Green. Newport, RI: Naval War College, 1998, https://ia801601.us.archive.org/1/items/lawofarmedconfli71schm/lawofarmedconfli71schm.pdf, accessed 9 June 2019.

"Shouldering (US DoD Definition)." *Military Factory* (2021), https://www.militaryfactory.com/dictionary/military-terms-defined.php?term_id=4876, accessed 19 October 2021.

South China Sea Arbitration. Memorial of the Philippines (30 March 2014). Annex 77. Memorandum from Col. Nathaniel Y. Casem, Philippine Navy, to Chief of Staff, Armed Forces of the Philippines, No. N2E-0412–008 (11 April 2012). Vol. IV, 131–46, http://www.pcacases.com/pcadocs/The%20Philippines%27%20Memorial%20-%20Volume%20IV%20%28Annexes%2061-102%29.pdf, accessed 9 June 2019.

———. Annex 211. Note Verbale from the Embassy of the People's Republic of China in Manila to the Department of Foreign Affairs of the Republic of the Philippines, No. (12) PG-239 (25 May 2012). Vol. VI, 401–4 http://www.pcacases.com/pcadocs/The%20Philippines%27%20Memorial%20-%20Volume%20VI%20%28Annexes%20158-221%29.pdf, accessed 9 June 2019.

———. Annex 239. Opinion of Craig H. Allen, Judson Falknor Professor of Law, University of Washington (19 March 2014). Vol. VII, 371–88, https://files.pca-cpa.org/pcadocs/The%20Philippines%27%20Memorial%20-%20Volume%20VII%20%28Annexes%20222-255%29.pdf, accessed 9 June 2019.

———. Annex 697. Affidavit of Mr. Crispen Talatagod (12 November 2015). Vol. II, 201–18, https://files.pca-cpa.org/pcadocs/The%20Philippines%27%20Supplemental%20Documents%20-%20Volume%20II%20%28Annexes%20608-709%29.pdf, accessed 9 June 2019.

———. Annex 698. Affidavit of Mr. Cecilio Taneo (12 November 2015). Vol. II, 219–34, https://files.pca-cpa.org/pcadocs/The%20Philippines%27%20Supplemental%20Documents%20-%20Volume%20II%20%28Annexes%20608-709%29.pdf, accessed 9 June 2019.

———. *Supplemental Documents of the Philippines* (19 November 2015). Annex 696. Affidavit of Mr. Jowe Legaspi (12 November 2015). Vol. II, 185–201, https://files.pca-cpa.org/pcadocs/The%20Philippines%27%20Supplemental%20Documents%20-%20Volume%20II%20%28Annexes%20608-709%29.pdf, accessed 9 June 2019.

S.S. "I'm Alone" Case (Canada/United States, 30 June 1933 and 5 January 1935). Reports of International Arbitral Awards. Vol. III, 1609–18. New York: United Nations, 2006, http://legal.un.org/riaa/cases/vol_III/1609-1618.pdf, accessed 9 June 2019.

"Strage del Venerdì Santo, i due comandanti condannati anche in Cassazione [The Good Friday Carnage: The Two Commanders Also Convicted on Appeal before the Supreme Court]." *Brindisi Report*, 12 May 2014, http://www.brindisireport.it/cronaca/strage-del-venerdi-santo-i-due-comandanti-condannati-anche-in-cassazione.html, accessed 9 June 2019.

Tanaka, Yoshifumi. "Navigational Rights and Freedoms." *The Oxford Handbook of the Law of the Sea*, 537–58. Eds. Donald Rothwell et al. Oxford: Oxford University Press, 2015.

Timsit, Gérard. "Le fonctionnement de la procédure d'enquête dans l'affaire du Red Crusader [The Functioning of the Procedure of Inquiry in the Red Crusader Case]." *Annuaire Français de Droit International* [French Yearbook of International Law] 9 (1963): 460–72, https://www.persee.fr/doc/afdi_0066-3085_1963_num_9_1_1040, accessed 9 June 2019.

Tondini, Matteo. "The Use of Force in the Course of Maritime Law Enforcement Operations." *Journal on the Use of Force and International Law* 4 (2017): 1–17.

Treves, Tullio. "La navigation [Navigation]." *Traité du Nouveau droit de la mer* [Treatise on the New Law of the Sea], 687–808. Eds. René-Jean Dupuy and Daniel Vignes. Paris: Éditions Économica, 1985.

Union of Soviet Socialist Republics-United States: Joint Statement with Attached Uniform Interpretation of Rules of International Law Governing Innocent Passage. Entered into at Jackson Hole, Wyoming, 23 September 1989, https://cil.nus.edu.sg/wp-content/uploads/formidable/18/1989-USA-USSR-Joint-Statement-with-Attached-Uniform-Interpretation-of-Rues-of-International-Law-Governing-Innocent-Passage.pdf, accessed 9 June 2019.

United Nations Convention on the Law of the Sea. Concluded at Montego Bay on 10 December 1982. Entered into force 16 November 1994, http://www.un.org/depts/los/convention_agreements/texts/unclos/unclos_e.pdf, accessed 6 June 2019.

United States. Department of the Navy. *United States Navy Regulations 1990*. Doc. PCN 50100370000. Washington, DC: Department of the Navy, 1990, https://www.marines.mil/Portals/59/Publications/United%20States%20Navy%20Regulations.pdf?ver=2012-10-11-164138-043, accessed 9 June 2019.

———. Navy; US Marine Corps; and US Coast Guard. *Commander's Handbook on the Law of Naval Operations Edition July 2007*. Doc. NWP1–14M/MCWP 5-12.1/COMDTPUB P5800.7A [Washington, DC:] Department of the Navy, Office of the Chief of Naval Operations and Headquarters, US Marine Corps, Department of Homeland Security, and US Coast Guard, 2007, http://www.jag.navy.mil/documents/NWP_1-14M_Commanders_Handbook.pdf, accessed 9 June 2019.

Viron Xhavara et quinze autres contre l'Italie et l'Albanie [Viron Xhavara and Fifteen Others v. Italy and Albania]. Requête [Application] n° 39473/98 (jugement) [Judgment] [2001] Cour européenne des droits de l'homme [European Court of Human Rights], http://hudoc.echr.coe.int/eng?i=001-31884, accessed 9 June 2019.

Vitányi, Béla. "L'immunité des navires d'État – I [The Immunity of Government Vessels—I]." *Netherlands International Law Review* 10 (1963): 33–61.

"The Whiskey Class." *Weapons and Warfare. History and Hardware of Warfare* (10 June 2017), https://weaponsandwarfare.com/2017/06/10/the-whiskey-class/, accessed 9 June 2019.

CHAPTER 7

Summary and Conclusions

Since 2010, the risks to the safety of navigation in the South China Sea have been increased by incidents, most of which involved different types of vessels from China (including Taiwan), on the one hand, and vessels from one or the other of Indonesia, the Philippines, and Vietnam, on the other. Incidents between Chinese and Philippine official vessels that occurred in the waters of Scarborough Shoal on 28 April and 26 May 2012 were the object of Submission No. 13 of the Philippines to the Arbitral Tribunal constituted under Annex VII of the United Nations Convention on the Law of the Sea ("Convention"). In its Award rendered on 12 July 2016, the Tribunal found that China's operation of its law enforcement vessels created serious risk of collision and danger to Philippine ships and personnel and violated Rules 2, 6, 7, 8, 15, and 16 of the Convention on the International Regulations for Preventing Collisions at Sea 1972 ("COLREGS 1972"). The decision is noteworthy, as this seems to be the first international judicial decision that specifically invokes the COLREGS as the legal basis for the decision. The decision is all the more remarkable, in that the Philippines was not a party to the COLREGS at the time of the incidents. Nevertheless, the Tribunal considered that the COLREGS were applicable to the Philippines as "generally accepted international regulations" referred to in Article 94(4)(a) and Article 94(5) of the Convention, which had the effect of incorporating the COLREGS

A. C. Robles Jr., *Vessel Collisions in the Law of the Sea*,
https://doi.org/10.1007/978-981-16-9793-7_7

into the Convention. As a result, violations of the COLREGS would be considered violations of the Convention.

Chapter 1 presented the uncontested factual background of Submission No. 13. On 28 April 2012, a Chinese law enforcement vessel approached two Philippine vessels, on separate occasions, at high speed and at a very short distance. On 26 May 2012, a Chinese law enforcement vessel attempted to cross the starboard bow of a Philippine official vessel twice, after which another Chinese vessel attempted the same maneuver. Subsequently, the Philippine vessel proceeding to Scarborough Shoal was pursued by three Chinese vessels. Two more attempts were made to cross its starboard bow, followed by an attempt to ram it.

China's failure to contest this factual account is in sharp contrast to its attempts made on several occasions to present its own version of the facts to prove that its construction activities at seven reefs in the South China Sea caused no harm to the marine environment. China stressed that all the activities of its vessels were law enforcement activities that were within the scope of China's sovereignty over Scarborough Shoal. The Chapter suggested that China did not contest the factual account presented by the Philippines in order to spare itself the embarrassment of being proved wrong. China had had such an experience in 2009, when its denials of the conduct of Chinese official and fishing vessels toward the US vessel *Impeccable* were proven to be untrue by video evidence put online by the US.

In view of the fact that the COLREGS were deemed to be incorporated into the Convention as "generally accepted international regulations," Chapter 2 analyzed the historical process through which the COLREGS came to be generally accepted by mariners and States. The origins of the COLREGS were traced to the practice of mariners in the UK in the eighteenth and nineteenth centuries, which came to be known as the "Rules of the Road." These Rules were codified by British legislation and extended to the vessels of other States who consented to have the regulations applicable to their vessels. One advantage of COLREGS for mariners is their simplicity. Since their aim is limited to collision avoidance, they cater for all levels of shipping technology, entail minimum interference to navigation and with other uses of the sea, and are easily comprehensible. States early on realized that for collision regulations to be effective, they had to be international in scope. At first, States merely accepted regulations adopted by the UK. From the late nineteenth century onward, States participated in the drafting of the regulations through international conferences. States understood that their obligation consisted in adopting domestic legislation consistent with the International Regulations and providing the legal and judicial machinery that would enable their enforcement. China has accepted all versions of the COLREGS that have been adopted since then (1889, 1910, 1948, 1960, and 1972).

Chapter 3 examined two issues relating to the Arbitral Tribunal's jurisdiction with respect to Submission No. 13. First, the Chapter argues that despite the scholarly debate on the notion of "generally accepted international regulations," analysis of the *travaux préparatoires* of the Geneva Convention on the High Seas 1958, on which Article 94 of the Convention was patterned, demonstrates that the COLREGS were the first "generally accepted international regulations" that the United Nations International Law Commission had in mind when it formulated the provision. In these circumstances, it is not too far-fetched to state that the COLREGS are the paradigmatic "generally accepted international regulations." Second, the Chapter addresses the post-arbitration denial of jurisdiction by the Chinese Society of International Law ("CSIL"), on the grounds that the Convention lacked an enabling provision that would render the COLREGS applicable in the territorial sea, specifically in the territorial sea of Scarborough Shoal. This argument is readily dismissed, for two reasons. First, it misunderstands the decision of the Tribunal, which stressed that the duty to comply with the COLREGS was the duty of the flag State, rendering superfluous any preliminary determination of sovereignty over the territorial sea. Second, it contradicts the text and history of the COLREGS. The latter applies to "all vessels upon the high seas and in all waters connected therewith navigable by seagoing vessels" and requires that States take measures to implement them. Moreover, the history of the COLREGS demonstrates that they have always been applicable in the territorial sea and even in the internal waters of States that adopt them.

Chapter 4, which is based on the assumption that violations of the COLREGS are violations of the Convention, discussed the violations of three sets of rules of the COLREGS attributable to the Chinese official vessels and to China. The first set is the general rule on responsibility, Rule 2. The Chinese vessels' conduct demonstrated a lack of understanding of the concept of good seamanship and could not be excused by special circumstances, which can only refer to immediate danger. The second set of rules, comprising Rules 6, 7, and 8, applies in all conditions of visibility. The Chinese vessels did not proceed at a safe speed, a circumstance that would have prevented them from taking action to avoid collision and being stopped at the appropriate distance in case of risk of collision (Rule 6). They failed to consider that the risk of collision existed (Rule 7). The maneuvers that they undertook did not result in passing at a safe distance (Rule 8). The third set of rules, consisting of Rules 15 and 16, is applicable to vessels that are in sight of one another. The Chinese and Philippine vessels found themselves in a crossing situation, in which the former would have been the give-way vessels and the latter the stand-alone vessels. The Chinese vessels failed to take action to keep out of the way of the Philippine vessels (Rule 15) as well as to take early and substantial action to keep clear (Rule 16).

Chapter 5 presented a critique of the CSIL's rationalizations of the conduct of China's vessels. These rationalizations, while drawing on international case law, omitted references in the latter to the need to fire warning shots and to resort to force having in mind considerations of humanity. The omission may be explained by the fact that neither requirement was met by the conduct of the Chinese vessels.

The CSIL referred to an incident that took place on 10 April 2012 involving Philippine warships and Chinese fishing vessels, in the course of which the Philippine vessels are said to have severely violated China's sovereignty and the human rights of the Chinese fishermen. This incident is dismissed as irrelevant, as there was no evidence that the Philippine vessels had conducted themselves in a way that created immediate danger and that justified departure from the COLREGS on the same day, or 18 days later, or 46 days later. Nor could the alleged human rights violations committed by the Philippine vessels, on which no details are provided, justify Chinese conduct that would have endangered the lives of Philippine mariners on the same day, or 18 days later, or 46 days later.

The attempts to justify the conduct of Chinese vessels on 28 April and 26 May as law enforcement activities against violations of China's laws and regulations relating to innocent passage in the territorial sea were analyzed from two further perspectives. The first considered that the Philippine vessels were warships that enjoyed sovereign immunity and could therefore not be the object of law enforcement activities by foreign States, contrary to the arguments of the CSIL. Even if foreign warships failed to fulfill the requirements of innocent passage in the territorial sea or the laws and regulations of the coastal State relating to innocent passage,

State practice demonstrates that States refrain from the use of force as far as possible and pay due regard to elementary considerations of humanity when they do decide to use force. The second perspective focused on the principles and rules applicable to the use of force in the conduct of maritime law enforcement activities. While States do provide for the use of force as a last resort, State practice demonstrates that even in the course of such activities, States are keen to avoid collisions. They instruct their vessels to follow the COLREGS. Furthermore, they present excuses even when vessels only brush against each other, and they prosecute their law enforcement officials who fail to comply with the COLREGS.

The decisions of the Arbitral Tribunal relating to the near-collision between Chinese and Philippine vessels confirm that the International Regulations for Preventing Collisions at Sea are an integral part of the United Nations Convention on the Law of the Sea. These decisions highlight the little-known fact that the COLREGS are among the oldest rules forming part of what is now known as the law of the sea to be accepted by States. In the 1950s, the United Nations International Law Commission, fearing that newly independent States would fail to adhere to the COLREGS, adopted the formula of "generally accepted international regulations" that permitted the incorporation of the COLREGS into the Geneva Convention on the High Seas 1958, the relevant provision of which was subsequently incorporated into the Convention. The result of this incorporation is that States that are not parties to the COLREGS 1972 but are parties to the Convention are bound by the COLREGS 1972.

Contrary to the scenario that was anticipated in the 1950s, it was a State that had long been bound by the COLREGS that was accused of breaches of the COLREGS. The formula adopted by the ILC redounded to the benefit of a State that was not party to the COLREGS at the time of the incidents of which it complained. It is a sad commentary on the conduct of China that after over a hundred years of being party to the COLREGS and of complying with them, it should now resort to breaches of the COLREGS as instruments of its foreign policy. One is saddened even more by the CSIL's rationalization of China's violations of the COLREGS, which provide China with tailor-made arguments for justifying collisions as instruments of foreign policy.

The Tribunal's decision that China has breached the COLREGS has unfortunately not been sufficient to dissuade China from continuing to operate its law enforcement vessels in ways that endanger the safety of human life and navigation in the South China Sea. Undoubtedly, China's conduct is a threat to the integrity of the COLREGS, which have ensured the safety of maritime navigation since the second half of the nineteenth century. China's conduct also represents a breach of a fundamental norm of international law, the prohibition of the threat or use of force. Not even the firm conviction that one has sovereignty over a disputed territory or maritime space can justify the recourse to collisions as instruments of foreign policy.

China's systematic breaches of the COLREGS feed the perception of a Chinese threat to the safety of human life and navigation in the South China Sea and indeed, give substance to it. They make a mockery of regional efforts to negotiate a Code of Conduct binding on the littoral States. They can only alienate other littoral States and heighten the interest of non-littoral States in ensuring the safety of human life and navigation in the South China Sea. It is to be hoped that a major disaster will not be required to convince China of the need to act in conformity with the COLREGS, the United Nations Convention on the Law of the Sea, and international law. It is to be regretted that there are few grounds for being so sanguine.

Index

A. C. Robles Jr., *Vessel Collisions in the Law of the Sea*,
https://doi.org/10.1007/978-981-16-9793-7

Y

Z

The manufacturer's authorised representative in the EU is Springer Nature Customer Service Centre GmbH, Europaplatz 3, 69115 Heidelberg, Germany. If you have any concerns regarding our products, please contact ProductSafety@springernature.com

Printed and bound by CPI Group (UK) Ltd, Croydon, CR0 4YY
30/09/2026
02225234-0001